Culture and Customs of Botswana

Botswana. Cartography by Bookcomp, Inc.

Culture and Customs
of Botswana

ᭇᴐᴐᴑᴑᴑᴑ

JAMES DENBOW AND PHENYO C. THEBE

Culture and Customs of Africa
Toyin Falola, Series Editor

GREENWOOD PRESS
Westport, Connecticut • London

Library of Congress Cataloging-in-Publication Data

Denbow, James R. (James Raymond), 1946–
    Culture and customs of Botswana / James Denbow and Phenyo C. Thebe.
        p. cm. — (Culture and customs of Africa, ISSN 1530–8367)
    Includes bibliographical references and index.
    ISBN 0–313–33178–2 (alk. paper)
    1. Botswana—Civilization. 2. Botswana—Social life and customs. I. Thebe,
Phenyo C. II. Title. III. Series.
DT2452.D46 2006
968.83—dc22   2005029680

British Library Cataloguing in Publication Data is available.

Library of Congress Catalog Card Number: 2005029680
ISBN: 0–313–33178–2
ISSN: 1530–8367

First published in 2006

Greenwood Press, 88 Post Road West, Westport, CT 06881
An imprint of Greenwood Publishing Group, Inc.
www.greenwood.com

Printed in the United States of America

The paper used in this book complies with the
Permanent Paper Standard issued by the National
Information Standards Organization (Z39.48–1984).

10 9 8 7 6 5 4 3 2 1

Copyright Acknowledgments

Contents

Series Foreword

Africa is a vast continent, the second largest, after Asia. It is four times the size of the United States, excluding Alaska. It is the cradle of human civilization. A diverse continent, Africa has more than fifty countries with a population of over 700 million people who speak over 1,000 languages. Ecological and cultural differences vary from one region to another. As an old continent, Africa is one of the richest in culture and customs, and its contributions to world civilization are impressive indeed.

Africans regard culture as essential to their lives and future development. Culture embodies their philosophy, worldview, behavior patterns, arts, and institutions. The books in this series intend to capture the comprehensiveness of African culture and customs, dwelling on such important aspects as religion, worldview, literature, media, art, housing, architecture, cuisine, traditional dress, gender, marriage, family, lifestyles, social customs, music, and dance.

The uses and definitions of "culture" vary, reflecting its prestigious association with civilization and social status, its restriction to attitude and behavior, its globalization, and the debates surrounding issues of tradition, modernity, and postmodernity. The participating authors have chosen a comprehensive meaning of culture while not ignoring the alternative uses of the term.

Each volume in the series focuses on a single country, and the format is uniform. The first chapter presents a historical overview, in addition to information on geography, economy, and politics. Each volume then proceeds to examine the various aspects of culture and customs. The series highlights the mechanisms for the transmission of tradition and culture across generations: the significance of orality, traditions, kinship rites, and family property distribution; the rise of print culture; and the impact of educational institutions. The series also explores the intersections between local, regional, national, and global bases for identity and social relations. While the volumes are organized nationally, they pay attention to ethnicity and language groups and the links between Africa and the wider world.

The books in the series capture the elements of continuity and change in culture and customs. Custom is represented not as static or as a museum artifact but as a dynamic phenomenon. Furthermore, the authors recognize the current challenges to traditional wisdom, which include gender relations, the negotiation of local identities in relation to the state, the significance of struggles for power at national and local levels and their impact on cultural traditions and community-based forms of authority, and the tensions between agrarian and industrial/manufacturing/oil-based economic modes of production.

Africa is a continent of great changes, instigated mainly by Africans but also through influences from other continents. The rise of youth culture, the penetration of the global media, and the challenges to generational stability are some of the components of modern changes explored in the series. The ways in which traditional (non-Western and nonimitative) African cultural forms continue to survive and thrive—that is, how they have taken advantage of the market system to enhance their influence and reproductions—also receive attention.

Through the books in this series, readers can see their own cultures in a different perspective, understand the habits of Africans, and educate themselves about the customs and cultures of other countries and people. The hope is that the readers will come to respect the cultures of others and see them not as inferior or superior to theirs but merely as different. Africa has always been important to Europe and the United States, essentially as a source of labor, raw materials, and markets. Blacks are in Europe and the Americas as part of the African diaspora, a migration that took place primarily because of the slave trade. Recent African migrants increasingly swell their number and visibility. It is important to understand the history of the diaspora and the newer migrants as well as the roots of the culture and customs of the places from where they come. It is equally important to understand others in order to be able to interact successfully in a world that keeps shrinking. The accessible nature of the books in this series will contribute to this understanding and enhance the quality of human interaction in a new millennium.

Toyin Falola
Frances Higginbothom, Nalle Centennial Professor in History
The University of Texas at Austin

Preface

Large deposits of gem-quality diamonds have made Botswana one of the richest countries in Africa on a per capita basis. While diamonds and minerals, combined with cattle and tourism, form the economic foundation of the country, what truly separates Botswana from most other African nations is its long tradition of democratic rule, respect for ethnic and racial differences, and freedom of the press. While no nation is perfect with respect to the balance struck between the ability for minority voices to be heard and the need for consensus in national governance, the political dialogue in Botswana is often closer to what is found in the Western world than it is to other parts of Africa. There have been no coups d'état, no bloody military put-downs of opposing political parties, and no massive losses of human life due to the poor management of resources that all too often lie at the root of starvation or suffering. Even though Botswana has had its share of problems, including ecological disasters such as drought, the spirit of its people and their willingness, despite differences in cultural background, to work together to overcome such setbacks is what makes this country so refreshing.

Some have attributed Botswana's economic and political success to a lack of ethnic diversity in the country. While this may be true on a certain level, we hope this book will illustrate just how rich and varied the cultures, customs, languages, and peoples of Botswana really are. For us, it has been a humbling experience to try to condense this diversity into a readable account, and it is perhaps inevitable that one is more conscious of what has been left out than what has been included. We have focused our detailed discussions and examples for the most part on the Tswana, widening it when possible to include other customs and practices as our knowledge and experience dictated. Our intention has not been to slight any particular group but rather to try to keep the text as accessible as possible to an audience new to the country. The complex interrelationships among dance, religion, healing, social harmony, and psychosocial wellness, for instance, strain separating these topics into different chapters headed as religion, dance, or gender and personhood. By providing more specific information and terminology, we hope to cut across some of these imposed divisions while at the same time providing those interested in developing a more in-depth view of the country and its cultural diversity with a starting point from which to begin.

Acknowledgments

This book could not have been written without the expertise and encouragement of many people, both in the United States and in Africa. To begin with, we are grateful to Professor Toyin Falola for suggesting that we take on this project and for his helpful encouragement and occasional prodding to get it done. We are also indebted to Wendi Schnaufer for her patience when things got slow and encouragement and advice when it was needed.

The book could not have been written without the invaluable aid of Morongwa Mosothwane, who used a great deal of her free time to critique the book as it was progressing. She also provided photographs and added a much-needed feminine critique on important issues. In many ways, she is a silent partner in this book along with my wife of 36 years, Jocelyne Denbow, who read and edited the chapters, contributing valuable comments and insights on many of the topics.

James Denbow would also like to acknowledge the friendship and support of Alec and Judy Campbell of Crocodile Pools and Mike and Kirsten Main of Gaborone, who have provided decades of good conversation, knowledge, and friendship. Mike graciously provided photographs from his large collection, as did my daughter, Jennifer Denbow. Much thanks are due to both for their generosity. Grateful appreciation also goes to Nonofho Mathibidi, Philip Segadika, and the late Alex Matseka of the National Museum of Botswana, who worked with me on many occasions and were always ready to interpret, give friendly advice, and provide support when needed. I am also grateful to

Hildi Hendrickson for reading and commenting on a draft of Chapter 5, and to Ed Wilmsen for comments on the manuscript.

Special gratitude goes to all the people at Bosutswe who for so many years cheerfully shared their precious water, firewood, and friendship with me. In many ways, they became like a second family by sharing their joys, troubles, stories, and delights in their children. It was truly a pleasure to hear your voices ringing, occasionally in song, across that valley in the early morning, and special thanks are owed to Elatetswe "Kaiser" Mangwedi, Bosutswe Ketsidile and his wife Lesego, Queen Seabelo, and Banthole "C4" Bantole. Finally, I am indebted to the students of the University of Botswana who, through their unfailing enthusiasm, contributed to the experiences that have made Botswana such a delight, in particular, Gadza Keatlholwtswe, Thato Masarwa, O'Boy Kalake, and Lawrence Masoga. *Ke a leboga thata.*

Phenyo Thebe would like to express his gratitude to his wife Thato and daughter Laone for their emotional support and understanding while he was preoccupied with the manuscript. In addition, he will always be grateful to his mother Ketsweletse Thebe and his late father Tichara Elias Mmolawa Thebe, both of whom have been his source of inspiration throughout his life. He also wishes to thank his extended Botswana family who helped in many different ways and to acknowledge the director and staff of the National Museum of Botswana for their support and encouragement. Special thanks are due to Berlinah Motswakhumo and Salalenna "Greek" Phaladi for their helpful discussions and criticism.

Finally, to all the sons and daughters of Botswana who have a passion for Botswana's culture and customs—we thank you all, named and unnamed! *Le ka moso bagaetsho.*

Chronology

40,000 years ago	Middle Stone Age hunters and gatherers occupy Tsodilo, ≠gi, and the shorelines of paleo-Lake Makgadikgadi.
20,000 years ago	Later Stone Age (LSA) groups occupy most of the country where permanent water supplies exist.
200 C.E.	A few LSA groups acquire cattle and possibly goats and sheep.
350	First Iron Age agropastoralists move into the eastern margins of county.
700	First agropastoralists occupy northwestern Botswana and the Tsodilo Hills.
900	Long-distance trade networks traverse the Kalahari as far as Tsodilo, connecting with early chiefdoms that controlled large cattle herds in the east and specularite mines in the northwest.
1000	Centralized chiefdoms form in the northeastern part of the country and direct ivory and other products to Swahili outlets on the coast.
1200	Gold mining in the interior intensifies the importance of long-distance trade to early kingdoms.

1300   Many settlements in northeastern Botswana fall under the control of Great Zimbabwe. Iron, copper, bronze, and gold manufacture become signatures of the elite in the Botswana. In Ngamiland, political restructuring of trade routes, perhaps coupled with environmental changes, lead to a collapse of early chiefdoms at Tsodilo.

1500   Rise of the Khami Empire in southwestern Zimbabwe leads to changes in the political economy of many sites in northeastern Botswana. Present Kalanga-speaking groups derive from these earlier chiefdoms in a triangle stretching from Francistown to Mahalapye to the Makgadikgadi pans.

1700   Present-day Batswana groups become recognizable in the historical record as the Ngwaketswe and Ngwato separate from the Kwena. Other South African groups also are said to have become established in the southeast of Botswana: the Rolong, Kgatla, and Tlaro.

1800   Batawana separate from the Bangwato and settle in northwestern Botswana.

1820–50   Mfecane (Difaqane)—a period of warfare—disrupted most of southern Africa, including Botswana. Raids by the Ndebele and the Kololo were especially troublesome.

1845   David Livingstone establishes a mission at Kolobeng, setting in train European exploration of the country in the 1850s–80s. Major trade routes to the coast were established across the country to carry ivory, ostrich feathers, root rubber, and other veld products out to world markets.

1867   First European gold mining in southern Africa begins in the Francistown region.

1885   Botswana made a British protectorate as part of Bechuanaland.

1890   Protectorate is extended northward to include the Tawana and Chobe regions north of 22 degrees south latitude.

1895	Three Tswana kings (Bothoen I of the Ngwaketse, Sebele I of the Kwena, and Khama III of the Ngwato) journey to England with the missionaries Edwin Lloyd and William C. Willoughby to protest possible incorporation of Bechuanaland by Cecil Rhodes into the British South Africa Company.
1896	Disastrous Jameson Raid is staged through Botswana in an attempt to assist English-speaking colonists in an overthrow of Paul Kruger's Afrikaner-dominated government in Johannesburg. An ongoing rinderpest epidemic continues to decimate Botswana's livestock herds and also kills approximately 75 percent of its wild game.
1899	Hut tax is introduced that forces Batswana into the European economy while offsetting the costs of the British protectorate.
1910	Union of South Africa. The Union Act considered the incorporation of the High Commission territories (Botswana, Lesotho, and Swaziland) into South Africa but in the end did not do so. Economic integration with South Africa, however, was effected through the establishment of the South African Customs Union. The small partners received only 2 percent of the total receipts, however, leading to dissatisfaction that continued right up through independence.
1918	Some Batswana participate in World War I.
1919	Native Tax is established to pay for the increased costs of administration of the protectorate.
1919–1920	African Advisory council and the European Advisory Council are established to deal separately with the affairs of Batswana and European residents.
1934–38	Through Proclamations 74 and 75, the British administration attempts to curb the power of local chiefs by cutting their authority, including their rights to local tax monies and the control and sale of stray cattle.

1940–45	Some Batswana participate in World War II.
1948	Sir Seretse Khama marries Ruth Williams.
1950	Seretse Khama is deposed by the colonial government as paramount chief of the Ngwato and sent into exile.
1956	Seretse Khama returns from exile and becomes involved in modern politics.
1959	First political party, the Bechuanaland Federal Party, is established by Leetile Raditladi. The copper mines at Selibe-Phikwe are opened.
1960	Bechuanaland Peoples Party (BPP) is formed by Motsami Mpho, Philip Matante, and Kgalemang Morsete.
1962	Botswana Democratic Party (BDP) is formed under Seretse Khama with support from the colonial administration.
1964	Bechuanaland Independence Party (BIP) is established under Motsami Mpho as a breakaway from the BPP.
1965	Botswana National Front (BNF), the major opposition party, is formed by Kenneth Koma. The District Council's Act is passed, establishing district and town councils in an attempt to further reduce the powers of traditional chiefs.
1966	Botswana Independence. At this point, Botswana was ranked as one of the world's poorest nations. Establishment of a parliament with elected officers, a house of chiefs, and a president, Sir Seretse Khama. Botswana Meat Commission established as the single marketer for Botswana beef exports.
1967	Diamonds discovered at Orapa. Copper deposits are also discovered at Selibi-Phikwe.
1968	Tribal Land Act created district land boards to oversee land distribution. Previously, land allocation had been a royal prerogative.

1971	Orapa diamond mine opens.
1973	Coal mining begins at Morupule mine, which supplies the country's principal electrical generating plant.
1975	Tribal Land Grazing Policy established to control overgrazing. Inadvertently, it also created a de facto land ownership through borehole rights on the fringes of the Kalahari.
1976	Botswana stops using the South African rand and launches its own currency, the pula.
1977	Botswana Defense Force (BDF) established with Sir Seretse Khama's eldest son, Ian Seretse Khama, appointed as deputy commander under Monmphati Merafhe, commander. Its principal purpose is to defend the country against aggression by white-ruled regimes in Rhodesia, South Africa, and Namibia as well as to counteract any problems arising from ongoing civil war in Angola.
1978	Forces under the rebel Rhodesian government of Ian Smith kill 15 BDF soldiers in a surprise attack at Leshoma, Botswana.
1980	Vice President Sir Kitumile Masire assumes the presidency of Botswana after the death of the first president, Sir Seretse Khama. The Southern African Development Cooperation Conference is formed with the intention of creating a unified market in southern Africa. Onset of a period of severe drought results in the introduction of drought-relief programs.
1981	Literacy rate stands at 34 percent.
1982	Jwaneng diamond mine, the richest in the world in terms of the value of recovered diamonds, begins operation. The University of Botswana established as independent from the combined University of Botswana, Lesotho, and Swaziland.
1984	BDP wins a majority in national elections, and Sir Kitumile Masire is reelected president.

1985	Botswana reports its first AIDS case.
1985 and 1986	South African army carries out raids on Gaborone, killing 15 civilians they allege were African National Congress "terrorists."
1988	Pope John Paul II visits.
1989	Soda ash plant at Sowa Salt Pan begins production.
1991	Unity Dow wins a constitutional court case that eventually allows children to become Botswana citizens through either their mother's or their father's birthright under the amended Citizenship Act of 1995.
1994	BDP captures 53 percent of the vote, and Masire is reelected as president. The ritual murder of a 14 year-old girl leads to social unrest, police and BDF intervention, and the temporary closing of the University of Botswana. The Directorate of Corruption and Economic Crime is established after the exposure of corruption among top-level civil servants.
1995	Government begins the relocation of thousands of Sarwa from the Central Kalahari Game Reserve. An outbreak of contagious bovine pleura pneumonia forces Botswana to destroy 320,000 head of cattle. The land tribunal is established to hear complaints arising from land allocations under the Tribal Land Boards.
1997	Constitutional amendment limits the president to two five-year terms in office. The voting age is lowered from 21 to 18.
1998	Botswana Congress Party is established after a split in the BNF. Unity Dow is appointed as the first woman High Court judge.
1999	BDF wins a majority after national elections. Festus Mogae elected president of Botswana after Sir Kitumile Masire announces his retirement. Border disputes occur between Namibia and Botswana

over a small amount of land in the Caprivi Strip. The trans-Kalahari highway between Gaborone and Namibia is completed.

2000   Botswana literacy increases to 72 percent. Botswana Television is launched.

2001   Tsodilo Hills are declared a World Heritage Site.

2002   United States Peace Corps returns to Botswana after a hiatus of five years to assist with the AIDS epidemic. Sarwa residents of the Kalahari take the government to court to protest alleged forced relocation. Their case is dismissed on a technicality.

2003   First female paramount chief, Mosadi Seboko, assumes the highest-ranking office of the Lete people.

2004   President Mogae wins a second term by a landslide vote. Botswana's HIV infection rate falls slightly, but enough to remove it as the top country in the world for HIV infection rates.

2005   Kenneth Good, an Australian professor of political science at the University of Botswana and long-time resident, is deported as an "undesirable inhabitant or visitor" under the Botswana Immigration Act after publishing works critical of the functioning of Botswana's democracy.

Pula is devalued by 12 percent in a move to control imports, promote exports, and combat rising inflation. This follows a 7.5 percent devaluation in 2004.

Kaone Kario of Maun is crowned Nokia's "Face of Africa."

Botswana government officials remove almost all of the remaining Basarwa residents from the Central Kalahari Game Reserve.

1

Introduction

The Republic of Botswana, approximately the size of Texas or France with an area of 231,803 square miles, is one of the most sparsely populated countries in Africa, with just 1.6 million inhabitants. The capital city, Gaborone (pronounced HA-bore-own), situated in the southeastern part of the country less than 20 miles from the South African border, was built from scratch at independence in 1966.[1] It is now home to 10 percent of the nation's population, while another 50 percent live within 60 miles of the capital. An additional 30 percent of the population lives along the eastern side of the country, clustered around the towns of Mahalapye, Palapye, Serowe, Selibe-Phikwe, and Francistown.

Although the total population is small, the growth rate has been among the highest in the world, averaging 4.7 percent per year during the decade from 1971 to 1981. Major improvements in heath care and village sanitation are among the principal reasons for the tripling in population since 1966, although in recent years the growth rate has declined to around 3 percent as families have begun to transition from rural to urban conditions where changes in the social and economic status of women have resulted in increased desire for and access to family-planning methods. Botswana also has the highest incidence of HIV/AIDS in the world, which affects more than 35 percent of the adult population. This has contributed to declining growth rates by dramatically lowering life expectancies from 71 years in 1991 to around 46 years today. Unless conditions change, the high HIV/AIDS infection rates are likely to severely diminish the economic gains of past decades by redirecting government resources and money to the care of HIV/AIDS victims.

Entrance to the Riverwalk, one of many modern shopping malls in Gaborone. Photo courtesy of Mike Main.

Economic growth rates for Botswana have also been among the highest in the world. Beginning in the early 1970s, when the first diamond mines became operational, the basis of the nation's economic wealth has shifted from an agrarian economy centered around animal husbandry to one heavily dependent on diamonds and other minerals, which now constitute more than 80 percent of the nation's export earnings. Agriculture, however, continues to provide some livelihood for more than three-quarters of the country's population. Forty years of peaceful parliamentary democracy have nurtured the impressive economic gains by creating a political climate of wise fiscal management and capital investment. As a result, since its independence in 1966, Botswana has transformed itself from one of the poorest nations on earth to a middle-income country with one of the highest sustained rates of economic growth in the world, boasting a per capita gross domestic product (GDP) of $7,800 in 2001. Much of this wealth has been invested in improvements in infrastructure, including the following:

1. The expansion of the national road system to link all the major urban areas in the country by tarmac
2. The extension of safe drinking-water facilities to almost all towns and villages
3. The expansion of health clinics to most rural areas and increased availability of both public and private hospitals in major centers
4. The expansion of the countries educational system to include more than 700 primary and 200 junior and senior secondary education facilities

With free elections held since 1966, Botswana is Africa's oldest multi-party democracy, with universal franchise for all citizens older than the age

Administrative districts and major urban areas, villages, and administrative centers.

of 18. In the decades since independence, this political stability has sustained one of the fastest rates of economic growth in the world over the past two decades (9.2 percent according to the World Bank), with a real GDP rate of 6.9 percent a year and a per capita growth rate stable at about 4.3 percent of annual growth. Rapid economic growth, combined with wise fiscal policies, has enabled Botswana to achieve one of the highest standards of living of any sub-Saharan country. Unusual for Africa is the low incidence of government corruption, which the Berlin-based Transparency International rates as the lowest in sub-Saharan Africa, just below Belgium on a ranking of 90 countries worldwide. Since independence, Botswana has consistently invested its resources to better the lives of its citizens through the extension of health, education, transportation, and communications infrastructure to all parts of the country.

Botswana is surrounded by countries plagued by civil unrest and war. First, the long Rhodesian war at times spilled over into Botswana. Second, the apartheid situation in South Africa affected the country in a variety of direct as well as subtle ways. In the 1980s, for instance, the South African Defense Force launched a number of military raids into Gaborone, setting off car bombs and murdering innocent Tswana as well as refugees, even though Botswana has always tried to maintain a stance of political freedom and neutrality. In addition, the governing of Namibia by South Africa through a discredited mandate from the League of Nations after the end of World War I fostered decades of generalized instability along the permeable northwestern border of Botswana. This was exacerbated by the South African army's recruitment of Khoisan (Sarwa or Bushman) trackers and guides to be used against Angolan troops and Namibian freedom fighters; some of these trackers came from western Botswana, and many more had relatives on both sides of these borders. Civil war in southern Angola, exacerbated by military operations by South African units covertly supported by the U.S. government, along with civil war in Zimbabwe, contributed to the influx of refugees into Botswana in the 1970s and 1980s. At one time or another, the refugee "camps" outside Francistown provided a primitive haven from political persecution and warfare for people from all the neighboring countries.

THE NATURAL ENVIRONMENT

A landlocked country, Botswana straddles the Tropic of Capricorn in the southern African region. It is bordered by Zimbabwe to the northeast, South Africa to the south and southeast, and Namibia to the west and north. While the country supports considerable environmental diversity, the Kalahari Desert (or Kgalagadi, in Tswana), which blankets almost 80 percent of the country, is composed of fairly monotonous, undulating, grass- and brush-covered plains with little physiographic relief. In contrast, papyrus-bordered lagoons and rivers in the Okavango Delta, the largest inland delta in the world, cover over 6,000 square miles in the northern part of the country. To the east of the Okavango, the Linyati and Chobe river systems empty into the Zambezi River just above Victoria Falls. This area, which includes the Moremi Game Reserve and Chobe National Park, supports some of the largest herds of elephant and other game in Africa. Diseases such as malaria, bilharzia, and sleeping sickness, along with low soil fertility, have historically limited agricultural settlement in this area.

Elephants *(ditlou)* drinking at a water hole at Savuti in the Chobe National Park. Botswana has some of the largest herds of elephants in Africa, and, unlike many places, their numbers are increasing, not decreasing. Game viewing, one of Botswana's major tourist attractions, brings significant income to rural areas.

As one moves southward, rainfall gradually decreases from a high of 800 millimeters per annum along the Chobe River in the north to a low of approximately 250 millimeters per annum in the Gemsbok National Park on the southwestern border of the country where windblown sand dunes slowly drift across a dry desert landscape interspersed with brush and grasses. Along the more heavily populated eastern side of the country, tertiary cycles of erosion have removed the overlying mantle of Kalahari sands, exposing more fertile and better-watered soils over a variety of geological substrates that include, near the capital of Gaborone, exposures of some of the oldest rocks on earth. These hardveld soils support most of the country's population.

The country's soils were formed through the interaction of four main factors: the parent rock from which the soil was derived, the relief of the land as it affects the drainage characteristics along hillsides and valleys, past climatic cycles that have facilitated or retarded weathering of parent materials, and time. Some of the ironstone and lacustrine formations found in central and eastern Botswana, for instance, reflect wetter climatic conditions in the past quite different from those of the present. The principal physiographic units of Botswana soils reflect the interactions of these factors.

This unusual grove of baobab trees in Nxai Pan National Park is a tourist attraction for those wishing to view game in the Makgadikgadi pans. The grove is little changed from when the famous artist Thomas Baines painted it in 1861 in a work titled *The Sleeping Five*.

The most widespread physiographic zone in the country is the sandveld, which is composed of windblown arenosols or sands that cover more than three-quarters of the country to the west and south of the Okavango Delta. The second physiographic zone includes extensive deposits of alluvial soils found throughout the Okavango Delta, the Linyati and Chobe Rivers, and along the Boteti River, which drains from the Okavango eastward into the Makgadikgadi pans, where it evaporates. The Makgadikgadi basin also contains lacustrine evaporates produced by the drying out of an enormous Pleistocene lake that covered an area the size of Lake Victoria approximately 40,000 years ago. Most of the area is unsuitable for agricultural settlement because the grasslands of this unit are of low nutritional value for livestock. However, the opening of a mine to exploit reserves of soda ash and salt extracted from the pans has created jobs and a new town—Sowa Town. A local rail line links the town with the main north-to-south rail line running from South Africa through Gaborone and Francistown to Zimbabwe.

The final zone, known as the hardveld, contains highly variable soils and physiographic subunits that include more fertile regosols, luvisols, and lixisols with better water-retaining characteristics than the arenosols of the Kalahari. The hardveld can be divided into two regions on the basis of the dominant tree vegetation, with mopane and mopane/acacia woodlands covering much of the east-central and northeastern hardveld, while a more mixed cover of acacia bushveld, void of mopane, is found in the southeast.

The availability of drinking water, along with differences in annual rainfall and vegetation cover, shapes the contemporary settlement patterns of Botswana. The Kalahari Desert in the center of the country is not so much a true desert of blowing sand dunes as it is a "thirstland" where supplies of surface water are scarce. Before the advent of boreholes, many of which reach hundreds of feet below the surface before encountering water, drinking water was available only in the rainy summer months at seasonally filled pans; in winter, animals and humans sometimes had only the moisture squeezed from wild Tsama melons to tide them through to the next rainy season. The average annual rainfall in the Ghanzi and Kgalagadi districts along the western side of the desert is too low (400 millimeters or less) for sustainable agriculture, and even with the advent of well-capitalized cattle posts with permanent boreholes, populations still average less than 0.2 persons per square mile.

Even though little rain falls over the Kalahari, the moisture-retaining characteristics of the fine-grained sand supports a mantle of grass, brush, and woodlands that sustains large herds of zebra, eland, wildebeest, springbok, gemsbok, buffalo, elephant, ostrich, and other wildlife. Small numbers of cattle and goats are also kept there. Game cordon fences built in the 1960s now control the movements of wild herds across the central Kalahari to the Makgadikgadi pans in an attempt to combat periodic outbreaks of game-borne diseases, such as foot-and-mouth disease, that periodically threaten the country's livestock industry.

The eastern hardveld, with its fertile soils and streams, supports 80 percent of Botswana's population—most centered around the major cities and towns of Gaborone, Lobatse, Kanye, Mahalapye, Palapye, Serowe, and Francistown. While privately owned land concessions dating from the colonial period are found in the Tuli block and along a narrow strip of the country's border with South Africa, most farming lands and cattle posts in the hardveld are on communally held land, with access controlled at the local level through a national system of Village Land Boards. Overgrazing, limited soil fertility, and soil erosion hamper efforts by small-scale farmers to produce adequate food. As a result, through the 1970s and 1980s the government has attempted to improve the sustainability of herding through the commercialization and privatization of communal area livestock production. In 1975, the Tribal Land Grazing Land Policy created managed, leasehold ranches in an attempt to improve and sustain better range conditions around boreholes in the Kalahari. More recently, fencing of some communal areas in the hardveld under the Agriculture Act of 1995 have resulted in further land privatization. While this can result in "good" range management, it is detrimental to the livelihood of those disenfranchised from the land through a lack of capital or political support.

PEOPLES AND LANGUAGES

Fossilized remains of some of the earliest ancestors of humankind, *Australopithecines* and *Homo erectus,* have been discovered in neighboring South Africa, so it is no surprise that stone tools covering more than 2 million years of human prehistory are common finds in Botswana as well. By 5,000 years ago, it is certain that the ancestors of present-day Khoisan-speaking peoples were the only inhabitants of the country. Today Botswana is a nation of more than 20 ethnic groups who speak languages belonging to two of the four major language families of Africa: Khoisan and the Bantu, a sub-branch of the Congo-Kordofanian family.

The Bantu language Setswana, spoken as a first language by more than 80 percent of the population, is the dominant national language; English, which is widely spoken, is the official language used in government documents.[2] The name "Botswana" means "the land of the Setswana-speaking peoples," reflecting the fact that most inhabitants speak a dialect of Setswana as their mother tongue. More than 20 other Bantu languages are also spoken in Botswana. These can be divided into two linguistic subdivisions: eastern and western Bantu. Speakers of western Bantu languages live in the northwestern sandveld, west of the Okavango Delta. They include the Herero, Mbanderu, and Mbukushu, with relatives in Namibia and Angola, as well as the Yeyi, who live in the Okavango and the neighboring Caprivi Strip of Namibia. Eighteenth-century oral traditions describe the arrival of Yeyi farmers and fishermen among the Khoisan of the Okavango as being like "a scattering of flies across a milk-pail" as they migrated southward from the upper Chobe River region. In more recent times, this dispersion may have been a response to slave raiding in southern Angola, but the presence of clicks in the Yeyi language argues for longer-term interactions with Khoisan speakers. Archaeological finds of pottery and metal artifacts dating to the last half of the first millennium C.E. in the Tsodilo Hills west of the Okavango Delta suggest that many oral traditions, including those of the Yeyi and Mbukushu, may have telescoped a longer chronology of agropastoral occupation than is currently retained in historical memory. The Mbukushu and Yeyi are two of the few groups in Botswana that use corporate matrilineages. In such matrilineal societies, chieftainship is hereditary through the female line so that the chieftainship is passed to the chief's sister's eldest son. Both groups are agriculturalists and fishermen whose chiefs, acting through their ancestors, are renowned for their rainmaking abilities.

The oral traditions of Herero and Mbanderu pastoralists who live interspersed among the Mbukushu, Khoisan, and Tswana to the south and west of the Okavango and into Namibia relate how their split from the Mbandu

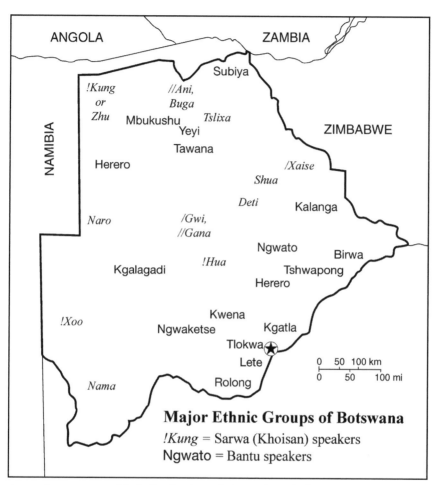

ANGOLA ZAMBIA

Subiya

!Kung *//Ani,*
or *Buga*
Zhu Mbukushu *Tslixa*
Yeyi

ZIMBABWE

Tawana

NAMIBIA

Herero

/Xaise

Shua

Deti Kalanga

Naro */Gwi,*
//Gana

Ngwato
Birwa
!Hua Tshwapong
Kgalagadi Herero

Kwena
!Xoo Kgatla
Ngwaketse
Tlokwa
Lete
0   50 100 km
0   50   100 mi
Nama Rolong

Major Ethnic Groups of Botswana
!Kung = Sarwa (Khoisan) speakers
Ngwato = Bantu speakers

Approximate geographical distribution of the major ethnic groups in Botswana. Regions are ethnically heterogeneous, however, and in most villages and towns one can expect to find individuals belonging to almost every ethnic group.

occurred in the seventeenth century as Tswana cattle raiding from the south caused turmoil. Today, smaller groups of Herero also live more widely scattered in rural communities along the Boteti River around Rakops, in Mahalapye in the eastern hardveld, as well as in Pilane near Mochudi and at Dikgatlhong in the Kweneng district in the southeast. They traditionally practice a bilateral form of descent, unusual for pastoralists in Africa. Although cattle are inherited through the mother's line (in fact, in the past, only women were allowed to milk cows), other beliefs, rights, and obligations pass through the father's line.

The remaining Bantu-speaking peoples in Botswana belong to the eastern Bantu subdivision and include, from north to south, the Subiya (in Tswana their language is called Sesubiya, but they call it Chikwahane), who live in the Chobe district, with a center at Kasane; the Tawana (an offshoot of the Ngwato subgroup of Tswana) with a capital at Maun in Ngamiland; and the Kalanga, relatives of the Shona of Zimbabwe, who are concentrated in the northern portions of Central and North-East districts, with a center at Francistown. Their language, Ikalanga, is the most widely spoken language in the country after Setswana and English.

The Tswana language is used as the principal medium of instruction in almost all primary schools during the first two years, and it is a compulsory subject for students in public and most private schools. In addition, it is the dominant medium of communication at the district administrative level. In the later years of primary school and in secondary and university education, English is the principal language used for instruction and exams. The Tswana language is closely related to Sotho. Both are widely spoken in neighboring South Africa, where there are twice as many Tswana speakers as in Botswana. The origin of the main Tswana dynasties—Hurutshe, Kwena, and Kgatla—is associated in oral tradition with the breakup of the Phofu dynasty in the western Transvaal of South Africa around 500 years ago. Drought is said to be the principal reason for this fragmentation, although political competition between junior brothers is also mentioned.

The Ngwato, the most populous of the Tswana-speaking groups, dominate the Central district, with a capital at Serowe. It is popularly believed that there are only a few true Ngwato, with the rest made up of different tribes that were forcefully incorporated into the Ngwato by Tshekedi Khama in the early or mid-twentieth century. A large proportion of the population of the Ngwato capital of Serowe, for instance, is made up of Kalaka or Kalanga people. Mahalapye has a large number of Herero, Xhosa, and other small groups, while Palapye is home to Talaote and Tswapong, among others. Other Tswana-speaking groups found in southeastern Botswana include the Kgatla, with a capital at Mochudi in Kgatleng district; the Kwena, with a capital at Molepolole in Kweneng district; and the Ngwaketse, with a capital at Kanye in the southern Kweneng district. Smaller Tswana-speaking groups include the Lete in Ramotswa; the Tlokwa in Tlokweng on the outskirts of Gaborone; the Rolong, who are concentrated along the southern border with South Africa; and the Hurutshe, who live in scattered small settlements in the Central and Northeast districts among the Kalanga and Ngwato. The Kgalagadi, who live scattered in small communities and cattle posts in the Kalahari Desert, speak a more divergent dialect of Tswana. This, along with their oral traditions, suggests that they have the greatest antiquity among Tswana speakers in Botswana.

Afrikaans, a language locally evolved from Dutch, is spoken around Ghanzi in Ngamiland in the northwest of the country. In 1897, the British government ceded the area around Ghanzi to Cecil Rhodes and the British South Africa Company, with little consideration for the wishes of the local people. The land was allocated to a small group of Afrikaans-speaking white farmers or Boers who trekked in their ox wagons across the Kalahari to develop freehold farms. Their descendants continue to live in this area today.

The non-Bantu Khoisan family of languages includes speakers of click languages belonging to both Khoi and San subgroupings. While Khoisan languages share the use of clicks as consonants and many elements of vocabulary, they are quite distinct from one another grammatically—an indication of the time depth that separates the histories of the various groups. Speakers of San languages include the Zhu/oasi or !Kung found in the far northwest of the country and across its borders in neighboring Namibia and Angola. Most of the Khoisan speakers belonging to the Khoi subgroup are concentrated in the central and western Kalahari and the Okavango Delta and are interspersed more widely among Bantu speakers in the eastern hardveld. They include the Nama, found in the western Kalahari and Ghanzi districts; the Buga and //ani in the Okavango; the G/wi and //Gana in the central Kalahari; and the Deti, Denesana, Shua, and Hietshware, who occupy the area from the Makgadikgadi pans eastward into the hardveld of Central district.[3]

While small numbers of Khoisan continue to live at least seasonally as hunters and gatherers, most have been assimilated into the rural cattle-post economy as herders and laborers. Although Khoisan hunters and gatherers, pejoratively known as Bushmen, are now an almost universal trope in the Western popular culture, all ethnic groups in Botswana make significant use of veld resources to sustain themselves; as a result, all have important economic and cultural ties to the wild plants and animals found in the country. Despite this, some social stigma still applies to peoples locally typed as "hunters and gatherers," even though they live side by side with their Bantu-speaking neighbors. In eastern Botswana, most Khoi are indistinguishable by economy, dress, or physical features unless they begin to speak Khoi languages. Many Khoisan languages are dying out, however, because of continuing prejudice and discrimination toward Khoisan peoples, who are called Sarwa in the Tswana language.

The discovery of rich diamond pipes in the central Kalahari in the 1960s has led to the development of new population centers at Orapa and Jwaneng. However, many of the jobs created require skills and training not easily obtainable by people living in the surrounding desert. More recently, government initiatives to resettle indigenous Khoisan speakers living in the central Kalahari have created considerable debate. From the government's point of view, it is not economically viable to provide community services such as education and health to small, dispersed populations in rural or undeveloped areas, such as the Central Kalahari Game Reserve. The government has therefore tried to encourage people to accept resettlement in less remote areas by providing them with small herds of goats and cattle for subsistence. Some international organizations have protested, arguing that it looks like forced resettlement undertaken to clear people away to make room for new diamond mines. The fact that high government officials have voiced the argument in atavistic terms has further fueled accusations of discrimination. President Festus Mogae, for instance, complained, "How can you have a Stone Age creature continue to exist in the age of computers? If the Bushmen want to survive, they must change or otherwise, like the dodo, they will perish."[4] No less atavistic, perhaps, are the comments of others who would highlight Sarwa culture as almost uniquely unchanging and static: "Diamonds, the curse of modern Africa, were discovered under their hunting grounds and, to President Mogae, *they are worth a great deal more than the human treasures of a culture lasting 10 millennia or more.*"[5] Surely, no culture has "lasted" substantially unchanged for 10,000 years.

During the 1970s, 1980s, and 1990s, wars of liberation and battles against apartheid brought many refugees to Botswana who sought asylum from political repression and racial intolerance in South Africa. Many became citizens, further contributing to Botswana's diversity and reputation for political freedom. More specialized languages familiar to segments of the population include slang languages such as *Tsotsitaal,* which is a mixture of Afrikaans and other Bantu languages. A "*Tsotsi*" is a colloquial term for a criminal or thief, and this street language had its origins in the youth gangs of Johannesburg and other large South African cities. During the 1980s, *Tsotsi* gangs claimed to be resisting apartheid by "redistributing wealth." Men returning from stints as migrant laborers in South Africa spread the language to Botswana, where it was adopted by some as part of an alternative lifestyle that included particular ways of walking, dress, dance, and music. *Fanagalo,* another hybrid language, has become a lingua franca for mine workers in Johannesburg and Pretoria; it was also introduced to Botswana by returning migrants and by individuals seeking political asylum from apartheid in the 1970s and 1980s.

POPULATION DISTRIBUTION

In the nineteenth century, Tswana communities were organized into a tripartite settlement pattern of towns surrounded by farming lands and, at a greater distance, cattle posts and hunting grounds. Two hundred years ago, these precolonial towns were some of the largest in Africa, often occupied by more than 10,000 inhabitants. As the Rev. John Campbell, an early missionary commissioned by the London Missionary Society to undertake exploratory travels into the interior of South Africa, described them in 1813,

> All at once we had a full view of Latakkoo, lying in a beautiful valley. The town being divided into a great many districts [wards], standing a little distance from each other, makes it cover a great deal of ground, perhaps five miles in circumference.... [W]e were much pleased to see fields enclosed with hedges.[6]

The population of these large villages fluctuated seasonally as people moved out to surrounding satellite homesteads and cattle posts to tend to planting, harvesting, and herding. This historical preference for "urban" living, even in a country so sparsely populated, continues today with more than 80 percent of the country's population living in towns of more than 10,000 inhabitants. Nonetheless, while more and more Tswana are building their homes in urban areas such as Gaborone and Francistown, most maintain connections with their home village *(ko gae)* by keeping a second residence there. Relationships between city and home village are further strengthened by marriages *(lenyalo)*, which usually take place in the home village, and funerals, as most people also prefer to be buried in their home village.

Modern urbanization has come about in a variety of ways, including the building of new towns at mining centers such as Orapa, Jwaneng, and Selibe-Phikwe; the growth of existing towns, especially the major centers of Gaborone, Lobatse, and Francistown; and the rapid growth of former villages, such as Molepolole, Kanye, Serowe, and Palapye, into towns. Six hundred miles of rail line along the eastern side of the country add to the transport infrastructure, while a digital telephone network links all but the most remote of villages.

As a counterpoint to the growth of urban centers, a second population trend has been the dispersal of people into parts of the country that were formerly uninhabited. This has been made possible with the drilling of deep boreholes that have allowed cattle posts to expand into the drier parts of the country. This rural migration was facilitated by the expansion of the country's national road network from just seven miles of tarmac at independence to more than 3,000 miles today; upgraded gravel roads and maintained tracks cover an additional 12,000 miles, while sandy "tracks" link even the most remote cattle posts with the national grid. All villages with a population of more than 100 are now connected to the national transportation grid. One can thus move throughout the country on well-maintained tarmac roads that include the trans-Kalahari route from Gaborone through Ghanzi to Gobabis in Namibia and the north-to-south route that runs from Gaborone to Francistown along the rail line and then turns west across the Makgadikgadi pans to Maun and Shakawe on the Okavango Delta and to Kasane on the Chobe River.

Since independence, government expenditures to upgrade roads throughout the country reflect not only an emphasis on improving the economic infrastructure of the country but also a reinforcement of cultural values as migration trends that have dispersed friends and family across widely spaced towns and villages are counterbalanced by the frequency with which people will travel sometimes large distances to visit. It is not uncommon for young people to travel 500 or 600 miles over a long weekend to visit friends and relatives in other cities. Good roads, private bus services, and ubiquitous pay-per-destination hitchhiking all facilitate easy movement throughout the country.[7]

A cultural emphasis on travel and mobility is further attested to by the heavy demand for low-interest government loans by civil servants for the purchase of cars and trucks. According to figures from the U.S. Federal Highway Administration, in 1996 southern Africa had by far the highest rate of vehicle ownership in Africa. South Africa led with 120 registered vehicles per 1,000 people, followed by Botswana with 55. If one factors out the large (and comparatively wealthy) white population of South Africa,

Botswana has a favorable business climate for the small entrepreneur. This defensive driving school takes advantage of the fact that the country has one of the highest rates of car ownership per capita in Africa. The country also has one of the highest automobile accident death rates on the continent, creating a demand for defensive driving schools. Photo courtesy of Mike Main.

which accounts for a high percentage of owned vehicles, then comparisons with the figures for the largely African ownership in Botswana would be much closer. In comparison, the highest rates of vehicle ownership in West Africa are found in Ghana, Nigeria, and Senegal, all with just 9 vehicles per 1,000 inhabitants. The fatality rates for motor vehicle accidents in Botswana are also the highest on the continent, at 31 deaths per 1,000 people.

Cities

Apart from Gaborone and Francistown, the major urban centers in Botswana have grown from the capitals of the traditional Tswana nations: Mochudi, Molepolole, Serowe, Kanye, Palapye, Maun, Kasane, and Shoshong. In addition to the district capitals, the other principal towns are Lobatse, Ghanzi, Palapye, and Tonota.[8] Others emerged during the colonial period as trading centers along the Cape-to-Salisbury (Harare) rail line built in the 1890s. Francistown, the country's second-largest city with a population of around 90,000, began in the 1870s as a gold mining camp, one of the first in southern Africa. Gaborone, the capital, was built from scratch in the 1960s on British Crown land technically controlled by the queen. The city is named after *Kgosi* (King) Gaborone, who led the Tlokwa *morafe* ("nation") into the area in the 1880s. This "neutral" site was chosen so as not to favor any single *morafe* by building the capital in its traditional territory. It was also chosen

A view of central Gaborone with the Parliament building in the right foreground. Orapa House, the Debswana (DeBeers/ Botswana) diamond-sorting facility, is the tall building in the middle background. Photo courtesy of Mike Main.

because of its strategic location next to the rail line, its nearness to South Africa, and, most important, its closeness to a major source of water. Laid out around the remains of a small colonial outpost that consisted of a fort, a prison, a post office, and expatriate housing, the small village has become one of the fastest-growing cities in the world and is now home to more than 200,000 people. Originally designed as a series concentric circles around a city center, much like the plan of a traditional village, the city has a number of widely spaced centers surrounded by dense urban housing and high-rise office buildings interspersed with small self-help and low-cost housing units that were characteristic of Gaborone's first stage of development in the 1960s and 1970s. New towns have also sprung up around mining ventures: Selibe-Phikwe, servicing the copper mine in Northeast district; Sowa city, the site of a soda ash mining plant on the Makgadikgadi pans; and the diamond towns of Orapa and Jwaneng. All these centers have been the focus for in-migration from rural areas.

EDUCATION

Education for young people in Botswana goes back to the traditional initiation schools termed *bojale* for girls and *bogwera* for boys. These schools, which lasted for many months, taught young people the responsibilities of adulthood, respect for elders and royalty, the virtues of obedience, and their rights and obligations in society. Traditional education included learning their history through praise poems and the teaching of acceptable behavior through games, riddles, puzzles, and proverbs; the fundamentals of Tswana religious beliefs and cosmology were also discussed. While such initiation rites were central to Tswana culture, perhaps because of the practice of male circumcision and the sexual instruction that took place, early missionaries perceived them as a threat to their authority and worked hard to ban what they saw as an indoctrination of young people "in all that is filthy, in all that is deceitful and unrighteous, and in all that is blasphemous and soul-destroying."[9]

Missionaries, the first and perhaps most renowned of whom was David Livingstone, started the first formal schools. Livingstone built a small school in the 1840s at his mission site at Kolobeng about 15 miles west of present-day Gaborone. As part of his missionary project, he, along with his father-in-law, Robert Moffat, translated the Bible into Setswana. This was completed in 1857. Apart from first-millennium C.E. Christian texts in Ethiopia, this was the first translation of the Bible into a sub-Saharan African language. Ironically, while Moffat, Livingstone, and other early missionaries were drawn from social backgrounds that emphasized labor over scripture, many Tswana still considered that early mission education was too centered on "reading, writing, and scripture instead of building, carpentry or any other practical subject." One of the unintended consequences was that a relatively high proportion of women were educated, in part because parents, eager to please the missionaries, sent their daughters to school but kept their sons at home where they provided more practical labor at the cattle post. Women were particularly attracted to the church because, according to some observers, "it raised them to equality with their husbands."[10] Other early followers (*badumedi,* "those who agree") were drawn in disproportionate numbers from the marginal and disempowered. These included not only serfs and social outcasts but also second sons and junior elite who had little authority in the traditional political structure.

As local evangelists were trained, mission schools expanded into other parts of the country. Tswana *dikgosi* (kings/chiefs), welcomed the missionaries because it was believed that their presence would provide some protection from attacks by neighboring Boers in South Africa. At the same time, the *dikgosi* generally made it their policy to allow only one missionary society to work in their territories because they (or their missionary advisers) feared the potential schisms that religious pluralism could bring. From the first, there were also concerns that missionaries were undercutting the traditional bases of Tswana society, which rested on spiritual as well as material foundations. Because of the Protestant orientation of early British missionaries with the London Missionary Society and, slightly later, the Hermannsburg Lutherans, the Roman Catholic Church did not gain a foothold in the country until the 1920s, when a Catholic mission was opened at Kgale Hill outside Gaborone. A primary school built there later became the first secondary school in the country—Saint Joseph's College. This school has produced a number of prominent leaders of Botswana, including the former vice president, the late Peter Mmusi. Missions also put out the first newspapers in Botswana published in Setswana, such as *Mahoko a Bechwana* (News of Batswana), published by the London Missionary Society from Moffat's station at Kuruman.[11]

PUBLIC EDUCATION

Basic school education is free for all citizens of the country through the first 12 years, from Standard 1 through Form 5. English is the recommended medium of instruction from Standard 2 (second grade) onward. While this accounts for a high literacy rate in Botswana, it is also true that access to primary education remains difficult for many who live in remote villages and cattle posts. In these areas, parents have to send their children to larger towns and villages for schooling. Even when living with relatives, the cost of boarding often makes schooling prohibitive for these parents; boarding also removes much-needed labor from the farmlands and cattle posts. As a result, in rural areas a significant number of people still cannot read or write. After completing Standard 7 and passing a national exam with English and Tswana components, students are awarded a Standard 7, or Primary School Leaving Examination, Certificate. Admission to secondary school education was formerly dependent on the pass level of a student on the Standard 7 exam. More recent initiatives have resulted in automatic promotion through Form 3, which the government has now set as the basic standard of education for every student.

The secondary school system is divided into two tiers. The first, Junior Secondary School, generally takes three years, after which a Junior Certificate exam is taken. Results on this standardized exam control access to a Senior Secondary School where the last two years of education are taken. At independence, there were seven secondary schools in the country that accommodated both Junior and Senior Certificate (General Certificate of Education) students. Today there are more than 27 Senior Secondary Schools for Forms 4 and 5, and every large town has a Community Junior Secondary School. At completion of their secondary school education, students must pass the Botswana General Certificate of Secondary Education as a prerequisite for admission to the university.

There are a number of training opportunities open to secondary school graduates who do not go on to university. These include vocational training

Primary-grade schoolchildren in their school uniforms lining up to wash their hands at one of the school taps. A typical classroom is in the background.

centers that provide three-year certificates in a broad variety of professional, technical, engineering, and business studies. Entry requirements consist of a minimum of a C pass on the Junior Certificate plus working experience in the area to be studied. Brigade centers in many parts of the country offer additional educational opportunities in trades such as agriculture, auto mechanics, building, and carpentry. These courses are especially useful for individuals whose Junior Certificate results prevent them from attending a senior secondary school.

The University of Botswana, formerly the University of Botswana, Lesotho and Swaziland, offers certificates, diplomas, and B.A. and B.S. degrees in the humanities, sciences, business, social sciences, engineering, and law. One-year postgraduate diplomas are offered in secondary education, library and information sciences, and education counseling. Master's degrees are also offered in a variety of fields, including the humanities and social sciences, sciences, education and business, and engineering and technology. Doctoral degrees are available in higher education and are under review for some other fields. University education is in practice free for qualified citizens, with the current student body almost equally divided between men and women.[12]

The University of Botswana, with an annual enrollment of over 12,000 students, including 1,000 postgraduates, supplies the country with much of the trained technical and social workforce to create, manage, and maintain the rapid development the country has experienced since independence. Like many other things in Botswana, the construction of the university was a community project *(ipeleng),* with significant funding coming from donations through projects such as *motho le motho ka kgomo* ("Everyone bring a cow"), where every individual who could afford to was asked to contribute a cow or cash equivalent to be used in the construction and upgrading of the university. Some people even contributed agricultural products such as sorghum and maize/corn, all of which are recognized in the University of Botswana coat of arms.

Botswana supports a number of nonformal education efforts, including the National Literacy Program initiated in 1980. The adult literacy rate is now approximately 70 percent, with women scoring slightly higher than men. Other programs include distance education initiatives to enable students and citizens with special needs to participate in Junior Certificate, General Certificate of Education, and Special Education programs so that they can become productive members of society. Over the next decade, a new government initiative, titled "Vision 2016" or "A Framework for a Long Term Vision for Botswana," plans to provide citizens with a choice of continued education, either in academic or in vocational and technical fields, with full access to the Internet and other communication media.[13]

RESOURCES, OCCUPATION, AND ECONOMY

Botswana is a dry land with low and unreliable rainfall. As a result, the livestock sector has always dominated the agricultural economy because herds are more resilient to the droughts that affect the country with regularity. Before 1970, livestock formed the economic backbone of the country, accounting for a vast majority of Botswana's export revenues. Although diamonds and copper now dominate the export economy, cattle are still important economically as a store of wealth and a source of milk, meat, and hides for most of the population. Europe has been one of the important importers of Botswana beef, which picked up in the 1970s as abattoirs were opened in Lobatse, Maun, and Francistown. One of the major constraints to cattle export has been periodic outbreaks of foot-and-mouth disease that have required strong measures, including continuously manned cordon fences that stretch across the country, to control it. The agricultural sector still provides the largest source of jobs in the country not only for farmers and herders but also for veterinarians, abattoir workers, and retailers. Unreliable rainfall and growing job opportunities in other sectors of the economy have impacted the agricultural sector, and there is some evidence that subsistence farming is on the decline.

With the opening of the diamond mines in Central District in 1970, the wealth-generating sector of the economy has shifted from agropastoralism to the mining sector, which now accounts for about 70 percent of export revenues. Revenues from the "clean" diamond industry have transformed Botswana from one of the poorest countries in the world to a middle-range economy that is one of the most stable on the continent. The country is now the largest exporter of gem-quality diamonds in the world, with an annual output of well over 17 million carats. The Botswana government and the DeBeers Mining Company own the mines jointly. Other minerals that occur in economic quantities include copper, nickel, and soda ash. Large deposits of coal also exist in the Serowe area, but the cost of transporting it through South Africa or Namibia to regional or overseas markets has so far been prohibitive, although coal is used to fuel the country's electrical generating plant at Morupule just outside Palapye.

Recent statistics indicate that tourism is now the third-highest foreign revenue earner after mining and cattle. A large part of this revenue is generated from within southern Africa, as tourists from South Africa and Botswana have begun to take advantage of the easier access to wildlife areas afforded by improved roads, lodges, safe water supplies, and other infrastructure. In addition, widespread use of Global Positioning Systems (GPS) has made it easier for tourists, both foreign and local alike, to travel to remote areas without the necessity of hiring expensive guides. Botswana has some of the largest national parks and herds of wild game in Africa, and wildlife management areas, parks, and reserves account for around 40 percent of the country's surface. Tourists are able to enjoy a variety of experiences that include photographic as well as hunting and trophy safaris. The main areas of attraction are located in the northern half of the country and include the Tsodilo Hills (a World Heritage rock art site), the Okavango Delta, the Moremi Game Reserve, Chobe National Park, the Makgadikgadi salt pans, and the Makgadikgadi Game Reserve. Smaller or less frequently visited parks include the Gaborone Game Reserve, Mokolodi Nature Sanctuary, the Khama Rhino Sanctuary, the Khustse Game Reserve in the central Kalahari, and the Gemsbok National Park in the southwestern corner of the country. In addition to its wildlife experiences, Botswana's political and economic stability make it an attractive and secure venue for tourists. More than 27,000 people are now directly employed in the tourism industry, which generates 70 percent of the jobs in rural areas where other sources of work and income are scarce. Although the government is largely responsible for the promotion and advertising of the industry, these costs are being increasingly shared by the private sector, which manages a number of private safari companies and wildlife reserves. Attractions such as the rock art at Tsodilo and medieval stone-walled ruins belonging to the Zimbabwe culture increasingly draw tourists interested in culture as well as those interested in wildlife and nature.

GOVERNMENT

Traditional Roots

In the nineteenth century, Tswana communities were governed through an institution known as the *kgotla,* where men discussed matters of economic or political importance to the family or community. Large towns were divided into segments called wards, which represented the major ethnic and family divisions within the community. Each segment usually arranged its houses around a central animal corral (kraal, *lesaka*) situated in front of the most senior homestead. These segments were in turn grouped around the most senior *kgotla,* that of the *kgosi* (king). The *kgotla,* symbolized by a semicircular fence of stout, upright logs, sometimes topped by skulls of cattle or, in the case of Shoshong, a rhinoceros skull, was located next to the central animal kraal. A specially "doctored" fire situated at the entrance had the purpose of preventing dangerous or harmful actions (such as lightning strikes) or people with personal jealousies or grudges *(baloi)* from entering the *kgotla* and interfering with its deliberations. The *kgotla* was the venue through which the chiefs *(dikgosi)*, communicated directly with their subjects, creating a some-what democratic institution that permitted (within limits) free speech while at the same time allowing the *kgosi* to test public acceptance of matters already discussed in private with his counselors and advisers. The people expect the *kgosi* to be modest, compassionate, and diligent while showing respect for tribal customs and practices in his daily life as exemplified in the often-recited proverb "*Kgosi ke kgosi ka batho*" (literally, "*kgosi* is a *kgosi* by the grace of the people").

In the past, with some exceptions (e.g., recently arrived immigrants and some lower-status commoners), the *kgotla* was open to all male members of the com-munity, with seating arrangements following the order of status or seniority. Women, minors, and unmarried men (considered as incompletely socialized beings and referred to as *Makope,* or "yellow locusts") were excluded from the deliberations.[14] Only males who were members of the dominant Tswana ethnic groups could participate in the *kgotla.* Subservient peoples, such as the Kgalagadi and Sarwa, had no right to voice an opinion or to take part in important deci-sions. Women were also excluded regardless of their ethnicity, and even in recent years some "traditional" *kgotla* meetings may be called that exclude women. Because women were often the de facto heads of households in communities where migrant labor opportunities attracted men to South Africa for work, their exclusion from the traditional *kgotla* system of governance impacted develop-ment work in the community. Although women were thus generally disenfran-chised in the traditional *kgotla* and proverbs such as "*ga di nke di etelelwa ke manamagadi pele*" ("households and nations cannot be headed by women") rein-force such notions, there are documented incidences when women have acted as regents (e.g., Queen Ntebogang Gaseitsiwe, who stood in as acting chief for *kgosi* Bathoen II of the Ngwaketse between 1924 and 1928).

Perhaps setting the stage for Botswana's later democracy, even in the early nineteenth century considerable freedom was allowed for individuals to discuss and criticize community affairs within the *kgotla,* as Campbell observed: "Such is the freedom of speech at those public meetings, that some of the captains [headmen] have said of the King, that he ... is not fit to rule over them."[15]

Almost a century and a half later, very similar criticisms made by an old man in the *kgotla* in Mochudi were broadcast over the radio when Vice President Sir Ketumile Quett Masire became president at the death of Sir Seretse Khama in 1980. More recently, another well-publicized incident occurred when the then minister of Local Government and Lands suspended *kgosi* Seepapitso IV of the Ngwaketse for "insubordination." The *morafe* requested that President Masire come to a *kgotla* meeting. During the meeting, an old man accused him of being a *mmina phiri* (literally, "one who dances the hyena"), meaning that he has a hyena as a totem and so by implication is from a junior *morafe* or origin

A *kgotla* meeting in Shoshong. The *kgotla,* identified by its semicircle of upright posts, is the political center of every Tswana community. While women may now attend these meetings, men still attend in larger numbers, organizing and seating themselves by seniority and age.

and thus not of a high enough social rank or caste to settle the dispute of an Ngwaketse king. A traditional right to freedom of expression was respected in all these cases, a right reflected in two Tswana proverbs: "*Mmualebe o a be a bua la gagwe*" ("Everyone has the right to say what he likes [in the *Kgotla*]") and "*Mafoko a kgosing a mantle otlhe*" ("Words spoken in the Kgotla are the most beautiful"). In all these cases, freedom of expression was respected, and there was no punishment for criticizing the highest government official. Another saying encapsulates this tolerance of opposing views: "*Ntwa kgolo ke ya molomo*" ("the highest form of war is dialogue").[16] The deep cultural embeddedness of such sayings helps explain why Botswana takes care to be one of the most democratic countries in the world.

At the conclusion of every *kgotla* meeting or *pitso,* the national cry *Pula, Pula* can be heard echoing through the community. Meaning "let there be rain," the cry of *Pula* resonates significantly with the inhabitants of such a dry country, and it is proclaimed at the conclusion of almost every public gathering and celebration. It is also the principal national unit of currency and is often used as a toast.

Independence

Many changes in governance occurred with independence in 1966 as Botswana adopted a modified Westminster constitutional framework that established a republic with strong executive, parliamentary, and judicial branches. Many of the postcolonial structures put in place had the effect of democratizing local government while at the same time reducing the powers of traditional, nonelected authorities such as the *dikgosi,* whose powers are now exercised mainly in local, customary courts still located at the *kgotla.* The executive branch of the government includes the president, who is head of state, and a cabinet composed of ministers appointed from members of the National Assembly or Parliament. The executive branch has control of government ministries and departments staffed by civil servants who implement government policy. Each political party selects its own president, who automatically becomes president of Botswana, after endorsement by the National Assembly, if his party wins the general election. The president has the power to appoint the secretary of the cabinet, known as the permanent secretary to the president, the speaker of the Parliament, and permanent secretaries who head the day-to-day affairs of ministries charged with specific administrative and developmental responsibilities. The president may dissolve Parliament; he may also appoint the chief justice and the commander of the Botswana Defense Force.

The National Assembly, which includes the president, is the supreme law-making body. It is composed of 40 members of parliament, one from each of the elective constituencies in the country; an additional four members are specially elected and include the attorney general and the speaker. Elective

The Botswana Parliament building, constructed in the 1960s, is typical of the "International Style" of architecture that characterized most of the early government buildings in Gaborone at independence.

constituencies are reviewed every 5 to 10 years to determine whether bound-ary changes due to population redistribution are necessary. All citizens older than the age of 18 may vote, provided they are of sound mind and have not been imprisoned for more than six months.

Where tribal or customary traditions are involved, Parliament must con-sult with another body representing more traditional interests—the *Ntlo ya Dikgosi* ("House of Chiefs")—which was initially composed of members rep-resenting the eight major Tswana *merafe* (literally, "nations"): the Rolong, Ngwato, Lete, Tlokwa, Kwena, Kgatla, Ngwaketse, and Tawana, along with seven additional members who are elected from persons holding the office of subchief in the Chobe, Francistown, Ghanzi, and Kgalagadi districts. In recent changes, the Kalaka (Kalanga) are now represented, but other groups, such as the Yeyi in the Okavango, continue to lobby for representation.

The country's electoral system is designed to take into account the input of rural communities. During the colonial period, a system of "indirect rule" through the *dikgosi* was instituted, but with independence more democratic political and administrative structures reduced the powers and functions of chiefs. One of the first changes was made with the District Councils Act of 1965, which established district councils composed of elected representatives. District commissioners (DCs), a post retained from the colonial era, head the district councils and work with the council secretary (administrative) and a council chairman/chairperson (political). The DC is expected to "supervise" the *dikgosi,* a responsibility not universally accepted by many chiefs. Other offices set in place under the DC include the District Land Boards, estab-lished in 1968 and headed by the District Officer for Lands, and the District Officer of Development, a post established in 1975. Although district land boards still report to the DC, land board secretaries (administration) and land board chairmen/chairpersons now head them. Almost all the district land boards are named after the dominant political faction in each district; for instance, the Ngwato Land Board in Serowe oversees the land affairs for Cen-tral District. But all districts, and indeed most communities, are composed of people from many different ethnic backgrounds, or *merafe,* some of whom believe their interests are not fairly represented by land boards with such "tribalized" names.

With the establishment of district land boards under the DC's office in 1968, yet another of the traditional rights (and benefits) of the *dikgosi* was taken away by government officers who make up local district development committees headed by the DC. These councils have taken over almost all the traditional functions of chieftainship, including authority to collect and dispose of stray cattle, one of the traditional sources of revenue for chiefs during the precolonial and colonial eras. District councils also have oversight of primary education and health care as well as community development projects that include roads, dams, and other public projects.

Botswana has had three presidents since independence, each of them appointed through a peaceful democratic process of elections; since 1999, terms of office are for five years, with a limit of two terms. Freedom of speech is highly respected in Botswana, and political parties have considerable freedom to critique the government both in Parliament and through independent newspapers and even street corner gatherings (sometimes referred to locally as "freedom squares"). At election time, impassioned candidates or their representatives roar out their platforms and merits through bullhorns. Voter turnout is high, with 77 percent of registered voters participating in the 1999 election. The Independent Electoral Commission administers elections, but opposition parties argue that this is not a nonpartisan body for two reasons. First, it is housed in government offices and funded by the Botswana government, which is dominated by the Botswana Democratic Party. Second, the president appoints the commissioner.

HISTORY

Prehistory

As with all countries in southern Africa, Botswana contains an abundance of Paleolithic artifacts dating back to the origins of humankind more than 2 million years ago. In some areas, such as the Makgadikgadi salt pans, the fossilized remains of prehistoric animals, some now extinct, can be found along with hand axes and spear points belonging to the Early and Middle Stone Ages that date between 2 million and 30,000 years ago. In more recent times, Botswana has become well known in the West as the home of some of the last peoples to supposedly subsist almost entirely by hunting and gathering—the Sarwa or Bushmen.[17] On the contrary, many Sarwa are nearly indistinguishable linguistically and economically from their rural, Bantu-speaking neighbors, and none rely solely on foraging for their living. Indeed, the first transitions from hunting and gathering to herding began in the Kalahari almost 2,000 years ago as the ancestors of some Sarwa began to acquire herds of sheep and cattle of their own. This processes accelerated after 500 C.E., when the first Bantu-speaking farmers and herders began to settle in northern and eastern Botswana.

Early Chiefdoms and Kingdoms

Between 700 and 1000 C.E., domestic herds of cattle, goats, and sheep increased rapidly on the dry, nutritious grasslands of eastern and northern

Botswana. As herds expanded, so did opportunities for some lineages to increase their political support by using cattle to make favorable marriages and political alliances as well as to attract followers by lending out animals in a system called *mafisa;* some Sarwa may also have been recruited to help with herd management. By the end of the first millennium c.e., control over cattle wealth resulted in the formation of some of the earliest chiefdoms in southern Africa. The introduction of trade goods from the Indian Ocean that included glass beads from India and chickens, with an ultimate origin in Indonesia, further enhanced social stratification after 700 c.e. In exchange, elephant ivory and other veld products were sent down the Limpopo valley to the Indian Ocean.

Initially, exploitation of local resources, including specularite, a form of hematite that was mixed with fat to make a sparkling hair dressing, along with iron and copper, linked emerging chiefdoms in the northern Kalahari with those on the eastern side of the country. Around 1200 c.e., however, the political economy of Botswana changed as gold began to be mined along the Limpopo and Motloutse Rivers. Political restructuring followed as new polit-ical alignments were created in response to the rise of Great Zimbabwe as a regional power. Families associated with the important sites of Mapungubwe, in the Limpopo valley, and Great Zimbabwe replaced the elite at older chiefly settlements, such as Bosutswe and Toutswe in Botswana. In the Northeast district around Francistown, many other stone-walled centers were built in the Zimbabwe pattern. The ruins follow a Zimbabwe plan of circular stone walls surrounding the houses of the elite; most contain graphite-burnished pottery and other commodities associated with Zimbabwe hegemony. These ruins, which run from the Motloutse River west to the Makgadikgadi pans, attest to the dominance of Kalanga-speaking peoples in this region between the fourteenth and eighteenth centuries. Yet these settlements undoubtedly served as a political and economic focus for a broader spectrum of peoples, both Bantu and Khoisan. Further south, the ancestors of the Kalanga- and Tswana-speaking peoples responded differently to the stimuli of outside trade and political competition by maintaining greater autonomy from Zimbabwe power. This is reflected in different styles of pottery and stone ruins. Drying climates after 1400 c.e. accelerated these processes of transition and change.

West of the Makgadikgadi, an earlier chiefdom in the Tsodilo Hills of northwestern Ngamiland controlled extensive specularite mines, but this chiefdom collapsed around 1200 c.e. as increased numbers of glass beads, cowry shells, and other east coast trade goods perhaps undercut demand for locally produced indices of wealth. Increased demand for gold after its discov-ery around 1200 c.e. would have also diminished the value of wild products such as ivory, rhinoceros horn, and leopard skins. Decreases in the value of hunted products would, in turn, have reduced the bargaining power and perhaps status of hunters in a luxury economy now focused on control over metal goods and cattle. In addition to iron, copper, and gold, bronze also began to be manufactured and worn by regional subelite. Contemporary descendants of hunters and gatherers may have thus been cycling in and out of agropastoral economies for centuries, complicating the seemingly "isolated" historical trajectories that led to the "survival" of hunting and gathering bands into the twentieth century.

Farther south, in the vicinity of Gaborone and Molepolole, there was no gold to be mined, and distances to the major east coast entrepôts of trade at Mapungubwe and Great Zimbabwe were greater. While a few glass beads and marine shells have been recovered from archaeological excavations here, the political economy seems to have been less impacted by this trade. Instead, the Iron Age Tswana communities in this region continued an earlier cattle-centric focus with frequent competition and raiding between communities. Many seventeenth- and eighteenth-century villages were therefore built in defensive positions on hilltops that were surrounded by defensive stone walls. The layout of these communities parallels the later Tswana pattern of housing clusters built in a semicircle around central animal kraals where the *kgotla* would also have been situated.

The *Mfecane (Difaquane)*

In the first two decades of the nineteenth century, wars, raids, and population dislocations known as the *Mfecane* or *Difaquane* (derived from Zulu words meaning "crushing" or "pushing and shoving") rolled across southern Africa. The reasons for this turmoil are diverse and include both indigenous and European factors. But the end result was a redistribution of peoples whose ultimate origins lie in South Africa. The Kololo, the Ndebele, the Ngoni, and others raided settlements in Botswana on their way north to Zimbabwe, Zambia, Malawi, and Tanzania. While historical memory resonates with the terror of these raids, they had a much less lasting effect on the peoples and cultures of Botswana than the more pervasive set of influences that followed the incursions of white missionaries, traders, adventurers, and settlers.

Missionaries, Hunters, and Adventurers

As part of a project to stem Boer advancement into the interior as well as to save souls, the London Missionary Society under Robert Moffat established a mission station and school in the 1820s at Kuruman, just outside the border of modern Botswana. In the mid-1840s, Moffat's son-in-law, David

Livingstone, moved farther into the interior to set up a new mission and school at Kolobeng, just 15 miles west of present-day Gaborone. Sechele, the chief of the Kwena on whose land Livingstone had settled, was his first convert. Convinced that Livingstone's preaching was not very productive, Sechele is said to have remarked, "Do you imagine that these people will ever believe you by your merely talking to them? I can make them do nothing except by threatening them; if you like, I shall call my head men, and with our rhinoceros-hide whips we shall soon make them believe all together."[18] Over the next 10 years Livingstone made several trips across the Kalahari with Tswana guides to "discover" what local people were already familiar with—Lake Ngami on the edge of the Okavango Delta and the Victoria Falls (*Mosi o a Thunya,* "smoke that thunders") on the Zambezi River. While at Kolobeng, Livingstone began correspondence with friends in England to help him produce a plow that would be strong enough to till the hard soil of Botswana.[19] There is no record that he was successful in his early endeavors, but by the end of the nineteenth century, Botswana farmers had adopted this device, which transformed both the technology and the economics of agriculture in the country. Livingstone's relationship with the Kwena people led to considerable distrust of him by the Boers, who accused him (rightly) of providing guns to the Kwena. During his absence from Kolobeng in 1852, the Boers destroyed the mission station. This, the subsequent death of his wife in 1862, and the fact that he clearly preferred exploring to preaching and conversion led him to abandon the station and embark on wider missionary explorations into the interior of Africa.

In the last half of the nineteenth century, lured by the profits (and adventure) to be made by supplying the elephant ivory and ostrich feathers in demand in Victorian salons and Western saloons, Europeans began to enter the country in increasing numbers. They included Cotton Oswall, a sometime traveling companion of Livingstone, along with explorers and traders such as Thomas Baines, Charles James Andersson, Frederick Green, James Chapman, and others who left no journals to record their exploits or ensure their memory.[20]

In the 1860s, gold was recovered from prehistoric workings in the Francistown area, leading to the first small-scale gold rush in southern Africa. The "discovery" of Great Zimbabwe by Carl Mauch not long afterward and finds of gold jewelry in some of the stone ruins that dot the granite country between Great Zimbabwe and the Motloutse River in Botswana led many prospectors into the region. In 1880, David Francis negotiated mining rights in northeastern Botswana with King Lobengula of the Ndebele, and in 1890 a town named after him became a railhead on the Cape-to-Bulawayo railway. The town quickly grew into Botswana's first "city" and by 1897 it boasted a hotel, three banks, and a few small cash-and-carry businesses. In addition to

Great Zimbabwe, gold-hungry miners quickly ransacked many of the small thirteenth- to seventeenth-century stone ruins that surrounded Francistown. Over the next decade, a company, registered in 1895 as the Ancient Ruins Company, burrowed through most of the prehistoric ruins in northeastern Botswana and adjacent Rhodesia, "mining" them for their metallic gold while discarding the more intangible gold of their history. At the time, the possibility that Africans had built the ruins was thought to be highly improbable, as it would have contradicted a fundamental construct of colonialism: that Africans were biologically and culturally incapable of creating an impressive civilization marked by long-distance trade and impressive architecture, hence their need for colonial "direction."

The Protectorate

The Boer attack on David Livingstone's mission in Kolobeng (the ruins of which are now a small site museum) was symptomatic of increasing encroachment into Tswana territories by white adventurers, traders, and settlers in the last half of the nineteenth century. Pleas to the British government for protection by Tswana chiefs and resident expatriate missionaries fell on deaf ears, however, until the German acquisition of South West Africa (Namibia) under the Treaty of Berlin in 1884. Almost immediately afterward, in 1885, the British government declared protection over Botswana lands lying between the Molopo River in the south and 22 degrees south latitude. In 1890, protection was extended north to 18 degrees south latitude, incorporating the region covered by present-day Botswana. While one incentive for this action was to block further expansion of German power in southern Africa, another factor was the desire to capture Bechuanaland as a reservoir to supply the growing demand for labor in the diamond and gold mines of South Africa.

Britain had no desire to spend money on the protectorate, and by 1894 plans were under way to transfer the administration of the territory to the privately held British South Africa Company (BSAC) managed by Cecil Rhodes. In protest, three Botswana kings—Bathoen I of the Ngwaketse, Sebele I of the Kwena, and Khama III of the Ngwato—along with their missionary advisers, E. Lloyd and W. C. Willoughby, traveled to Britain to petition in person against the transfer. At the same time, Cecil Rhodes, then prime minister of the British Cape Colony, was plotting to support a rebellion of English-speaking residents against the Afrikaans-speaking Boer Republic of the Transvaal under Paul Krueger. In 1896, a secret raid from Rhodesia through Botswana by a band of British adventurers, led by Starr Jameson, was launched that was intended to coincide with an uprising of the English-speaking *Uitlanders* in Johannesburg. The small band of 600 men was quickly defeated, however, and the BSAC was forced to pay the Boer government almost 1 million pounds in compensation. The failure of the rebellion embarrassed the British government, and demands to transfer Bechuanaland to the control of Rhodes's company were put on indefinite hold. In 1899, the British administration instituted a hut tax to help pay for the administration of the protectorate; a "native tax" to be collected by local authorities on behalf of the British administration followed in 1919. Both had the effect of forcing the Tswana into wage labor in the European-dominated sector of the economy so that they could earn the cash needed to pay for their own "administration." The British administration of the protectorate was based outside present-day Botswana at Mafikeng in South Africa. As a result, the Bechuanaland Protectorate was the only colonial territory in the world whose administrative center, Mafikeng, lay outside its boundaries.

A system of parallel or indirect rule was developed that left African kings to rule their own people, but their powers to tax, conduct trials and wars, and other matters were either eliminated or closely regulated by the resident magistrate. White missionaries and traders found themselves caught between these two forces, indigenous and British, as "advisers." In 1919 and 1920, the parallel system of governance was formalized and separate African and European Advisory Councils were created, each dealing with the affairs of their own people while under the supervisory eye of the resident magistrate. The result was inexpensive administration for the British while leaving African authorities under the inaccurate impression that they maintained control over their own affairs. Much of this was illusion, and the British attitude of sufferance and disdain are well illustrated by the comments of Sir Charles Rey, resident commissioner from 1930 to 1937, who noted in his private at diary on June 24, 1931, that he "went to the *kgotla* meeting of all the tribe at 10 A.M. That little snake Tsekedi is away (with my permission) conducting some investigations in the north as to the value of land concerning which we propose to do a 'deal' in regard to mining so as to buy off his opposition to mining in his Reserve—it will be a great thing if it comes off."[21]

An attempt to incorporate Bechuanaland into the Union of South Africa failed in 1910, although Botswana, along with the other High Commission territories of Lesotho and Swaziland, were integrated economically with South Africa as part of the South African Customs Union. But Botswana received only a fixed 2 percent share of Customs Union revenues right up to and beyond independence in 1966. Otherwise, the territory was left to fend for itself as a poor, sandy wasteland with no resources of note other than to serve as a labor pool for its wealthier South African neighbor. Throughout the 1930s and 1940s, local kings, such as Tshekedi Khama of the Ngwato, tested and protested the right of British administrators to intervene in their internal affairs, but little notice was generally paid outside the region. Given Colonel Rey's eye for mining profits, it is perhaps fortunate that the diamond mines that would later fuel one of the most rapid economic growth rates in the world were not discovered until after independence.

While distanced neglect on the part of its resident commissioners and the British government might have meant that, at least in material terms, there was little change from the precolonial to colonial periods, European dominance did result in many profound changes in Botswana society. The economics of agriculture, for instance, were transformed as plows and oxen were introduced into agricultural production, perhaps facilitating in some small way the abandonment of polygyny. The commoditization of labor, with young migrant workers leaving their wives and communities to travel to the South African mines, created other transformations in family structure as women were often left as the de facto heads of households in their husbands' absence. Many times, these were younger sons with little claim to wealth and status in the traditional economy but who returned home with a greater ability to challenge traditional structures and purchase cattle in their own right. Finally, Christianity was grafted onto an embedded structure of traditional belief and practice, resulting in profound changes in the cosmology and worldview of many Tswana.

Independence Movements

The emergence of formal political parties to voice dissatisfaction with British rule emerged only in the late 1950s with the establishment of the short-lived Bechuanaland Federal Party under Leetile Raditladi. In 1960, Motsami Mpho and Philip Matante, both members of the African National Congress in South Africa and active in antiapartheid protests there, formed the Bechuanaland Peoples Party (BPP). In 1965, Mpho broke from the BPP to form the Bechuanaland Independence Party (BIP). What was then viewed as the radical stance of this party among more conservative Tswana led to the formation of the Bechuanaland Democratic Party (BDP) in 1962 under the leadership of the Ngwato *Kgosi,* Sir Seretse Khama. Although Sir Seretse had come under political and social criticism among some of his followers, as well as segments of British society, for marrying an English woman, the BDP enjoyed the support of the colonial administration. Even though Khama "renounced" his kingship *(bokgosi)* to head the BDP, some still accused him of using his traditional position to solicit political support. In the country's first election, the BDP won a dominating 28 seats in the general assembly, followed by three seats for the BPP and none for the BIP. In late 1965, another party, the Botswana National Front (BNF), was formed with the intention of uniting resistance to the BDP under one opposition front. While Parliament is still dominated by the Botswana Democratic Party, representatives of the major opposition party, the BNF, won 13 of 40 seats in 1994. The elections of 1999, however, reversed those gains, and the Botswana Democratic Party now controls 33 seats, with those of the BNF falling to six. The Botswana Congress Party currently has one seat.

CULTURAL ISSUES

Because almost 80 percent of the population are the descendants of the Tswana-speaking nations that began to fragment in the fifteenth to sixteenth centuries, with another 11 percent being Kalanga, on the one hand there is a kind of homogeneity of cultural beliefs and customs in the country. Yet at the same time, there are sometimes wide differences between Tswana customs and beliefs and those of the smaller, minority *merafe,* who make up the remaining 9 percent (i.e., Sarwa, Mbukushu, Herero, Yeyi, and Subiya). This produces a social context with ample opportunities for cultural arbitrage. All but the smallest of communities in Botswana are multiethnic, and historical and archaeological evidence indicates that this has been the case for hundreds if not thousands of years. In the northwest of the country, Tswana, Herero, Mbukushu, and Yeyi are intermixed with one another and with Khoisan speakers in almost every community. One of the results is that multilingual fluency is common, as is knowledge of differing cultural beliefs. Many Mbukushu, for instance, are familiar with the trance dances of the Zhu/oasi even if they seldom participate in them, and most Zhu/oasi speak some Herero, Tswana, or Mbukushu, depending on the ethnic makeup of the people with whom they interact most on a daily basis.

The system of governance that Botswana has evolved from the pluralistic roots of the traditional *kgotla* and the social mechanisms to cope with the multiethnic context of even the smallest of Botswana communities appears robust enough to work with such ongoing historical realities while providing protections for the freedom of speech of minority groups. This respect for democracy, perhaps as much as the numerical dominance of the Tswana, has shaped the oldest and most stable democratic government in Africa. But the establishment of a functioning pluralistic democracy is not an easy task, and there are many issues yet to be resolved in a complex balancing act that attempts to unite all of Botswana's ethnic groups into a single nation while at the same time respecting and extending rights of expression and representation to those varying cultures. As one author summarizes the current dilemma,

> The terms *minority* and *majority* have, by definition, no numerical significance
> in Botswana. What determines whether a tribe is major or minor is whether it

belongs to one of the eight Setswana tribes and speak one of the eight Setswana dialects. For instance, the Bakalaka are believed to be the largest tribe in the Central District, and yet they are regarded as a minority tribe because they speak Ikalanga, which is not related to Setswana. The Wayeyi constitute about 40% of the population of the Ngamiland district.... By contrast, the Batawana constitute one per cent of the population and yet the former are regarded as a minority tribe and the latter as a majority tribe. The Batawana rule over the Wayeyi, and the Batawana Paramount Chief represents the Wayeyi in the House of Chiefs. The government does not recognise the Wayeyi Paramount Chief.... The Balete and Batlokwa have small populations occupying one village, and yet they are regarded as majority tribes and are represented by their Paramount Chiefs in the House of Chiefs. The general pattern is that Setswana speaking groups rule over all the non-Setswana tribes. Minority languages and cultures are suppressed and their use in public domains is discouraged. These policies are meant to foster national unity and a national cultural identity. They are congruent with an assimilationist model and are underpinned by an orientation that views linguistic and cultural diversity as a problem and a threat to national unity.[22]

NOTES

1. The written "g" is pronounced as an "h" in the Tswana language. This is true of all Tswana spelling.

2. The Bantu prefix "Ba" denoting people, which occurs in a variety of forms in Botswana (e.g., Ova-Herero, Ha-Mbukushu), will not be used hereafter. The term "Batswana," however, will be used to refer to all the people of Botswana, not just to the Tswana ethnic groups. Similarly, the prefix "Se," which denotes "language" in many Botswana languages, will not be used because of the variety of forms found in the country (e.g., Oji-Herero, Ochi-Herero, Tsi-mbukushu, I-Kalanga).

3. The orthography for various consonantal clicks in the Sarwa or Khoisan languages and some Bantu languages varies. In general, Khoisan orthographies follow the International Phonetic Alphabet (IPA) terminology, while the equivalent "click" sounds in some Bantu languages are usually written using the standard text symbols of Q, X, and C to stand for the three most common clicks: the lateral alveolar or "side click" is written // in the IPA format or as an "X" in Bantu languages such Xhosa and Zulu (the sound is something like the noise used by riders to urge horses on); the dental or "frontal click" written as / would correspond to "C," as in the "c" in *Mfecane;* and the postalveolar click "!" as in *!Kung,* produced by a sucking action from the top of the palate. It is written as "Q" in some Bantu languages in words such as *Difaquane.* The palatal click ≠ has no simple text equivalent. It is made in a manner similar to the ! or Q click by sucking the back part of the tongue down from the back of the hard palate. Naturally, most non-Sarwa speakers, including many Batswana, have difficulties with these sounds, and so they just revert to the easiest one for most people to make—the lateral alveolar or "//" or "X"—to stand for them all. For this

reason, most of the Sarwa place-names on Botswana maps (since they are not made by Sarwa speakers) are wrong because they almost always use the "X" symbol to stand for all clicks. For instance, the safari camp Xugana in northeastern Okavango should really be spelled Qogana or !Ogana if the correct click notations are to be used.

4. John Simpson, "Diamonds Are Curse of Ancient Bushmen," *Daily Telegraph*, November 8, 2002.

5. Ibid. (emphasis added).

6. J. Campbell, *Travels in Southern Africa, undertaken at the Request of the London Missionary Society* (London: Francis Westley, 1822).

7. Hitchhiking prices are generally slightly higher than bus fares.

8. Cities such as Gaborone are gradually engulfing neighboring villages such as Tlokweng and Mogoditshane that were once separate towns.

9. John Mackenzie, *Ten Years North of the Orange River 1859–69* (London: Frank Cass, 1871), p. 378.

10. Emil Holub and E. E. Frewer, *Seven Years in South Africa: Travels, Researches, and Hunting Adventures, between the Diamond Fields and the Zambesi (1872–79)*, vol. 1 (Boston: Houghton Mifflin, 1881), p. 296.

11. N. Parsons, *King Khama, Emperor Joe, and the Great White Queen: Victorian Britain through African Eyes* (Chicago: University of Chicago Press, 1998), pp. 244–46.

12. University students are given a bursary from the government that is supposed to be paid back after graduation. But the government has not followed up on this, and no students are known to have paid back their bursary.

13. Botswana Presidential Task Group for a Long Term Vision for Botswana, *A Framework for a Long Term Vision for Botswana* (Gaborone: Government Printer, 1996).

14. Until men became independent from their families by marrying, having children, and taking responsibility for their household, lands, and cattle, their lives were still considered "incomplete."

15. Campbell, *Travels in Southern Africa*, vol. 2, p. 157.

16. In the nineteenth century, accounts indicate that some disputes between warriors were settled through contests where praise poetry was recited (see chapter 3).

17. The term Bushman has many pejorative connotations, so its use is generally frowned on in southern Africa, as is the term "native."

18. J. Comaroff and J.L. Comaroff, *Of Revelation and Revolution*, vol. 1 (Chicago: University of Chicago Press, 1991). Copyright vol. 1, 1991 by the University of Chicago Press. Reprinted by permission from University of Chicago Press and the authors John and Jean Comaroff.

19. David Livingstone wrote to his sister, Janet, in 1849 that "if I had the money . . . I propose to order two [ploughs], one for the chief & the other for ourselves. Of extra strength every way, though they should cost 6 pounds each. The Boers use an immense wooden thing, which is a weight by itself to the twelve oxen which draw it. From its length & only one handle with two wheels the Natives call them camelopards [*thutwa*, or giraffe]." D. Livingstone and I. Schapera, *Family Letters, 1841–1856*, vol. 2 (Westport, Conn.: Greenwood Press, 1975), p. 36.

20. Thomas Baines, *Explorations in South-West Africa: Being an Account of a Journey in the Years 1861 and 1862 from Walvisch Bay, on the Western Coast, to Lake Ngami and the Victoria Falls* (London: Longman, Green, Longman, Roberts, and Green, 1864); James Chapman, *Travels in the Interior of South Africa: Comprising Fifteen Years' Hunting and Trading: With Journeys across the Continent from Natal to Walvisch Bay, and Visits to Lake Ngami and the Victoria Falls* (London: Bell and Daldy, Edward Stanford, 1868); Frederick Green, C. H. Hahn, and J. Rath, "Account of an Expedition from Damaraland to the Ovampo, in Search of the River Cunene," in *Proceedings of the Royal Geographic Society,* 2, no. 6 (1858): 350–54. Green carved his name and the date "1858–59" on a large baobab tree at Gusta Pan south of Gweta.

21. Charles Rey in N. Parsons et al., *Monarch of All I Survey: Bechuanaland Diaries, 1929–37* (Gaborone: Botswana Society; New York: L. Barber Press, 1988).

22. L. Nyati-Ramahobo, "The Language Situation in Botswana," *Current Issues in Language* 1 (2, 2000): 253–54.

2

Religion and Worldview

Bantu life is essentially religious.... Religion so pervades the life of the people that it regulates their doing and governs their leisure to an extent that is hard for Europeans to imagine. Materialistic influences from Europe are playing upon Africa at a thousand points and may break up Bantu life, but the Bantu are hardly likely to be secularized, for they will never be contented without a religion that is not able to touch every phase of life and to interpret the divine in terms of humanity.[1]

Only when the Sotho-Tswana have regained pride in their past, in the ways in which their fathers conducted themselves and their affairs, shall we be able to assess how "Christian"—in the Western sense—they have been through the ages and even now.[2]

TRADITIONAL RELIGION

Religious ideas affect in fundamental ways how people in Botswana perceive themselves, their relationships with their families, their friends and neighbors, and their interpretations of daily events. Among the Tswana—as indeed generally for most Bantu-speaking societies—traditional religious beliefs often inform the events, actions, and practices of contemporary life. Like the air one breathes, religious cosmology and a belief that the ancestors (*badimo*) participate in the daily affairs of the living are part of the taken-for-granted matrix within which life is lived and understood. Almost all aspects of personhood—success or failure, health or sickness, charisma or repulsiveness, wealth or poverty—are understood to have spiritual dimensions.

It has been noted that "the intimate presence of 'badimo' [is reflected] at every point of life."[3] The implication is that the cause of both bad and good fortune lies in interpersonal, community, and spiritual relationships—the jealousy of a neighbor, the displeasure of a slighted ancestor *(badimo)*, or the workings of witchcraft *(boloi)*. Thus, the well-being of an individual is not a personal affair but is a function of his or her relationship with other people, ancestral spirits, and even nature. In addition, the health and survival of the community can also, in consequence, be affected by the social behavior of a single individual. For Batswana, then, the world is composed of a complex set of inseparable relations between social, religious, and psycho-physiological realms in which "the greatest good for all can be achieved if all live according to the basic virtue of harmony; the harmony between people, nature, ancestors and Modimo [God]. If the harmony is disrupted, it is explained as illness."[4] Cosmological and spiritual beliefs are thus central to daily life and practice and not reserved only for special religious places or rites. Perhaps as a result, most people in Botswana consider themselves followers of traditional religions.

Most Batswana would probably describe themselves as following traditional religious beliefs, but a substantial number are also affiliated with one of the denominations of Christianity. But even the most westernized Christian sects incorporate rites, such as the first fruits ceremonies and prayers for rain, that have been adapted from traditional practices. Botswana churches can be divided into two basic types: African independent churches and Pentecostal churches. African independent churches combine biblical teachings with traditional beliefs. The most popular of these is the Zionist Christian Church (ZCC). It prohibits polygyny, but allows marriage payments *(bogadi)*. Another example, the Spiritual Healing Church, was formed by a Tswana man, Jacob Mokaleng Motswasele, with a headquarters in Matsiloje west of Francistown. On a personal level, traditional cosmologies saw the progress of a person's life as a series of "rebirths" and changes in status were often associated with changes in name and clothing as well as responsibilities and obligations. For the Spiritual Healing Church, after baptism women wear blue skirts; white shirts, hats, and shoes; and a blue waist band. The parallels between old rites of passage, new rituals of baptism, and spiritual and social rebirth and renewal are notable since, as one authority writes,

> at the traditional initiation ceremony, the fact that the initiate becomes a new person is symbolized ... by the discarding of old clothes and the putting on of new ones. At Christian Confirmation the catechumens are also draped in new clothes, long white robes for the girls and dark suits for the young men. Noticeable in particular is the change in clothing habits of the girls after the ceremony.

They, as it were, graduate from wearing short, school-girl type skirts to "dressing like grown-up people," i.e. wearing skirts at least covering the knee. Even their deportment, carriage and manners change, showing that they have passed from childhood to adulthood.[5]

Missionaries of the London Missionary Society and the Wesleyan Methodist Missionary Society introduced some of the most widespread Christian sects in the early nineteenth century. These churches still have a large number of followers. During the colonial era, they received considerable external funding and built churches and hospitals countrywide.[6] As a result, they were able to attract a significant number of followers. These churches remain popular among the middle and upper classes, but with the lessening of funding from colonial sources, their membership decreased after independence as many Batswana sought new spiritual homes. The two most active churches in Botswana today are the Catholic Church and the South African–based ZCC, with its headquarters in Moria about 800 miles northeast of Johannesburg. The latter church is especially active among the working class. Anglican, Seventh-Day Adventist, and numerous other small Zionist and Apostolic churches are found in rural areas along with Methodist, Lutheran, and Dutch Reformed churches.[7] In the past decade, the International Pentecostal Christian Church (IPCC), based at Silo in South Africa, has gained considerable popularity through its releases of choral music on CD. The women wear red, white, and blue uniforms and openly promote polygyny from their center in Mochudi. Islamic, Quaker, Hindu, and Bahai churches can be found in major towns, although these congregations are predominantly expatriate. Despite its late introduction to Botswana, Islam is gradually gaining a significant number of followers in the country in part because, compared with Christianity, some people find it more compatible with the more patriarchal tenets of traditional life where men dominate family and community power structures.

At the other end of the religious continuum are those whose faith focuses more on traditional beliefs in the powers of ancestral spirits *(badimo)*. These congregations, which vary widely in size and specific beliefs, can be loosely grouped together as African traditional religion. In between these two extremes lies a highly varied collection of sects that combine, to greater or lesser degrees, Christian beliefs with more traditionally inspired practices of revelation, divination, prophecy, and charismatic healing. Some, such as the ZCC, have thousands of followers; others are no larger than an extended family led by a member who has had divinely inspired "dreams" that purport to reveal hidden meanings behind everyday events or biblical passages that can then be used to solve social and economic problems. The ZCC has an Easter pilgrimage to Moria, its headquarters, that is the largest Easter service in Africa. Members of the church from throughout Africa are expected to attend the ceremony at least once in their lifetime, and Batswana members attend in large numbers every year. Overall, more than 2 million people attend this service each year.

Even though they often incorporate traditional beliefs, the religious and worldviews of the Tswana are not static but undergo redefinition and transformation in the context of a changing world. Tswana—and indeed all African—religious practice has always been open to appropriating new ideas, knowledge, and techniques that seem useful in daily life. During their initial encounters with European missionaries at the beginning of the nineteenth century, for instance, there was not an immediate rejection of Europeans and their Christian preaching but rather a desire to harness to traditional ends what was seen as the power of those beliefs:

> Because Tswana recognized no sharp boundary between the sacred and the secular, what struck them most about the whites were their goods, their knowledge, and their technical skills.... Tswana endeavor[ed] to empower themselves by appropriating these techniques ... to discover their hidden bases ... to persuade Europeans to part with the "medicines" that appeared to instill superhuman powers, medicines that might infuse them [Tswana] with new skills or even make their hearts pure.[8]

EASTERN BANTU SPEAKERS

Eighty percent of the people living in Botswana belong to one of the Tswana tribes (*merafhe*) and speak dialects of SeTswana, an eastern Bantu language the speakers of which moved into southern Africa around 1,000 years ago.[9] Another 11 percent speak Kalanga, a dialect of the Shona languages, the speakers of which also belong to the eastern Bantu language family that also settled in southern Africa in the first millennium C.E.; today the Kalanga are concentrated in the northeastern part of Botswana. The Herero, Yeyi, and Mbukusu live in northwestern Botswana and speak less closely related western Bantu languages. The earliest speakers of western Bantu to settle in northern Botswana did so around the middle of the first millennium C.E.[10] The Subiya, who speak another western Bantu dialect, live in the far northeastern corner of the country. Together, these groups make up approximately 95 percent of Botswana's population. As one might expect, their traditional worldviews and cosmologies are more closely related than those of the remaining segment of Botswana's population, the Khoisan. Given the numerical dominance of the Tswana and Kalanga in Botswana, this chapter will focus more on these peoples, with briefer consideration of western Bantu and Khoisan peoples.

The Tswana

In the first decades of the nineteenth century, such well-known figures as Robert Moffat and his son-in-law David Livingston, both affiliated with the London Missionary Society, settled in Tswana communities. Initially, missionaries placed their faith in the power of "intellectual" approaches to conversion through "preaching" and "listening" in religiously dedicated church buildings. The Tswana, however, were more interested in actions than words and "were not easily interpolated into the dialogic triangle of preacher, listener, and divine truth."[11] Once missionary dreams of mass conversions diminished, they turned to more indirect methods to gain converts to Christianity (and capitalism) by intervening in the daily life of the Tswana and encouraging them to wear European clothing, build square houses in imitation of those erected by the missionaries, and organize their houses in lines along streets bordered by "properly" enclosed fields planted in geometric design. In other words, salvation was to begin by changing the physical dimensions of daily life. The degree to which Tswana rejected, accepted, or modified their beliefs in response to these early missionary endeavors varied according to social class, gender, and age. The first converts were often those who expected to gain benefits not available to them within the existing political and social structure: members of subservient ethnic groups or social classes, younger sons of chiefs marginalized from power by primogeniture, and, importantly, women.

The principal God, whose name was once thought to be too sacred to speak aloud, is *Modimo,* which is related to the word for ancestral spirits, *Badimo*—a term translated in early editions of the Bible by Robert Moffat as "devils" who "possessed" people during spiritual and healing ceremonies. Through such biased translations as well as attacks on rites of initiation and rainmaking, missionaries struck at the heart of traditional governance where the power to rule, to make rain, to regulate the planting and harvest seasons, and to conduct rites of passage were seen as being divinely invested in kingship. The cultural importance of rain and those who claimed to control it—the kings *(dikgosi)* and rainmaking specialists known as *baroka*—were viewed as a threat to Christian principles by early missionaries. The power of *dingaka,* more "spiritually inspired" traditional doctors (the term is derived from *dinaka,* the small animal "horns" filled with medicines that they wear around their necks), was also a matter of contestation by early missionaries. In his book *Missionary Travels,* Livingston, who established a residence at Kolobeng just outside Gaborone in the 1840s, recorded one of his conversations with a "witch doctor" in which both he and the *moroka* shared the belief that the spirits, or God, was ultimately responsible for making rain; but they fundamentally disagreed over whether God or the *moroka* should take credit for making it fall. Prayers for rain are now almost universally incorporated into church services, both Christian and traditional, as the dry season ends and the time for planting begins. In many areas, harvest ceremonies *(dikgafela)*, traditionally used to thank the ancestors *(badimo)* for the harvest, are still conducted each August as families bring a bit of their harvest in special baskets to the *Kgosi*. This grain was often stored centrally near the Kgotla and was intended for redistribution during times of drought. The grain (usually sorghum) is put into a central granary *(difalana)* under his supervision, and a month later the *Kgosi* calls the *morafe* to a rainmaking ceremony where he announces that plowing of the fields can begin. Offerings of sorghum also accompany some ancestral "cleansing" *(phekolo)* or "healing" ceremonies as well. Prayers to the ancestors or God usually accompany these rites.

The *Kgotla* was the forum for the traditional court, and in the nineteenth century, accusations of witchcraft were often settled there as traditional doctors identified the offending parties by "smelling" them out by supernatural means. Unusual events, such as bolts of lightning striking houses or people, cattle falling sick, and a myriad of other problems deemed to be outside the usual norms of occurrence, would initiate action on the part of the *Kgosi* and *Dingaka* to protect the community from the evildoers thought to be responsible for such events. According to local folklore, "witches" *(baloi)* discovered in this manner were thrown into caves. The locations of two of these, Kgwakgwe in Kanye and Kobokwe (Livingstone's Cave) in Molepolole, are still known.

But the relationships between religion, healing, witchcraft, and divination are complex among the Tswana. A traditional *ngaka,* for instance, is not only a rainmaker and an antidote to witchcraft, which in some ways can be defined as "disharmony" in the community, but also a combination faith healer, detective, marriage counselor, and social worker.[12] As a result, the conceptual fields of African thought and cosmology do not always fit well in the categories familiar to westerners. Even within the category of *ngaka,* there are divisions between those who are diviners *(e e dingaka),* those who able to use spiritual forces to determine the causes of illness or other problems, and those who have acquired a knowledge of herbs that can be used for both good and evil purposes *(e tshotswa).* While both are healers, the former does not equate directly with the Western concept of "doctor." In addition, the spiritually inspired practitioners are generally thought to be the most powerful and effective because they address the underlying causes of disharmony and illness, or *bolwetse.*

A type of spiritual diviner and healer known as a *sangoma* is also becoming more common in Botswana. *Sangoma* originates in Nguni custom, but the practice has been most highly developed in the socially troubled context of mine life in South Africa. As miners have returned home to Botswana, the practice has spread, and there are now schools outside Gaborone where one can be initiated into its knowledge and practice. The final type of religious practitioner is the "faith healer" or prophet who usually combines divination and healing under a loose rubric of Christianity. In some cases, they may even refer to the Bible as a divination tool *(taolo)*.

Interestingly, while almost all *dingaka* (plural of *ngaka*) are men, women and even whites now practice as *sangoma* in Botswana. Women are often singled out as witches and associated with witchcraft because, according to the patriarchal stereotypes that empower men in the country, (1) they are short tempered and so likely to misuse the powers of *bonkgaka* for evil purposes; (2) they are the cooks and so could kill people or make them ill by adding poisonous substances to their food; (3) they act as midwives and so are in a position to acquire human body parts, especially afterbirth used for witchcraft; and (4) they are believed to be weak and lacking in the social character needed to act as diviner-healers.[13]

The Kalanga

The Kalanga, who are concentrated in the northeastern parts of the country, have very similar beliefs in the power of ancestral spirits to affect the living and in the relationship between the spiritual world and physical and mental well-being. The ancestors are thought to live underground in a land of the dead where they keep watch over the living. If they become upset or feel slighted, they are able to send sickness to the living as a sign of their displeasure. In addition to these spirits, there is a High God, called *Mwari* or *Ngwale,* who can be contacted through spirit mediums. Spirits reveal themselves through droughts, illnesses, or other calamities and may be appeased through worship, usually with the mediation of a spirit medium through whom *Mwari* and the ancestral spirits speak at shrines and caves where candles are burned and offerings of money and other materials are left. Drumming and dancing are often used to summon the spirit, who may take possession of a participant and speak in voices and other sounds through them. Many Kalanga-based sects such as the Zezuru combine a belief in *Mwari* with Christian tenets and believe that the essential element of healing is prayer rather than medicines.[14] These beliefs in the power of prayer have led some to resist government health campaigns such as the recent polio immunization program in 2004. As one man belonging to the Johane Church of God put it, "We were completely shocked when health officials and some law enforcement officers pounced on us, compelling our children to take the anti-polio drops ... the prophets guide us on how we should pray to achieve certain things. The sick are healed through prayer. That is how we live, and will continue living."[15]

Cosmology

Other aspects of traditional belief mark various stages of life from birth through marriage to death. Two important rites of passage known as *Bogwera* for boys and *Bojale* for girls play both religious and educational roles.[16] In the past, these ceremonies took many months and, for boys, involved circumcision; the female rites did not involve genital cutting. During these rites, songs and dances were used as an instructional medium through which young men and women learned the responsibilities of community life. Rainmaking rites are also carried out in some regions, such as the *nzeze* rites carried out at the site of a waterfall in Moremi Gorge in the Tswapong Hills not far from Palapye.[17] Another important rainmaking shrine is located in Ramokgwebana. While these are notable locations, rites are carried out in a wide variety of places in rural areas as rural farmers ask for rain.

From the time of the earliest missionaries, one of the central conflicts between Christianity, chieftainship, and traditional religion had to do with the responsibility of the chief to beseech his ancestors, sometimes with the assistance of specialist rain doctors known as *moroka ya pula,* to bring rain to the community fields and pastures so that his people would prosper. Even after conversion to Christianity, many continued to believe that it was the chief's responsibility to ensure that rain would fall. After a severe drought in the 1930s, for instance, one of the speakers at a Kgotla meeting in Mochudi claimed that it was Christianity—and especially the church building itself— that was causing the rain not to fall. As one of the participants expressed it,

> Let Christianity be suppressed, it is driving away the rain; let the building of a church be abandoned, there is no God for whom a house has to be built. We regard you, Lentswe, ... as our Saviour and our Jesus Christ, the rainmaker (moroka) who can bless our tribe; and now by allowing Christianity here you simply deny that you have the power to make rain.[18]

In another instance, the women in the community rose up to protest the fact that rainmaking ceremonies had been abandoned by *Kgosi* Molefi. Taking affairs into their own hands they marched to the *kgotla* brandishing sticks,

> dancing and singing, and whipping any man who came within reach. The following morning they went to Molefi's home ... and thrashed every man they

came across, so that the men used to run away from them. On getting there they danced and sang continuously in and around the courtyard, "wearing down its surface and scattering lots of branches about the place." They came again the next morning. That afternoon it rained heavily. Most of them returned to their fields. On Sunday Mr Reyneke preached in church against this "heathen revival." He was very sad about it; he said [former] Chief Lentswe had told them to abandon such practices, but now they seemed to be going back; the women were great obstacles to the progress of the tribe.[19]

Today Christianity has taken on a number of blended forms as modern prophets and priests combine elements of traditional belief in ancestors and spirit possession with prophetic interpretations of Christian doctrine while seeking advice, guidance, and spiritual inspiration to help people cope with their problems. The AIDS crisis, for instance, has led to a rapid expansion in the provision of Western medicine to rural areas, the development of private hospitals to supplement government-run ones, the provision of educational and health programs by churches and other community groups, and the broadcasting and printing of AIDS-related materials and advice on radio, on television, and in newspapers. But at the same time, there has been a concomitant resurgence in ancestral cleansing ceremonies *(phekolo)* led by prophets *(baporofiti)* who claim to communicate with ancestral sprits *(badimo)* who help them treat *(go alafa)* diseases such as AIDS that appear to lie outside the capabilities of Western medicine. Roadside stands selling traditional medicines *(ditlhare,* literally, "trees or bushes") are now much more common than before the AIDS epidemic as people search for alternatives to help them cope with what seems an unending epidemic. As people come to see Western medicine as too expensive or ineffective, they have turned in increasing numbers to their ancestors and divinely inspired prophets for relief.

Another response to the increasing death toll due to AIDS is also grounded in traditional belief. With death has come an increasing elaboration of funerals as more and more expensive coffins, accompanied by tents to shade the grave site, and feasts to console the living are used to both honor the dead and reinforce the status of the living. Because ancestral spirits are still widely seen as possible causes of sickness and misfortune, the increasingly elaborate funeral preparations may be thought of as a cosmological counterbalance to tragedy, with the consequence that "impoverishment by funeral" is now recognized as a serious problem facing working-class Tswana families.[20] In addition, funerals are now sometimes seen less as somber occasions and more as occasions to exhibit wealth and status. In the early part of the twentieth century, the dead were usually wrapped in black cattle skins and buried; simple food with no salt or other seasonings was served. Now, in addition to spending on increasingly elaborate caskets and grave shades, a wide range of

Zionist Christian Church (ZCC) members in their khaki uniforms ride to the Tsodilo Hills to collect "healing waters" from a sacred spring in the rocks. Photo courtesy of National Museum of Botswana.

spiced food is served at funerals. The relationship between religion, cosmology, and everyday life thus involves complex and often contradictory cultural syntheses and transformations of religion, health, and psychology.

WESTERN BANTU SPEAKERS

Herero, Mbukushu, Yeyi, and Subiya

Like the eastern Bantu speakers, western Bantu also revere ancestral spirits who, among the Herero, are often approached around a sacred fire *(okuruo)*, located on the eastern side of the homestead. Prayers for help or advice are offered up to ancestral spirits rather than to God *(Ndjambi)*, who is seen as a more distant figure associated with the clouds and heaven. In some areas, cairns of stones are believed to be inhabited by spirits, and those who pass by them must add a stone to the cairn to show respect.[21] Similar cairns can also be found in eastern Botswana.

Examples of rock paintings from the Tsodilo Hills in northwestern Botswana. There are more than 2,000 naturalistic and
geometric paintings in the hills done in red ocher and white pigments. This painting depicts the eland, an especially powerful
spiritual symbol among contemporary Sarwa. Cattle, possibly
shown at the top of the painting, were introduced into the area
about 1,500 years ago.

The Mbukushu, Dxeriku, and Yeyi live along the waterways of the
Okavango Delta in northern Botswana.[22] Like the Tswana and Kalanga, they
also place considerable importance on a spiritual connection with their ancestors. Mbukushu rainmakers, in particular, are especially renowned for their
ability to make rain—a precious commodity for farmers in this arid environment. Rainmakers enjoy significant religious and political authority not only
among their own people but among the Tawana and Herero as well.

Common to all the western Bantu peoples and to the eastern Bantu as well
is the belief that physical and emotional health are facets of spirituality and that
traditional healers and shamans are able to mediate with the spiritual or ancestral world to effect healing and spiritual balance. In the Okavango, Mbukusu
and Yeyi shamans are believed to be especially powerful and are sought out for
help. And as is the case elsewhere in Botswana, contemporary religions beliefs
are often combined with elements of Christianity. Indigenous sects such as the
ZCC have become the largest denomination in many communities around the
margins of the Okavango. The ZCC's regalia is unique. The police-like khaki
outfits, caps, and silver stars worn by men symbolize the church's reputation for
uprightness and order, as do the blue uniforms the women wear.[23] In theory,
ZCC members may not smoke, drink, gamble, or engage in premarital sex,
although there are of course exceptions in practice. As a religious community,
they are now an important voting bloc in the Okavango region.

In the Okavango, the Yeyi and Mbukushu live among Khoi speakers, sometimes known as "River Bushmen," who call themselves the Buga-khwe and //Ani-khwe—"khwe" being a local form of "khoi" denoting "people." They have traditionally practiced fishing along with hunting and gathering, and their traditional religious practices, more closely related to those of Khoisan speakers, place less emphasis on ancestors and more on trickster gods and a reverence for the power inherent in the natural world.

KHOISAN SPEAKERS

The Khoisan (or Sarwa in contemporary Botswana usage) can be divided into northern, central, and southern groupings. The northern Sarwa or San include the Zhu/oasi, a group related to the !Kung of Angola, who live in northwestern Botswana. The central Khoisan include the Buga and //Aani of the Okavango Delta as well as the Nama, who live along the Namibian border south of the Zhu/oasi, and the /Gwi and //Gana of the Central Kalahari Game Reserve.[24] Several smaller groups of central Khoi live to the east of them along edges of the Botletli River near the Makgadikgadi salt pans. They include the Denessana, the Deti, and the Hietsware. Because Khoisan peoples, along with Kgalagadi, in the central Kalahari, occupy some of the most arid and remote parts of the country, in that area most rely on hunting, gathering, goat herding, and poorly paid wage labor for their livelihood. In the Okavango and along the Botletli River, fishing is also important for all the people living there. In both places, Khoisan have been employed for generations as herders on rural cattle posts run by Tswana, Herero, and Europeans.[25]

Khoisan peoples are sometimes associated in the popular mind with a Stone Age life as hunters and gatherers.[26] Although some Khoisan beliefs and practices distinguish them from their Bantu neighbors and overseers, many others are shared with their Kgalagadi and other neighbors. One aspect of Khoisan religious and artistic practice that has disappeared is the painting and engraving of animals and human figures on rock outcrops and shelters. The individual species of animals depicted varies from region to region, with eland and humans accounting for the vast majority of the rock paintings in the Drakensburg Mountains of South Africa. In the Tsodilo Hills of northern Botswana, humans are rarely depicted, while animals such as giraffe, eland, rhinoceros, zebra, and elephant are more common.[27] In traditional belief, all these animals, with the exception of zebra, elephant, and rhinoceros, are thought to contain supernatural curing potency or power *(n/um)* that can be harnessed by shamans to cure sickness and other problems. While no one paints as part of religious performance today, a belief in the spiritual power of

A Sarwa man dancing in a typical "bent forward" posture during a trance dance. The dance is intended to activate spiritual power, or *n/um,* that men use to heal those who are ill. During the dance, men going into trance may feel spiritual connections with animals, such as the eland, giraffe, or gemsbok, that they believe possess supernatural potency.

these paintings has led some to vandalize them by pecking on them with stones to "activate" their potency. Interestingly, this vandalism seems to be carried out mostly by Bantu peoples, indicating that in the contemporary world even historically Khoisan religious symbols find wider validation as potent religious objects by non-Sarwa.

The most widespread medicine or healing songs in the Kalahari are the Giraffe song and the Sun and Rain songs. The Eland song (and dance) celebrates fertility and the coming of age of young women. In this dance, men raise their hands to their heads in imitation of the horns of eland bulls while trying to separate the young women from the "herd." This song appears, along with the Rain song, to incorporate archaic linguistic terms that suggest origins reaching deep into the past.[28] The power to heal, *n/um,* is associated with a creator god known variously as = Gao N!a or = Gaishi, who is distant from humanity but may create or take life according to his whim. A second spirit, //Gauwa, associated with spirits of the dead (//gauwa-si), is also thought to cause sickness and misfortune.[29] Terms vary somewhat in the central Kalahari, where the creator God, N!adima, has a trickster associate called G//awama, who, along with spirits of the dead (G/ama dzi), is believed to spread disease and misfortune. Despite widespread prejudice against the Sarwa in Tswana society, they are believed to be powerful healers and diviners. San dances are also becoming popular in school dance competitions televised on Botswana Television; they are also incorporated by some local musicians into their acts.[30] Some Sarwa healing dances, such as *Mogwana*, are also being performed in Gaborone and other urban centers as tenets of Sarwa cosmology are woven into changing Tswana culture and practice.

Social and medical problems were treated by medicine dances as men danced through the night and entered into trance states accompanied by songs named for the wild animals from whom they acquired *n/um*, or healing power. In some areas, all adult men participate in these curing dances, each entering into trance states that vary in intensity from individual to individual. While in trance, they attempt to draw out the "arrows of sickness" that //Gauwa and other spirits have "shot" into those who are ailing. On the Ghanzi farms and more settled communities, such egalitarian healing through trance dance has given way to "specialists" who claim to possess unique knowledge and abilities in the art of curing; they usually charge fees for their services.[31]

RELIGION, HEALING, AND AIDS

As discussed, the events of everyday life are often filtered through a lens of religious belief centered on the ancestors. This provides contextual meaning for events such as good fortune, success in a job search, or even the passing of an examination in school. But there is another dimension in which supernatural forces are believed to be intimately involved: misfortune, sickness, and disease. In this regard, almost a decade of widespread death associated with the AIDS pandemic, in the terminology of Western medicine, is framed in the eyes of many as being caused by witchcraft, sorcery, and ancestral displeasure. In response, a bevy of healers has emerged who, basing themselves loosely on personal revelations of tradition, claim to be able to cure what Western medicine cannot. As one healer put it, "The *badimo* are in the blood. It is they that make it possible for Western medicines to work. If *badimo* are not involved, no hospital can cure them."[32] Other long-standing churches, such as Guta Ra Mwari, also claim to be able to cure AIDS, polio, and other diseases through prophetic healing, claims that have occasionally been voiced even in the Botswana Parliament.[33] Some argue that traditional healers should be brought on board in the fight against HIV/AIDS, but precisely how to do this is complicated by the variety of traditional healers and by the fact that many healing-based churches and societies motivated by profit and power are not prepared to cooperate with government regulation or oversight. One of the concerns is to promote hygienic practices, as some healers often work by cutting slits into the skin for the insertion of medicines. In the past, they might use the same razor blade for many patients, increasing the chance of transmitting infection and disease. Through educational initiatives, most of these healers now wear disposable latex gloves for their consultations. Yet many patients forsake modern medical knowledge and measures in desperate appeals to the ancestors for help; it is mostly the prophets *(baporofiti)* who profit.

NOTES

1. William Willoughby, *The Soul of the Bantu: A Sympathetic Study of the Magico-Religious Practices and Beliefs of the Bantu Tribes of Africa* (Garden City, N.Y.: Doubleday, Doran & Company, 1928), p. 1.

2. Gabriel Setiloane, *The Image of God among the Sotho-Tswana* (Rotterdam: A.A. Balkema, 1976), p. 183.

3. Ibid., p. 77.

4. G. Ntloedibe-Kuswani, *Bongaka, Women and Witchcraft,* Women's Worlds 99: The 7th International Interdisciplinary Congress on Women, Session VII: Gendering the Past, Tromso, Norway, 1999, p. 5.

5. Setiloane, *The Image of God among the Sotho-Tswana,* p. 189.

6. Hospitals include the DRM hospital in Mochudi sponsored by the Dutch Reformed Church, the SDA hospital in Kanye, and the London Missionary Society hospital in Serowe.

7. The term "Apostolic churches" is used to mean churches founded and headed by leaders who consider themselves divinely inspired prophets.

8. John Comaroff and J.L. Comaroff, *Of Revelation and Revolution,* vol. 2 (Chicago: University of Chicago Press, 1997), p. 77. Copyright vol. 2, 1997 by the University of Chicago Press. Reprinted by permission from the University of Chicago Press and the authors John and Jean Comaroff.

9. Christopher Ehret, *An African Classical Age: Eastern and Southern Africa in World History, 1000 B.C. to A.D. 400* (Charlottesville: University Press of Virginia, 1998).

10. Jan Vansina, *How Societies Are Born: Governance in West Central Africa before 1600* (Charlottesville: University Press of Virginia, 2004).

11. Comaroff and Comaroff, *Of Revelation and Revolution,* p. 66. Copyright vol. 2, 1997 by the University of Chicago Press. Reprinted by permission from the University of Chicago Press and the authors John and Jean Comaroff.

12. Ntloedibe-Kuswani, *Bongaka, Women and Witchcraft*, p. 5.

13. Ibid., p. 10.

14. Zezeru is the Tswana term for these Shona speakers. Those who live in Zimbabwe call themselves *Vapostori*.

15. Ryder Gabathuse, "In God's Name," *Mmegi wa Dikgang*, June 29, 2004.

16. I. Schapera, *Bogwera, Kgatla Initiation* (Mochudi, Botswana: Phuthadikobo Museum, 1978; distributed by the Botswana Book Centre). See also M. N. Mosothwane, "An Ethnographic Study of Initiation Schools among the Bakgatla bo ga Kgafela in Mochudi (1874–1988)," *Pula: Botswana Journal of African Studies* 15 (1, 2001): 144–65.

17. I. Schapera, *Rainmaking Rites of Tswana Tribes* (Leiden: Afrika-Studiecentrum, 1971).

18. Ibid., p. 19.

19. Ibid., p. 7.

20. On the other hand, expensive coffins and funerary rites do convey prestige, and some people think that elaborate displays of respect for the dead have some economic and social benefit.

21. Carl Hahn, H. Vedder, and L. Fourie, *The Native Tribes of South West Africa* (Cape Town: Cape Times, 1928).

22. There are many alternative orthographies and spellings for these names, especially for those with clicks, which are symbolized by a wide diversity of symbols. The "x" in Dxeriku, for instance, may be spelled as Dceriku, Diriku, Gciriku, Gceriku, Giriku, Niriku, or even D/eriku, depending on the author and the orthography followed. Mbukushu is somewhat more common than Mumbukushu, Bukushu, Bukusu, and Mbukuschu. Yeyi is also sometimes spelled Yei. In all cases, as with the terms Tswana and Kalanga, we have chosen not to use the Bantu prefix "Ba-" to denote an ethnic group because the form of this prefix varies from language to language.

23. It has been argued that "Tswana rulers ... when seeking to reassert authority in the face of growing European incursion, often enjoined ceremonial costume and its attendant public ritual. The potency ascribed to ritual attire probably contributed to the enthusiasm with which many Tswana took to church uniforms later introduced with much the same intention; namely, to regain a measure of control over a universe endangered by alien forces." Comaroff and Comaroff, *Of Revelation and Revolution*, p. 230. Copyright vol. 2, 1997 by the University of Chicago Press. Reprinted by permission from the University of Chicago Press and the authors John and Jean Comaroff.

24. *Kgalagadi* in Tswana.

25. Edwin Wilmsen, *Land Filled with Flies: A Political Economy of the Kalahari* (Chicago: University of Chicago Press, 1989).

26. Mathias Guenther, *Tricksters and Trancers: Bushman Religion and Society* (Bloomington: Indiana University Press, 1999).

27. A. Campbell, J. Denbow, and E. Wilmsen, "Paintings Like Engravings: Rock Art at Tsodilo," in *Contested Images: Diversity in Southern African Rock Art Research*,

ed. T. Dowson and D. Lewis-Williams (Johannesburg: Witwatersrand University Press, 1994), pp. 131–58.

28. N. England, *Music among the Ju/'hoasi and Related Peoples of Namibia, Botswana and Angola* (New York: Garland Publishing, 1992).

29. I. Schapera, *The Khoisan Peoples of South Africa: Bushmen and Hottentots* (London: G. Routledge, 1930).

30. One group is led by the performer Maxy.

31. Mathias Gunther, "The Trance Dancer as an Agent of Social Change among the Farm Bushmen of the Ghanzi District," *Botswana Notes and Records* 7 (1975): 161–66. For a fuller discussion of Bushman religion, see Guenther, *Tricksters and Trancers.*

32. Interview with Motofela Molato, Khubu la Dintsa, July 2002.

33. *Botswana Daily News,* November 27, 2001.

3

Literature and Media

Praise Poem to Cows

Heavy wooden bowl of my father
When I have eaten from it, my heart is glad
For it is the bowl of my parents
Wooden bowl for sweet gravy of the cow
Lovely cow of our home
One, alone, is sweetness
Missing one, alone, is sorrow
Dark, blue-grey cow—one who robs of sleep
Cow with the many spots
One with the melodious tongue
Stout-one of weapons
Preparer of liquid food
God, with the wet nose[1]

The baquana [Kwena], when they perform any feats of what they consider importance or prowess, compose a history of the circumstances and introduce a number of facts or supposed facts bearing upon the points. These they recite on various occasions, either when alone or in company with their fellows or at pechos [*dipitso*, "kgotla meetings"]. When they dispute with each other, they often settle their quarrels by a recitation of all their compositions. . . . The great warriors and hunters are generally most ready with such speeches, and give utterance to them with the greatest glee and force. Their custom in their disputes is to make the contending party repeat the speech, and that is done alternately. First one speaks, and after it is repeated; then the repeater begins his, and the late speaker repeats it.[2]

Until very recently, almost all the poetry and literature about Botswana that has been accorded international recognition has been written in English by those who have come to visit, to work, or to seek refuge in the country. Bessie Head (1937–1986), an acclaimed novelist sometimes referred to as an indigenous Tolstoy or Gorki, sought refuge in the rural village of Serowe from the persecution she experienced as a child born of "mixed" parentage in apartheid South Africa.[3] More recently, the novels of Alexander McCall Smith have made Botswana well known in the West through the detective adventures of Precious Ramotswa, his heroine of *The Ladies No. 1 Detective Agency* and other novels.[4] While Head's work is often permeated by dark social critique, pertaining especially to the daily struggles of women in Africa, McCall Smith presents a lighter view of Botswana culture and the strategies through which gender and custom are negotiated by middle-class protagonists in contemporary rural and urban settings. These books have generated great interest in Botswana culture and tourism, and some safari tours now advertise that visitors can "come and have tea on the hotel veranda of the President Hotel where Precious Ramotswa first met her fiancé, Mr. Matekoni." More recent novels, such as *Juggling Truths* and *Far and Beyon'* by Unity Dow, Botswana's first and only female High Court justice, give readers an insider's view of growing up in Botswana. Her books, in particular, use a wealth of local color and cultural detail to provide insight into how family, community, and religion contribute to mold individuals caught in the daily tug-of-war between modernity and tradition.

Less well known to the outside world is the long tradition of oral literature in Botswana that goes under the name "praise poetry," although sometimes it is hardly praise, and many examples would not be considered "poetry" in a strict Western literary sense of having fixed stanzas and rhyming set verses. Perhaps because of its complexity of metaphor and detailed historical referents, southern African praise poetry is often overlooked in more general studies of African oral literature where it has "tended to be ignored, or ... mentioned only in passing under the heading of 'Briefer Forms,' which is an odd way of classifying such elaborate and lengthy poems."[5] Yet in the early nineteenth century, the rhetorical strength of such creations was powerful enough that it could be used to resolve disputes between warriors.

The written word in the Tswana language also has a long history that goes back to the first translations of the Old and New Testaments by Robert Moffat and his son-in-law David Livingstone published between 1830 and 1857. Moffat brought his own printing press with him to his mission station at Kuruman in what became the Bechuanaland Protectorate, and on it he published scripture lessons in Tswana as well as his early translations of the gospels. In 1857, he also published Tswana translations of John Bunyan's *The Pilgrim's Progress,* a hymnbook, and a Tswana dictionary. By the end of the nineteenth century, mission publishers were widely distributing Bible tracts and stories in the Tswana language.

While these writings represent some of the earliest translations of the Bible and other Western classics into African languages anywhere on the subcontinent, the decision of whether to publish in English or in indigenous languages still concerns newer Batswana authors who want to disseminate their work in printed form or on radio or television. Language and its relationship to identity are deeply embedded in the political terrain of daily life. This is true in most places in the world, but it is especially so in Africa, where countries often encompass speakers of dozens of indigenous languages. Barolong Seboni, a Tswana poet, has expressed the complications of language choice thusly:

> I am acutely aware of the debates amongst African writers over the question of language that have polarized them into two camps; one side declaring that our first allegiance is to our native tongue, and the other arguing that English is as much our language as it is anyone else's; it is part of our historical (albeit colonial) heritage. The two camps are represented by [Nigerian author Chinua] Achebe on the one side, who embraces the English language, manipulates it and makes it speak in what can only be his native Igbo, and [Kenyan writer] Ngugi [wa Thiong'o] who rejects the colonial tongue and calls for a radical decolonialization.... My experience is that ... [African] voices are translatable into a foreign language by the creative act of writing.[6]

As Seboni implies, questions of power and authority are deeply embedded in language choice. Most of the work discussed in this chapter is either written in or has been translated into English. Seboni's point, however, encompasses only one aspect of the politics of language use. For instance, the government-controlled newspaper *Botswana Daily News* and other government publications are published only in Tswana and English. Radio Botswana and Botswana television similarly restrict themselves to these two languages, leaving Kalanga, Herero, and other minorities few alternatives but to write and produce in these languages. Government orders for non-English textbooks are also for books only in Tswana—there is no official instruction in other indigenous languages. Finally, the financial realities imposed on both government and private publishing houses means that demand for material in Botswana's other languages is too low to make publishing in them profitable. The dominance of English, followed by Tswana, in Botswana government publications, radio, and television broadcasts thus lends credence to the charge that in the interests of fostering national unity, a form of "linguistic imperialism has penetrated the social and economic lives of those tribes which do not speak Setswana as a first language."[7] In the international arena, most of the attention and recognition has been given to Botswana authors who have published in English; inside the country, Tswana-speaking voices find somewhat easier access to publishing and broadcasting venues.

ORAL LITERATURE

All the peoples of Botswana had creative forms of oral and visual expression long before the arrival of Europeans. The rock art of southern Africa, some of which has been dated to almost 30,000 years ago, is replete with pictographic and painted expressions of both literal and metaphorical vision.[8] Stories told around campfires for thousands of years doubtless featured in and set the context for many of these depictions. They include tales of shaman seeking the aid of the supernatural to benefit their communities, stories of more ordinary hunting adventures, and even the exploits of animal and human protagonists invented to characterize such universal qualities as envy, greed, vanity, and duplicity that are so commonly attributed to "human nature" by southern African peoples.

Praise Poetry

In the nineteenth century, praise poems *(maboko)* were composed not only for kings and people of high rank but also for and by almost everyone. The composition of an individual praise poem, for instance, was one of the tasks required of all young male cadets during their initiation school *(bogwera)*. As David Livingstone noted, "Each one is expected to compose an oration in praise of himself, called a *'leina'* or name, and to be able to repeat it with sufficient fluency."[9] As a result, most young men a century and a half ago were "familiar with the art of composing and memorizing praise-poems (just as English schoolboys were at one time commonly taught to write Greek or Latin verse)."[10] Poems were composed not only to flatter the powerful and commemorate the prowess and skill of great warriors and hunters but also to describe experiences such as work in the mines or other adventures about which men might desire to boast.[11] Over the course of his life, a man would continue to add to the *"leina"* he composed during his initiation, and as a result, poetic self-expression was "a prerequisite for acquiring a proper adult social personality."[12] A "praise-name," then, is something, "a person thinks a lot about because it is constantly being affected by what a person does and says and what a person has done to him or said about him."[13]

Because praise poetry was essentially oral literature until the beginning of the twentieth century, remembered praises to ancient chiefs have tended to become shorter and shorter as verses are condensed or forgotten over time. Another aspect of their orality was that they were intended to be performed at public gatherings where interaction between the speaker and the audience was an important factor. During the recitation, the ordering of the stanzas—and even their exact wording and the nature of their alliteration—was changed as the speaker improvised and elaborated around a theme, much as modern jazz performers do with music.[14]

Many poets wove inventive references to common proverbs, adages, and sayings into their stanzas, thereby evoking multiple layers of imagery and meaning. The historical and metaphorical nature of some poems, particularly the older ones in praise of ancient chiefs and other cultural "heroes," makes many of them extremely difficult for modern audiences and even their narrators to understand. Praise poems are still recited during the installation of a *kgosi*—or a president—and the poet, as a representative of the people, may use this occasion to send a message. The imagery is often elliptical with obscure allusions, as in this example about Kgosi Kgamanyane, who ruled the Kgatla between 1848 and 1874:

Home Affairs

Majestic slow walker,
Young tortoise, shun the burning grass.
Who am I to shun the burning grass?
They are like hail falling on me always,
The sparks of grass from the hills.
I shun the man with an axe,
One with a club I do not shun;
Should he smite I draw back,
Young tortoise I draw back into my shell.[15]

"Tortoise" was one of the personal names of Kgmanyane. In lines 6 and 7, the poem refers to an incident that occurred when Boer commandos took him captive in South Africa. They brought him into a room, intending to beat him. To protect himself, he dived under a table, much like a tortoise pulls back into its shell, as a defensive measure. Whether the sparks of burning grass falling all around refer to the harassment of Boer raiders, to troubles with his own people, or to both is now unclear.

In addition to poems in praise of bravery and intelligence or those dealing with ethnic conflicts and civil war are poems composed as critiques rather than praise, such as this one written about Molefi Kgafela, who was installed as chief of the Kgatla in 1929. His reign was marred by conflict and internal political dissention, and in the beginning stanzas of this poem, he is berated for attending to the needs of strangers, probably European traders, ahead of those of his own people, who long for him to provide the basics of life—a clean, well-kept town and sufficient food to eat:

Watchman of derelict homes
guardian of his mother's old ruin . . .
Molefi, sweep the town free of refuse
that old men may go where it is clean.
Fill up the holes and choke them; also smash the stones
they trip us and always make us turn up our toes
when we go across to the chief's place.
He sends away the prime beasts
the oxen with large hoofs
with hoofs that will fill the food-bowls
that fill the servants' bowls
so that a servant may eat and leave some over.
Molefi doesn't slaughter big oxen
he slaughters young ones and pregnant cows
he slaughters animals in calf
so that old men may eat the fetuses. . . .
He considers those living far away
he also hastens for strangers
strangers are those first given food
local folk he gives afterwards
People returned hungry from the chief
from the great court of the chief.[16]

In a contemporary poem of critique, Kgosi Toto of Kgalagadi district is censured for allowing Europeans too much influence in his district. The references to saliva and "milk" indicate that the poet suspects that the "white man" has bewitched him:

Nna tota kare o loilwe
O loilwe ka more wa Makgowa
Ba go siela mashi ka dikomoki
Ba go kgwela mathe ganong ba go ithatisa[17]
[Personally, I think you have been bewitched
I say you have been bewitched with the white man's medicine

They give you milk [milky substances] in cups
They put salvia in your mouth so that you will do them favors]

In the past, women rarely rose to political prominence, and there were no praise poems to them. This is changing, however, as Botswana women come to hold more prominent positions in Botswana society. The following praise stanza is one exception that honors Gaositwe Chiepe, one of Botswana's most respected politicians and former minister of Mineral Resources and Water Affairs:

Kana Batswana bare mosadi ga a ke a bokwa
Ba re bonatla jwa mosadi e a bo e le sope-le-wele
Tota MmaChiepe ene o natlafetse rotlhe re mo labile
O supile bonatla jwa gagwe ka go dira meepo
Mme le jaana ga a ise a fetse[18]
[Batswana say a woman is never cited in poetry
They say her hard works are like a ruined kraal
But Miss Chiepe has worked hard and is successful, as all can see
She shows her good works by establishing mines
Which even now, she continues]

Today, initiation rites are no longer held, and the art of poetic oratory and praise is not part of the westernized school curriculum. Nonetheless, Batswana continue to place high value and civic pride on public speaking. The ability to speak eloquently and to express one's thoughts, deeds, and prayers in met- aphorical and poetic language is seen as one of the most important constitu- ents of Botswana's culture and customs. As one author so elegantly phrases it, "The Tswana language is the granary of its culture" (pou ya Setswana ke sefalana sa ngwao ya Setswana).[19]

Folktales

Folktales are an important form of entertainment and education for all Batswana. Many of the stories and tales are almost identical across cultures, while others share similar themes if not identical ways of telling. Among the Bantu-speaking groups, most stories have a moral or teaching dimension and relate how clever animals such as the hare, while poor and seemingly power- less, can overcome obstacles by using their wits. In such tales, hyenas are generally seen as stupid and cowardly, while the Boers (white, Afrikaans- speaking South Africans) are portrayed as cruel. Some authorities have argued that the underlying structure of such tales represents attempts to cope with submerged, internal conflicts and contradictions within society—"inner psychic experiences that have characterized mankind throughout its history."[20] Others see the tales as providing useful conceptual metaphors for dealing with and resisting the strains caused by discrimination, colonialism, urbanization, and other daily conflicts brought about by modernity in general. The way to achieve success while coping with frustration is to adopt, "superficial conformity and docility, as a mask for cunning and careful, strategic thinking ... [in] a world where amoral social forces, opportunities and risks are met by cunning and opportunism ... precisely the world of the animal fables and their hero the trickster."[21] As one old man put it, in simpler language,

> These stories are told to children. They are just for their amusement. But when we live in town, we sometimes have to act just like Mr. Rabbit. We Tswana are small; we are hunted by everyone; sometimes *ditrikinyana* [English borrowing: literally, "little tricks"] are our only means of survival. We tell our children to behave in town. But they must often become rogues just to eat. Among the Europeans people are spoiled. There's no humanity, just as with Rabbit and his friends.[22]

Many folktales deal with tricksters, particularly hares or rabbits, as the original prehistoric underdogs and "con men" who use their wits and clever tricks to overcome adversity. While such performances are entertaining, they also reinforce traditional values, explain changes in cultural life, and provide models of courage in uncertain times. As one young girl was counseled by her father, "All right, you must listen carefully, because in my story, in everyone's story, there is always a lesson. If you miss the lesson, then you might as well have blocked your ears to the story."[23]

The telling of stories, many with moral lessons, remains a popular form of family entertainment, especially in rural areas poorly serviced by libraries, radio, and television. Storytelling is an important skill that children are sometimes instructed in as they are growing up. Unity Dow catches the process in these passages as her heroine, Nei, is instructed by her grandmother in the art of telling a story properly:

> "Nei, I have told you that story many times. In fact, I have an idea. Why don't you tell me the story? Let's hear if you have been listening to me all this time."
>
> "Grandmother, that is not fair. How can I possibly tell your story? I can't tell it right."
>
> "One day you will have to tell all these stories to your own children. This will give you practice. So tell me about the key and if you tell the story well, I will open that chest on a Saturday when you have no school and I will show you what is in there."
>
> I scooped handfuls of warm water and ran it over her back and began, "My grandmother had a brown key around her waist ..."

"No, Nei, you must start at the beginning."

"Let me start again, Nkoko. My grandmother was a beautiful young woman. Her name was Lelegaisang, meaning the greatest love of all ..."

I paused and asked, "Am I telling it right grandmother?"

"Yes, child of my child. Imagine that you are bathing your own child. She is six years old, and has never met me. I was gone long before she was born. What would you tell her? And remember, it is a long story that cannot be told at one sitting. You must not rush it, or she will not take it seriously."[24]

After the evening meal, which for most rural families is still eaten outside under the stars around a wood fire, the cooking pots are cleared away, extra logs are piled on the fire, and the area becomes a flickering stage for lively performances. Storytellers rise and move about the fire telling their tales while mimicking the movements, sounds, and behavior of the people, animals, or other characters in their story. In addition to telling true stories about travels to faraway places or of encounters with wild animals, teachers, or Europeans, this is the time for tales of ghosts, giants, flying snakes, and other supernatural creatures put on earth to encourage the good and moral behavior of children and their parents by portraying what happens to those who transgress society's norms.[25]

The Sarwa story of the marriage between a quagga (an extinct form of zebra) and a jackal, for instance, carries with it the message that individuals should stick with or marry their own kind—in this case, grazers with grazers and carnivores with carnivores. But the wider implications of the story are not lost on the audience. This nineteenth-century rendition is set in the mythic time when the world first began—a time when the rocks of the earth were still soft and "the identities of animals and humans were merged."[26] It begins,

The Quagga, who is married to a Jackal, gives one of her children some of her own liver to eat. A tortoise steals the piece of liver and takes it to the old Jackals who eat it with relish and declare that their relative had married meat. When the Quagga's husband joins them they tell him that he has married a Quagga and should kill his wife. So the Jackal poisons some sharp bones, hides them in his hut and encourages his wife to lie down on them. She is pierced by the bones and the poison soon begins to work. The Quagga, followed by her children, then goes to the water and attempts to drink before she dies. Having drunk, she collapses at the water's edge and is soon tracked down by the Jackals who skin her, cut her up and begin to boil her in a large pot. The Quagga's daughter, however, climbs an overhanging tree and, as she watches the horrible scene beneath, her tears fall onto the pot and split it open. Although surprised at the apparently inexplicable breakage, the Jackals still manage to consume all of the meat. The daughter then runs off to tell her mother's family about what has happened, and these old Quaggas, with the pretence of making a social visit, wait for an opportune moment and then trample the husband to death.[27]

Other folktales offer explanations about how the world got to be the way it is today. A Sarwa story from the Tsodilo Hills, for instance, relates how human reproduction began. The myth centers on a rock, *N/u//goridao*—the place of sex—in the hills:

> When the earth was young, people were all youths; they did not grow old and were not born. One day, three girls went up the hill to collect water from a well named */hokgam*—Medicine Mouth. On their way home they met three boys who had been told by God to meet them. God told them that they must have sex so there would be life and death. They did not understand sex, so God shaped the rock into three vaginas and showed them what to do.[28]

Another story that is very widely spread across the central Kalahari "explains" why some Sarwa have had cattle for a very long time while others remained as hunters and gatherers until the recent past. While this version seems on the surface to relate to historical events, other versions of it suggest it is a kind of "just so" story to explain how different peoples—foragers and herders—came from a common stock. This version, told by a very old Deti man, Braai Segaisi, who lived on the banks of the Boteti River in Tsienyane, relates how

> there were once two brothers, Tsum Tsumyei and Choro Chai. Choro Chai was the oldest and Tsum Tsumyei the youngest. One day when they were out hunting they heard a melodious sound. They crept quietly through the forest to see what was making it, and when they came to a clearing they saw some beautiful animals there. The older brother, Choro Chai, said, "Let's not kill them. Why don't we build a fence and put the animals inside it?" So, the two brothers worked together very hard and built a kraal of thorn bushes to hold the cattle. Then they went back and started running and shouting to chase the animals into the kraal they had made. But along the way Choro Chai tripped and fell. And so it was that the younger brother Tsum Tsumyei drove the cattle into the kraal by himself and closed the gate. He separated the calves from the cows and the next morning he milked them. Later on he gave his older brother the watery whey, while keeping the thicker sour milk for himself. Choro Chai said, "This is fine, little brother. I tripped and fell on the ground while you chased the cattle into the kraal. You can keep the cattle to live from since there are only a few of them. I fell on the ground so I will be the owner of the land and its wild game. I will continue to live by hunting."[29]

Both archaeological and linguistic evidence indicate that Late Stone Age pastor-foragers began to live along the banks of the Boteti River almost 1,500 years ago.[30] Today, the term that the Deti and many other Khoisan speakers use for cattle is *'b'e*, a word very different from the terms for cattle (*kgomo, koma/xama, ongombe, gumi, goma,* and so on) used by their Bantu and Nama neighbors. While Brai's story may be simply a story told to shore up the Deti peoples' historical legitimacy as cattle herders, it is interesting that the tale correlates with archaeological information.

EARLY MISSION AND COLONIAL LITERATURE

When the Bible Society was established in South Africa in 1820, no complete Bible was available in any of the indigenous languages of southern Africa. Beginning in 1817, Robert Moffat began to translate the Bible into the Tswana language, completing the Gospel of Luke in 1830 and the entire New Testament by 1840. As each section was completed, it was printed on a printing press at his mission station in Kuruman in present-day South Africa. By 1857, a complete Tswana Bible, with Old and New Testaments, was available.

In 1842, Moffat also published his *Labours and Scenes in South Africa,* one of the first works in what was to later become a flood of European diaries and accounts authored by missionaries, travelers, adventurers, and hunters who described their lives and adventures in Botswana. Notable among the earliest works are David Livingstone's *Missionary Travels and Researches in South Africa,* first published in 1858; James Chapman's *Travels in the Interior of Africa, 1849–1863;* R. Gordon Cumming's *The Lion Hunter of South Africa;* and William Cotton Oswell's *Hunter and Explorer.*[31] Lesser-known works that describe Botswana at the end of the nineteenth century include E. F. Sandeman's *Eight Months in an Ox-Wagon* and H. Anderson Bryden's *Gun and Camera in Southern Africa.*[32] These early accounts of adventures and travels in Botswana fueled popular interest in Africa among generations of readers in the United Kingdom, the United States, and South Africa.

In the early twentieth century, a number of expatriate diaries and memoirs extolled the virtues and vices of colonial Africa. One of the most lively and often acerbic of these is the running commentary on both black and white society in colonial Bechuanaland by Sir Charles Rey, resident commissioner of the Bechuanaland Protectorate between 1929 and 1937. On the visit of a party of researchers from Witwatersrand University, for instance, he wrote,

> Then back to the Renekes where I found that verminous Ballinger-Barnes party waiting to see me. They are from the Witwatersrand University, wretched people who are carrying out an "Investigation into the economic effect of the Impact of Industrialism on Natives in Africa"! My heavens, how can fools give people like this money to waste. They go about disturbing the natives by talking to all the scallywags—and all the decent natives hate them ... they'll lose a lot of money and fail in their beastly job if I turn them back now. So I gave them a limited permit for certain districts and sent them away—they

comprise Ballinger, an ex-trade unionist from the Clyde; Miss Hedgson, a flat-footed, flat-chested history lecturer from the University with a face like a horse; Barnes, one of the sub-editors of the "Star"—and his wife, a rabbit.[33]

Edited excerpts from Rey's diaries have been published as *Monarch of All I Survey: Bechuanaland Diaries 1929–37*.[34] These include accounts of his dealings (and deposings) of Botswana chiefs. The colonial-era flogging of an Englishman in Tshekedi Khama's court, for instance, provided an excuse for Rey to arrange for a naval detachment to come from Cape Town to depose "that little snake" Khama from his position as *kgosi* of the Ngwato. The political repercussions of the incident are the subject of the book *The Flogging of Phineas McIntosh, a Tale of Colonial Folly, Bechuanaland 1933*.[35]

NOVELISTS

Apart from the sometimes fanciful and one-sided accounts of hunting and exploring adventures published in the last half of the nineteenth and early twentieth centuries, there is very little in the way of literature about Botswana (as opposed to anthropological, scientific writings and colonial diaries) until the late 1960s.[36] Since independence, however, a few Botswana-based authors have made a reputation on the international literary scene. Foremost among these is Bessie Head, who moved to the small village of Serowe in 1964 to escape from a traumatic and unhappy existence in South Africa. The child of an "illicit" union between a wealthy white woman and an unidentified black man in apartheid South Africa, she was born in an asylum for the insane to which her mother had been committed as a result of her unrepentant transgression.

Head was raised in a foster home until she was 13, when she left to attend a mission school. During her early years, she worked as a journalist for *Drum* magazine and other publications in Cape Town and Johannesburg. At one point, she even published her own newsletter, *The Citizen*. Soon after entering into an unhappy marriage, in her mid-thirties, she emigrated with her two-year-old son to Botswana to escape the racist oppression of apartheid experienced by "a person of color" in South Africa. She lived in Botswana as a refugee for the next 15 years before she was finally granted Botswana citizenship. Initially settled in the Ngwato capital of Serowe to teach at Tshekedi Memorial School, she moved for a brief period to Francistown, where she spent an unhappy three years in a government-sponsored refugee community. After her return to Serowe, she wrote her three best-known novels—*When Rain Clouds Gather, Maru*, and *A Question of Power*—as well as a book of short stories, *The Collector of Treasures*.[37]

Although she was initially shunned by the villagers in Serowe, over time they came to accept her, and she established a special bond with many residents. She wrote, "I took an obscure and almost unknown village in the southern Africa bush and made it my own hallowed ground."[38] Her poetic description of the village in *Serowe: Village of Rain Wind* illustrates her love for the place:

> A ring of blue hills partly surrounds the village; at least they look blue, misty, from a distance. But if sunlight and shadow strike them at a certain angle, you can quite clearly see their flat and unmysterious surfaces. They look like the uncombed heads of old Batswana men, dotted here and there with dark shapes of thorn trees.[39]

In spite of her growing international fame as a writer, Head remained poor and lived her life in Serowe in humble circumstances, dwelling in a mud hut appropriately named "Rain Clouds." To supplement her uncertain income from writing, she sold garden produce from the Boiteko Garden, where she began working in 1974. In *Serowe: Village of Rain Wind,* she collected oral histories from people who had contributed to the development of the community. As she was too poor to be able to pay her informants, she promised all who contributed a complimentary copy of her book when it was published. This did not go down well with her publishers, who expected her to pay for the free copies from her royalties. Nonetheless, she fulfilled her promise—and even distributed the copies personally. In the notes for her collection of short stories, *The Collector of Treasures*, which chronicles marriage, witchcraft, funerals, infidelity, and other facets of village life, she gives further credit to the people of Serowe for her inspiration because "the richness of every detail came from the ... physical daily contact with people and sitting around in their yards. I can hardly take credit for the feeling of the work. It is just what people are like here. They are classics. A bit of Ancient Africa was retained intact in this community."[40]

Her final work, *A Bewitched Crossroad*, is a semi-fictionalized history of *Kgosi* Khama III, who ruled the Ngwato at the end of the nineteenth century. She wrote that "no matter where I turn the stuff on him I have read ... had the effect of pulling my life together."[41]

Head's untimely death from hepatitis complicated by alcoholism at the age of 49 caused distress at local, national, and international levels. She was laid to rest in the Botalaote cemetery in Serowe, with her grave marked by a piece of natural stone taken from the hills nearby. After her death, the Khama III Memorial Museum acquired her large collection of letters and papers. She kept carbon copies of almost everything she wrote, and the collection contains more than 2,000 letters that continue to attract researchers to Serowe. There are also 23 short stories in typescript form, some of them unpublished, as well as short articles and essays, a series of comments and book reviews, background notes for her novels, and a variety of other materials, including Christmas cards.

The difficult circumstances of her life provided the material for her insightful examination of wealth, power, gender, ethnicity, and the conflicts between tradition and modernity that feature in her novels. Throughout it all, she never lost sight of the fact that healing, renewal, and freedom are as much a part of life as humiliation and despair. Thinking of the future and of her unhappy past in South Africa, near the end of life she wrote in her private journal that "it is impossible to guess how the revolution will come one day in South Africa. But in a world where all ordinary people are insisting on their rights, it is inevitable. It is hoped that great leaders will arise there who remember the suffering of racial hatred and out of it formulate a common language of love for all people."[42]

In the decades after Head's death, a number of newer Botswana poets and novelists have appeared, many of whom also provide commentary on Batswana values, social injustice, and discrimination. Poet Barolong Seboni, for instance, spent his formative years in London, where, through contacts with southern African writers and refugees, he "caught the revolutionary spirit that was then blowing across southern Africa in search of self-determination and self-actualization."[43] Batswana writers whose work is less widely published and so more difficult to obtain internationally include Andrew Sesinyi and Mositi Torontle, who convey images of urban life in Botswana in the 1980s, and Moteane Melamu and Caitlin Davies, who provide more contemporary portrayals of the problems of modern urban life in Botswana.

Perhaps the most prominent new author in terms of international recognition is Unity Dow. Her novels provide local insight into the juxtaposition of tradition and modernity in themes that range from growing up in the village of Mochudi in the 1960s *(Juggling Truths)* to ritual murder *(The Screaming of the Innocent)*. In *Far and Beyon'*, she deals with the difficulties of growing up in a world where young people are forced to confront the daily specter of the AIDS pandemic in their lives and the conflicted and crosscutting ambiguities of personal relationships that result.[44] In a particularly poignant passage from *Far and Beyon'*, the narrator, a young woman named Mora, tries through a parable to get her mother to come to grips with the reality of AIDS and its affects on her family. Her two eldest brothers have died from the disease, but her mother has been convinced by a series of traditional "doctors" that they had died because they had been bewitched by her best friend. The parable begins thusly:

> A long time ago, there were two women who were great friends. They could pick each other's teeth without fear of harm, as the saying goes.... Then, one day, one of the two friends started going through a series of misfortunes. First, one child got sick. Then another.... Desperate and confused, the friend went from diviner to diviner, from prophet to prophet, from priest to priest. She was told that she had been bewitched. This woman was at first not convinced, but then, two of her children withered away and died.... This woman, in her hour of need, did not go to her only friend because the friend was responsible for her misery. Yes, her friend, ... was now killing them off. The friendship died; there was no more laughter, no more sharing of food, no more love. Instead there was anguish. The children of the two women were confused. Should they talk to each other? Should they play together? Should they even greet each other? ... Then the witch became the victim. Her daughter fell ill. She, too, like her friend, hopped from diviner to diviner.... The victim had become the witch.... But the truth was that the daughter was dying of AIDS. Just like her friend's two sons had died of AIDS.... That was the simple truth.... A truth exploited by many diviners, priests and false prophets, for their own financial gain.[45]

Tswana Literature

While writers in the Tswana language writers are faced with the problem of small markets for their works, some of the better known include Mokgomotso Mogapi, Ray Molomo, Tiroentle Pheto, Sederick Thobega, R. D. Molefhe, and L. D. Raditladi. Pheto's novel titled *Botlhodi jwa Nta ya Tlhogo* (Miracles of Head Lice) uses the coexistence of head lice with the human body as a metaphor to examine the historical friction between Christianity and African traditional religion. Some Tswana who accepted Christianity came to despise their traditional beliefs. They also give preference to English over Tswana, looking down on their native language. Rather than engaging in a confrontation between these two ways of life, however, he calls for the harmonization of these different cultures "just like head lice and the body have come to co-exist."

NEWSPAPERS AND THE INFORMATION MEDIA

Between 1856 and 1930, a number of Christian newsletters were published in Tswana. These included *Molekodi wa Batswana* (Batswana Information, 1856–57) and *Mahoko a Botswana* (Words of Botswana, 1833–89).[46] The first commercial newspaper in the Tswana language was published in 1901 by Sol Plaaje in the Bechuanaland Protectorate as the *Korante oa Bechoana* (Newspaper of Batswana). The Tswana writer and son of the founder of Mafikeng, Silas Molema, personally financed the paper. Later Tswana news publications published in the Bechuanaland Protectorate included, from about 1930 onward, *Lesedi la Botswana* (Light of Botswana), *Lesedi la Setshaba* (Light of the Nation), *Lebone la Bechuana* (Lamp of the Bechuana), and *Naledi ya Batswana* (Star of the Batswana). Sir Ketumile Masire, the second president of Botswana, was the Kanye correspondent for *Naledi* (The Star).[47]

Early newspapers published at the turn of the twentieth century by the Bechuanaland colonial government in Mafeking included the *Bechuanaland News,* the *Vryburg Chronicle,* and the *Bechuanaland Gazette.* In 1962, the colonial government's Department of Information also introduced a monthly magazine called *Kutlwano* (Mutual Understanding), which, in keeping with its name, was intended to promote harmony, goodwill, and mutual understanding among its readers. The magazine, which is still in print, publishes articles in Tswana and English that keep its readers informed about cultural affairs.

In 1963, the protectorate government based in Mafikeng also began publishing the *Bechuanaland Newsletter.* It did not carry independent news but was instead intended to be a mouthpiece of the colonial government and its policies. This newsletter was succeeded in 1965 by the *Bechuanaland Daily News,* which in turn became the *Botswana Daily News* at independence. For many years, the weekly "newspaper" was simply a collection of mimeographed sheets distributed free in small quantities to bars and other public venues in major villages across the country. Today the paper is a daily (Monday–Friday) and is still distributed throughout Botswana for free, although street vendors usually charge a small fee for their service, but they may be subject to legal action if they are caught selling the paper. Because the *Botswana Daily News* is owned and controlled by the government, its reporting tends to focus on government projects and programs, without much analysis or interpretation. The paper contains six pages in English, followed by two pages where the significant articles in the English section are translated into Tswana. The paper is not distributed in rural areas, so its primary audience is people living in large villages and towns. The only newspaper published entirely in Tswana is the popular, biweekly *Mokgosi;* there are no news publications in other indigenous languages.

Political newsletters also began to appear in the 1960s. The monthly newsletter *Therisanyo* (Consultation) was the mouthpiece for the Botswana Democratic Party (BDP) headed by the first president, Sir Seretse Khama. It began publication in 1962 from its headquarters in Kanye, the home of its editor and later vice president and president, Sir Ketumile Masire. The modest publication advocated a nonracial policy and had a well-organized distribution network. In 1964, the principal opposition party, the Botswana National Front (BNF), produced its own monthly newsletter, *Puo-Phaa,* from Mahalapye. The hope of the BNF party secretary and founder, Kenneth Koma, was that the BNF would be able to consolidate Botswana's more radical nationalist and traditionalist opposition under the party's banner.

Since its independence in 1966, Botswana has cherished the principal of freedom of the press, unlike many African countries where such freedoms do not extend to criticism of the government. Although the constitutional laws of Botswana are quite democratic in terms of freedom of information, journalists can still be sued if their reporting is libelous or factually in error; freedom of speech is not akin to trampling on an individual's human rights. The fact that the government ran or controlled all the early news outlets, including the *Botswana Daily News* and *Kultwano* magazine, however, did put implicit constraints on freedom of expression in the press. In response, independent newspapers and magazines began to appear in the early 1980s with a goal of more freely setting their own agendas while providing greater critique of government policy. *Dumela* magazine, one of the first to appear in 1981, disappeared after only four issues. The *Botswana Guardian,* an offshoot of the *Mafikeng Mail,* followed in 1982 but was later overtaken by its rival, *Mmegi wa Dikgang* (The Reporter), in 1984.

Mmegi is the oldest private newspaper in the country and has been one of the most successful because of its willingness to focus critical attention on social, economic, and political issues. As a result, it has become known for its thoughtful and sometimes courageous reporting. The *Gazette,* another independent newspaper, is more closely aligned with the policies of the ruling BDP party and rarely criticizes the government. Other privately owned newspapers include the *Guardian,* the *Sunday Standard,* the *Voice,* and the *Mirror.* Finally, one cannot ignore the controversial and short-lived paper *Newslink,* which appeared briefly in 1990. Soon after it opened, the editors of *Mmegi* unmasked it as an operation of the South Africa Intelligence Agency.[48] As a result of the *Mmegi* exposure, the publishers fled the country in 1992. This—and other hard-hitting investigative reports by Botswana's independent weekly papers—supports the positive assessment that a healthy independent press is alive and well in the country—in stark contrast to the lack of freedom in most other parts of the continent. As one author notes, "The private press in Botswana offers a noteworthy exception. Consisting of four weeklies and enjoying a degree of tolerance from government that is rare in Africa, Botswana's private press has earned credibility for its critical and investigative journalism, especially following its reporting of the 'Botswana Housing Corporation scandal' and the 'Newslink Africa' affair."[49]

Minority Voices

The Kuru Development Trust has become one of the mouthpieces for Sarwa communities in Botswana. They have recently published a book titled *Voices of the San,* which takes readers on a journey of learning about and appreciating the history and lifestyle of the Sarwa. The book is organized into four chapters that cover themes that the Sarwa themselves have identified as reflecting their current lifestyle: "1) Hunters turned Herders—the effects of contact and change; 2) Our Past Life—insight into their traditional cultures; 3) They say the land is like this, this, this—[illustrating] their close link with nature and land, and; 4) Those who are 'Deep down'—the surge for survival from a 'traditional' to a 'modern' economy."[50]

Cartoonists and Public Commentary

Billy Chiepe, originally of the Gaborone newspaper *Mmegi,* is a well-known Batswana cartoonist who presents his perspectives on Botswana's culture in a light-humored manner. He believes that it is good for people to laugh at themselves, even though some may become angry at his caricatures of them. Another popular cartoonist is Tebogo Motswetla, nicknamed *Mabijo* after the character he draws. His cartoons display a strongly Christian orientation, but he keeps his audience laughing with popular cartoons that both address and skewer cultural issues. Other satirical artists include Vusi Nyoni, a graphic designer at the Botswana Technology Centre in Gaborone, and Lazarous Chanda, who works in watercolors. Micco Samu is a regular contributor of comic strips to *Kutlwano* magazine and the weekly newspaper *Mirror.*

RADIO AND TELEVISION

There are two state-controlled radio stations in the country—Radio Botswana 1 (RB1) and Radio Botswana 2 (RB2); privately owned radio stations include Ya Rona FM and Gabz FM. The Voice of America also broadcasts from Selibe-Phikwe. For many years, the government resisted attempts to create independent stations by controlling broadcast licensing; it was only in 1994, after a young lawyer took the government to court, that the Botswana Telecommunications Corporation was charged with the responsibility of issuing licenses. While this opened the way for private stations, the lawyer who first brought the case did not receive one because, according to one report, "his application indicated the intended use of minority languages."[51]

Using government revenue, RB 1 can afford to broadcast 24 hours a day. But because it is a government outlet, its content is conservative and serves mainly to uncritically present information favorable to government programs and policies. In addition, it has sometimes been alleged that government ministers have attempted, through intimidation and threats of firing, to interfere with the editorial work of the government-owned stations. (Similar charges of government interference are also occasionally heard about Botswana Television and the Botswana Daily News.) While RB 1 is totally run with government funding, RB 2 is a commercial station controlled by the government. This has led the privately owned stations to complain of unfair, subsidized competition.

An analysis of the two government radio stations found that approximately 43 percent of their programming was in Tswana, with 22 percent in English and the remainder in both languages. In comparison with the government-run stations, English was found to be the language medium in more than 70 percent of the private station broadcasts, the focus of which is on a more youthful audience.[52] No stations in Botswana broadcast in Kalanga, Yeyi, Herero, or other minority languages. Although it is certainly true that most Batswana have a working understanding of the Tswana language, some have suggested that the lack of inclusion of other indigenous languages in Botswana media—whether print, radio, or television—has contributed to the spread of HIV/AIDS because language-appropriate educational materials were not equally available to all ethnic groups.

Soon after South African television began broadcasting four hours of evening programming in English and Afrikaans in 1976, television antennas began popping up on rooftops throughout Gaborone. After 1984, the number of television sets in Botswana took another jump as the apartheid-era "homeland" of Bophuthatswana began its own, quasi-independent programming in English and Tswana from its station—BOP TV—in Mafiking. For many years, Batswana received essentially free television from South Africa via a repeating transmitter on the top of Kgale Hill on the outskirts of Gaborone. These developments caused some concern, however, because some felt that Botswana citizens were being unduly influenced by news and entertainment originating from outside the country. Concern was especially high when ad hoc interviews with schoolchildren in Gaborone indicated that many of them believed that Lucas Mangope, the president of the Bophuthatswana homeland, was actually the president of Botswana. Nonetheless, television stations are expensive to build and run, and it was not until 2000, well after the end of apartheid, that Botswana built its own national station.

Currently, there are two television stations in Botswana: the Gaborone Broadcasting Company (GBC) and Botswana Television (BTV). GBC is a closed-circuit service with distribution limited to Gaborone. A third alternative, digital satellite television, is a commercial venture from South Africa that brings in international programming, particularly from the United States, via satellite. The establishment of BTV was a major endeavor for Botswana, and with its modern equipment, it can now be received in approximately 50 percent of the country. Expectations for it are high among local people, many of whom are anxious to take part in the variety of local programming the station is undertaking. It is their own station, and for the first time, the people of Botswana are seeing themselves rather than foreign cultures portrayed. BTV has become an overnight success as a new symbol of nationhood. People are already beginning to take pride in creating and watching programming that reflects their own people and cultures. Although the government wholly owns BTV, it has so far enjoyed the same degree of editorial independence and freedom experienced by the press and radio—a freedom of expression congruent with Botswana's democratic principles.[53]

NOTES

1. H. Alverson, *Mind in the Heart of Darkness: Value and Self-Identity among the Tswana of Southern Africa* (New Haven, Conn.: Yale University Press, 1978), pp. 125–26.

2. Andrew Smith (1835), quoted in I. Schapera, *Praise-Poems of Tswana Chiefs* (Oxford: Clarendon Press, 1965), p. 3.

3. Cover notes in B. Head, *The Collector of Treasures, and Other Botswana Village Tales* (London: Heinemann Educational, 1977).

4. A. McCall Smith, *The No. 1 Ladies Detective Agency* (Cape Town: D. Philip, 1998). See also A. McCall Smith, *Morality for Beautiful Girls* (New York: Anchor Books, 2002); *Tears of the Giraffe* (New York: Anchor Books, 2002); and *The Kalahari Typing School for Men* (New York: Pantheon Books, 2003).

5. R. H. Finnegan, *Oral Literature in Africa* (London: Clarendon Press, 1970), p. 121.

6. B. Seboni, "Why I Write What I Write," http://www.uiowa.edu/~iwp/EVEN/documents/SeboniWhyIWrite.pdf, p. 2.

7. L. Nyati-Ramahobo, "The Language Situation in Botswana," *Current Issues in Language* 1 (2, 2000): 254.

8. J. D. Lewis-Williams, *Believing and Seeing: Symbolic Meanings in Southern San Rock Paintings* (London: Academic Press, 1981); A. Campbell, J. Denbow, and E. Wilmsen, "Paintings Like Engravings: Rock Art at Tsodilo," in *Contested Images: Diversity in Southern African Rock Art Research*, ed. T. Dowson and D. Lewis-Williams (Johannesburg: Witwatersrand University Press, 1994), 131–58.

9. D. Livingstone, *Missionary Travels and Researches in South Africa* (New York: Harper and Brothers, 1858), p. 147.

10. Schapera, *Praise-Poems of Tswana Chiefs,* p. 3.

11. A praise song composed around J. Denbow's archaeological excavations at Bosutswe, for instance, was a hit at a local bar in 2001.

12. Alverson, *Mind in the Heart of Darkness,* p. 194.

13. Ibid., p. 195.

14. Performance of oral literature is an important skill in many societies; even Homer's epic poems, the *Illiad* and the *Odyssey,* were remembered and performed orally for generations before they were committed to paper.

15. Schapera, *Praise-Poems of Tswana Chiefs*, p. 75. Schapera attributes this poem to Kgamanyane himself.

16. From a praise poem to Molefi Kgafela (1909–56). His reign was marred by misconduct, and he was deposed from office by the Bechuanaland protectorate administration for several years. The poem was composed by Klaas Segogwane and was first recited at a kgotla meeting in 1931, soon after Molefi was installed as chief. Schapera, *Praise-Poems of Tswana Chiefs,* pp. 112–16.

17. K. Mogapi, *Ngwao ya Setswana* (Gaborone: Mmampodi Publishers, 1986), p. 76. Perhaps for obvious reasons, the author of this poem is not named.

18. Ibid., p. 73.

19. Ibid., p. 48.

20. Alverson, *Mind in the Heart of Darkness,* p. 56. C. Jung, ed., *The Trickster: A Study in American Indian Mythology* (New York: American Philosophical Library, 1956).

21. Alverson, *Mind in the Heart of Darkness,* pp. 210–11.

22. Ibid., p. 209.

23. U. Dow, *Juggling Truths* (North Melbourne: Spinifex Press, 2003), p. 130. Reproduced with permission from *Juggling Truths* by Unity Dow (2003). Published by Spinifex Press.

24. Ibid., p. 113. Reproduced with permission from *Juggling Truths* by Unity Dow (2003). Published by Spinifex Press.

25. For examples of stories about Kgwanyape, the rain snake, see I. Schapera, *Rainmaking Rites of Tswana Tribes* (Leiden: Afrika-Studiecentrum, 1971), pp. 35–42.

26. M. Biesele, *Women Like Meat: The Folklore and Foraging Ideology of the Kalahari Ju/oan* (Indianapolis: Indiana University Press, 1993), p. 33.

27. R. Hewitt, *Structure, Meaning and Ritual in the Narratives of the Southern San* (Hamburg: H. Buske 1986), p. 112.

28. E-mail from Edwin Wilmsen to J. Denbow, June 9, 2005.

29. Story told to J. Denbow, Tsienyane, July 25, 1980. Braai claimed to be able to remember the rinderpest epidemic of 1896, which, if true, would have made him over 90 years old at the time of this telling.

30. J. Denbow, *After the Flood: A Preliminary Account of Recent Geological, Archaeological and Linguistic Investigations in the Okavango Region of Northern Botswana. Contemporary Studies on Khoisan: In Honour of Oswin Köehler on the Occasion of His 75th Birthday.* Edited by R. Vossen and K. Keuthmann (Hamburg: H. Buske, 1986), 5.1, pp. 181–214.

31. R. Moffat, *Missionary Labours and Scenes in Southern Africa* (London: J. Snow, 1842); Livingstone, *Missionary Travels and Researches in South Africa;* J. Chapman

and Theodore Roosevelt Hunting, *Travels in the Interior of South Africa: Comprising Fifteen Years' Hunting and Trading: With Journeys across the Continent from Natal to Walvisch Bay, and Visits to Lake Ngami and the Victoria Falls* (London: Bell & Daldy, 1868); R. Gordon Cumming, *The Lion Hunter of South Africa: Five Years' Adventures in the Far Interior of South Africa, with Notices of the Native Tribes and Savage Animals* (London: John Murray, 1911); W. E. Oswell and D. Livingstone, *William Cotton Oswell, Hunter and Explorer: The Story of His Life with Certain Correspondance and Extracts from the Private Journal of David Livingstone, hitherto Unpublished* (London: W. Heinemann, 1900).

32. E. F. Sandeman, *Eight Months in an Ox-Wagon: Reminiscences of Boer Life* (Johannesburg: African Book Society, 1975); H. A. Bryden, *Gun and Camera in Southern Africa: A Year of Wanderings in Bechuanaland, the Kalahari Desert, and the Lake River Country, Ngamiland* (London: E. Stanford, 1893).

33. Charles Rey diary, June 15, 1931. Copy in possession of J. Denbow.

34. C. F. Rey et al., *Monarch of All I Survey: Bechuanaland Diaries, 1929–37* (New York:L. Barber Press, 1988).

35. M. Crowder, *The Flogging of Phineas McIntosh: A Tale of Colonial Folly and Injustice: Bechuanaland, 1933* (New Haven, Conn.: Yale University Press, 1988).

36. One exception is a novel by Naomi Mitchison that includes some information on Kgatla culture and customs. N. Mitchison, *Return to the Fairy Hill* (London: Heinemann, 1966).

37. B. Head, *When Rain Clouds Gather: A Novel* (London: Gollancz, 1969); *Maru: A Novel* (London: Gollancz, 1971); *A Question of Power: A Novel* (London: Davis-Poynter, 1973:); *The Collector of Treasures, and Other Botswana Village Tales* (London: Heinemann Educational, 1977); *Serowe, Village of the Rain Wind* (London: Heinemann, 1981).

38. H. Vorting, *Lekgapho Khama Memorial Museum Review 1988–1989* (Serowe: Serowe Printers, 1990), p. 63.

39. Ibid., p. 64.

40. Bessie Head Papers, File 44, 12.1.75. Khama III Memorial Museum, Serowe.

41. B. Head, *A Bewitched Crossroad: An African Saga* (New York: Paragon House., 1986).Bessie Head Papers, File 44, 5.1.1974. Bessie Head Papers, File 44, 5.1.1974.

42. Bessie Head, personal journal, 1985.

43. Seboni, "Why I Write What I Write."

44. U. Dow, *Juggling Truths* (North Melbourne: Spinifex Press, 2003); U. Dow, *Far and Beyon'* (San Francisco: Aunt Lute Books, 2000); U. Dow, *Screaming of the Innocent* (North Melbourne: Spinifex Press, 2000). Reproduced with permission from *Juggling Truths* by Unity Dow (2003). Published by Spinifex Press; Reproduced with permission from *Far and Beyon'* by Unity Dow (2000). Originally published by Spinifex Press. North American rights held by Aunt Lute.

45. Dow, *Far and Beyon'*, pp. 162–63. Reproduced with permission from *Far and Beyon'* by Unity Dow (2000). Originally published by Spinifex Press. North American rights held by Aunt Lute.

46. P. Rantao, ed., *Botswana Media and Democracy* (Gaborone: Mmegi Publishing House, 1996).

47. L. Nyati-Ramahobo, "The Language Situation in Botswana," *Current Issues in Language* 1 (2, 2000): 243–300.

48. J. J. Zaffiro, "Mass Media, Politics and Society in Botswana: The 1990s and Beyond," *Africa Today* 40 (1, 1993): 7–25.

49. F. B. Nyamnjoh, "West Africa: Unprofessional and Unethical Journalism," in *Ethics in Journalism: A Reader on Their Perception in the Third World*, ed. Michael Kunczik (Bonn: Division for International Development Cooperation of Friedrich-Ebert-Stiftung, 1999), p. 40.

50. Kuru Family of Organizations, Annual Report 2004, p. 6; W. le Roux and A. White, eds., *Voices of the San* (Cape Town: Kwela Books, 2004).

51. L. Nyati-Ramahobo, "The Language Situation in Botswana," 272–73.

52. Ibid.

53. P. Rantao, in M. Leepile, ed., *Botswana Media and Democracy* (Gaborone: Mmegi Publishing House, 1996).

4

Art and Architecture

[Nineteenth century] evangelists took it for granted that houses, and the routines they inscribed, constructed their inhabitants. The architecture of civilization should, therefore, be an effectual means of insinuating hygienic, Godly habits into heathen life. . . . The Europeans assumed one cardinal principle above all others: that the gauge of a civilized abode was the degree to which its interior spaces were rendered functionally specific and distinct. A residence with no internal divisions, no rooms given over to particular kinds of activity, signified savagery . . . all the more so if that residence was not enclosed on its own grounds. On the other hand, the making of decent dwellings—with living and dining rooms, bedrooms, kitchens, pantries— might give access to the Mansion of the Lord.[1]

ART

The traditional art forms of Botswana are as rich and varied as its people. Little has been written about Botswana crafts, and the Western distinction between art and craft is in any case blurred in the African context. Most traditional artworks in Botswana are made for both aesthetic and utilitarian purposes. For instance, wooden stools, spoons, bowls, mortars, and pestles are usually decorated by burning the object with heated metal tools. Although many of these designs are intended to carry meaning, others are purely decorative and done simply for the pleasure and enjoyment of the producer and user. In addition to the artist's or craftperson's creativity, the motifs, designs, and subject matter of Botswana art are influenced by the materials available to them in the natural environment.

Art in the form of rock paintings and engravings thousands of years old can be found in most parts of Botswana where there are suitable rock outcrops. One of the most visited rock art sites surrounds a spring on the outskirts of Mochudi, 15 miles north of Gaborone. Here human footprints have been pecked into the rock. They are associated by local tradition with the emergence of the first Tswana groups, led by a man known as Matsieng, from the underworld. According to local legend, Matsieng had only one leg because the footprints around the spring all seem to be of the left foot. He brought with him the domesticated animals that formed the basis of Tswana wealth.[2] There are other sites across the country, especially around springs, where similar animal and human footprints are carved into the rock. Although these engravings are undated, most archaeologists associate them, including those at Matsieng, with Late Stone Age hunters and gatherers rather than Iron Age herders and farmers. Their meanings and possible use in ritual are unclear.

The most important area for rock art in Botswana is the Tsodilo Hills in northwestern Ngamiland, where more than 3,000 paintings at more then 500 sites depict a variety of wildlife, human figures, and geometric designs.[3] The hills, home to both Sarwa (Zhu/oasi) and Mbukushu peoples today, were declared a World Heritage Site in 2001. Another important group of rock paintings is found at Manyana rock shelter about 20 miles west of Gaborone. This small shelter contains red-painted naturalistic figures of rhinoceros, giraffe, and humans along with geometric designs. A few of the human paintings and animals have elements that associate them with the out-of-body trance experiences of shaman during healing dances.

Early examples of Botswana art were included in nineteenth-century missionary and traveler's journals and diaries, such as those of John Campbell, David Livingstone, and John Mackenzie. For the most part, the art depicted consists of geometric and naturalistic motifs burned onto the surfaces of gourds, wooden bowls, spoons, and other utilitarian items. Men were renowned for their skill in sewing karosses (skin and fur blankets) and mats fashioned from tanned animal hides.[4] The most elaborate of these contained beautiful patterns and designs made by using the skins of animals with contrasting colors and textures of fur and hair. Women produced baskets, and pottery, while decorative beadwork of iron, copper, glass, and shells adorned their skin aprons and carrying bags. Much of this art is now gone, as these handcrafted everyday objects have been replaced by mass-produced goods. One area of Botswana art that has flourished, however, is basketry. Botswana baskets are the quintessential tourist commodity because they are not only beautiful and well made but also sturdy and lightweight and come in convenient sizes for packing in airline luggage.

Basketry

Woven baskets are perhaps the most famous of Botswana's crafts. They have played an important part in the country's agricultural sector because of their traditional use in agricultural and household tasks over thousands of years. Traditionally, baskets performed a wide variety of functions from huge grain storage baskets over two meters in diameter *(sesigo* or *sefalana)* to baskets used for straining traditional beer *(motlhotlho)* and containers used to hold and display products such as peanuts and mopane worms in the local market *(ditlatlana);* the shape and construction of the basket varied by function.[5]

Baskets can be divided into three main categories: closed baskets; large, open, bowl-shaped baskets *(ditlatlana);* and smaller, plate-shaped baskets *(maselo).* Closed baskets with lids are used for storing grain, seeds, and sometimes even sorghum beer. Women also use them to carry items on their heads. For winnowing grain after it has been thrashed, they usually use large, open, bowl-shaped baskets. Smaller, plate-shaped baskets are used for winnowing grain after it has been pounded. The *sefalana* or *sesigo,* a type of basket that is becoming something of a rarity, is a large grain storage basket that is made exclusively by men. Some of these were almost three meters in diameter, and in the past they were very valuable, with the traditional payment being a cow for a small one. Because the grain baskets were so large and needed to be very strong, they were made of coils of grass approximately one inch in diameter sewn together with strips of strong bark taken from the *morethwa* tree.

The main raw material used to produce other baskets is the fiber of the "vegetable ivory" palm tree *(Hyphaene petersiana,* called *mokola* in Setswana), which grows around the fringes of islands in the Okavango Delta and around pans in the Makgadikgadi; other plants are used in eastern Botswana where palm trees do not grow. The fronds are cut, boiled, and kept soft in a container of water from which the weaver draws as she wraps them around a palm fiber core to form a coil that is sewn together using a metal needle. To create designs, the cream-colored fiber is dyed using natural materials such as the roots or bark of the *motlhakola (Euclea divinorum)* and *motsentsela (Berchemia discolor)* trees to produce varying shades of brown. Basket makers are highly creative in their use of natural dyes because many people now buy baskets for decorative purposes rather than as functional containers. Although there is extensive use of baskets in the country, most are now produced for export, and Botswana's baskets are equal to the finest of art forms found anywhere in the world. There are now a number of established design traditions, some telling a story or with symbolic meaning.

The main producers of baskets in Botswana are women of the Yeyi and Mbukushu communities living in the northwestern part of the country. They

Baskets, one of Botswana's most developed
art forms, bring significant income to
their weavers, who often live in rural areas.
While their shapes still preserve their utilitarian function, the cost of more elaborate examples makes them too expensive
for people to use on a daily basis.

have passed the skill of basket weaving from one generation to the next. The
intricate abstract designs they produce require considerable geometric calcu-
lation to produce symmetrically, and many of them are reminiscent of the
beaded aprons worn in earlier times. Before international marketing co-ops
established in the early 1970s created a tourist demand for baskets, their
designs were more asymmetric and less complex and used fewer natural colors.
The involvement of Botswana Craft in the marketing of high-quality baskets
has led to more professionalism on the part of weavers, and the design art
they produce has become increasingly complex as they have incorporated new
materials such as the use of the leaves of a shrub (*Indigofera* sp.) to produce a
mauve color and the husks of fungus-infected sorghum to create a lovely pink
shade. In recognition of this important craft, a national basket exhibition and
competition has been held for more than two decades at the National Museum

in Gaborone. Judges select the best baskets, and their makers receive recognition along with cash awards and other prizes. This cooperation between private and government organizations and local weavers has made Botswana baskets some of the finest in Africa. While increased prices and marketability benefit the rural economy, this has resulted in a decline in the production of some shapes and styles as tourists demand "suitcase-size" baskets. Of course, the art of basket making, like all others, constantly changes in response to new market demands and the opportunities to experiment provided by new technologies and raw materials. To meet the need for strong baskets for everyday use, for instance, some weavers are recycling the ubiquitous plastic bag in lieu of palm fronds to make more inexpensive baskets for daily use.

Pottery

Clay pots have been produced in Botswana for almost 2,000 years, but it is one of the vanishing crafts in the country. Traditional pottery was crafted by hand using coils that were built up by hand to form jars, bowls, and other shapes demanded for household tasks such as cooking, food and water storage, and serving vessels. In all groups except the Mbukushu, where men are the potters, the art of pot making was passed down from mother to daughter. But pottery making is a complex industry requiring considerable skill and knowledge. Not every woman made pots, and a single potter often supplied the needs of many families. Clays vary widely in their suitability for making pots, and they have to be carefully prepared, with the appropriate percentage of tempering material added to ensure that they are strong and do not crack. After molding, the pots are burnished with a smooth stone to produce a polished surface to which decoration is applied. Pottery shapes and styles of decoration varied from region to region, although most pots made after about 1700 CE used design motifs worked in contrasting colors using natural ocher and graphite. After decorating and drying, the pots were covered with wood and brush and fired to temperatures around 700 to 800 degrees centigrade. Today, few people make or use clay pots for cooking, beer making, or storage because they are complicated and time consuming to make and more fragile and expensive than mass-produced alternatives. One may occasionally see a large beer-making pot in a village, but these are usually kept more as heirlooms than for everyday use.

A few cottage industries have emerged in Gaborone and Thamaga to produce pots for the tourist trade. Gabane Pottery, started in 1982, uses clay from the hills surrounding the village to create animal figures, masks, bowls, and jewelry pieces. It has developed its own style that incorporates traditional designs in a distinctive dark red color. Thamaga Pottery, another ceramic

Unusual for Africa, among the Mbukushu
of Ngamiland it is the men who make
the pots.

center, produces more utilitarian products, including dishware, ashtrays, and
other objects, using modern designs, glazes, and styles. All modern ceramics
are kiln fired, giving them greater durability than the traditional, wood-fired
vessels.

Weaving

Tapestry weaving is another cottage industry that combines craft skills with
artistic designs to help women earn an income. The Oodi weavers' cooperative, established in 1975, trained local women to dye, spin, and weave a variety of products, including wall hangings, hand-woven bedspreads, tablecloths,
table runners, and mats, in a variety of colors and designs, mainly for the
tourist trade. Some of their large tapestries incorporate village scenes that
often tell the story of a historical event. The tapestries and rugs are woven on
hand looms using karakul wool from Tswana herds, and the quality of the
designs they weave has gained them an international reputation. The weavers
at Tiro ya Diatla also fashion scrap wool into tourist goods. They are especially

well known for producing personalized teddy bears, complete with passports, for export.

Woodworking

Wood carving represents another important arts-and-craft sector. Generally, people in northern Botswana are more skilled at wood carving, whereas those in the southern region are better potters. Wood-carvers from the Shashe area in northeastern Botswana carve animals and toys from wood and animal horn. In past times, when travel by steam train required many stops to take on water, the trains were met by craftspeople selling their wares through the train windows, along with dry-roasted peanuts and hard-boiled eggs. Many of the carvings were of birds and other animals, along with wood bowls and lidded jars fashioned from Mopane heartwood on homemade, foot-operated lathes. Other popular items included an imaginary half-human, half-hare-like creature that in some parts of the country figures in folklore as a trickster; *Tokolosi,* a tiny creature that can be used for good and evil intentions, was also carved in a variety of shapes. These products and others, such as wooden carvings of birds, animals, and walking sticks, have not gained the same international market as baskets. Only occasionally available as they are produced by herders at the cattle posts and lands in their spare time, they are generally made for personal enjoyment and an occasional roadside sale. As a result, these items are often idiosyncratic, retaining considerable individuality and personality.

Leather Work

Tanned skin mats, often sewn into complex patterns using the skins of a variety of wild and domestic animals, are a traditional art form that is now rarely seen in most homes. One of these mats, approximately 15 by 25 feet in area and crafted with the skins of lions and leopards and other animals sewn into it, was produced by the men of Serowe in 1953 as a gift for Queen Elizabeth II on her coronation. While these products of Tswana craftsmen are now rare, in contrast to the commercialized game skins mounted on felt found in tourist shops, many Sarwa living in the Kalahari Desert and western Ngamiland continue to make skin aprons, karosses, and carrying bags for their own use and for sale. Their crafts, which are associated with aspects of their daily lives, include items used in hunting and gathering, dancing, healing, entertainment, and personal adornment. In addition, they now produce in bulk crafts such as bows and arrows, quivers, skin bags, and loincloths for tourists. Tiny sets of bows and arrows used by a suitor to "shoot" the woman he loves are also popular items produced for sale. According to tradition, after shooting his "game," he must wait to see whether she will signal her interest in him by picking up the arrow. Men do the hunting, tan the skins using indigenous plants, and sew them into bags and other items. Women then decorate the items with beadwork.

Beadwork

Beads made from ostrich eggshells have been found in archaeological deposits in Botswana dating to more than 10,000 years ago. Carefully emptied whole ostrich eggs are also used as water canteens that are sometimes decorated with geometric and naturalistic designs scratched into their surface and then darkened with charcoal. To make beads, the eggs are broken into angular fragments and then chipped into a rough, round shape using a stone hammer and a bone or horn punch. These are then drilled and strung onto a long sinew or bark string, which is drawn along a grinding stone that smoothes them to a uniform size. These are the sorts of beads generally found in tourist shops. Over time, bead strings worn around the neck and waist become highly polished and are prized as heirlooms. Beads produced for the tourist trade are more irregular and have seldom been worn long enough to develop a patina or polish. Ostrich eggshell beads continue to be an important aspect of Sarwa material culture. Strings of ostrich eggshell beads, often intermixed with glass beads, are sewn with sinew onto aprons, bags, and headbands. Headbands, especially, are important gifts traditionally exchanged between Sarwa trading partners in a system known as *hxaro*. A few of the more common motifs included on them are known by such evocative names as "bull's piss" for a zigzag line with alternating spots on either side that represent the footprints of the ox as it walks and urinates or "owl's eyes" for a motif of concentric circles. Mbukushu women are also excellent bead workers who sew zigzag designs of black and white beads onto the skin aprons they tie around their waist.

MBUKUSHU CRAFTS

The Mbukushu of Etsha are Angolan refugees who brought with them a variety of craft skills. They live in settlements on the western edge of the Okavango Delta. Mbukushu men, known for their blacksmithing and woodcarving skills, fashion decorative and functional tools such as axes, hoes, adzes, and knives in wooden sheaths for local use and for sale to tourists. They make musical instruments such as thumb pianos that have metal keys attached to a wooden resonator and are played by striking the keys with the thumbs. They also manufacture a variety of sizes and shapes of drums carved from the trunks of large trees. They burn designs of interlocking triangles onto the soft wood surfaces of these instruments using metal tools that have been heated red hot in the fire. Some men, also skilled weavers, make decorated carrying bags from palm fibers and sleeping mats from Okavango reeds. Their skills are matched by the women, who use natural resources of the Okavango area to fashion baskets and bracelets from palm fronds, necklaces from ostrich egg-shell beads and aromatic woods, and sitting mats from papyrus.

HERERO CRAFTS

The Herero of northwestern Botswana are renowned pastoralists, and much of their crafts and artwork center around cattle herding and milking. These include milk jugs carved with sharp-bladed adzes from a single piece of hardwood and used for storing milk. These are sometimes decorated with triangular motifs that are burned into their surfaces. Deep wooden bowls were also carved, usually with raised rims and decorated lugs carved into their surfaces for suspension; containers for storing fat are made from pieces of wet cowhide hardened into round shapes. Herero women also make small dolls dressed in traditional clothing for the tourist trade.

Herero women in their traditional clothing. They are holding dolls that they sell to tourists to make extra income.

CONTEMPORARY ARTS

The visual arts play an important role in the cultural identity of the country. In realization of this role, the government of Botswana has committed itself to promoting, supporting, and preserving the art of all its peoples as part of its goal to reinforce "unity in diversity." To stimulate the visual arts, the Botswana government has created an infrastructure to protect national art collections, most of which are housed at the National Museum, Monuments and Art Gallery in Gaborone and in regional museums such as those in Mochudi, Serowe, and Francistown.

The Botswana National Museum, Monuments and Art Gallery

One of the primary aims of the Botswana National Museum, Monuments and Art Gallery is to promote Botswana art and artists at the national and international levels. To this end, it hosts a number of important exhibitions, including the Artists in Botswana Show, the National Basket and Craft Exhibition, the National Children's Art Exhibition, and the Thapong International Artists Workshop and Exhibition. These exhibitions are produced in collaboration with the private sector. The National Basket and Craft Exhibition, for instance, is organized by the National Museum in collaboration with Botswana Craft and has been running for more than 20 years. Through its cooperation with Botswana Craft, the major private marketer of crafts and baskets in the country, the National Museum has been able to expand its holdings of Botswana baskets and other items while at the same time helping to promote the marketing of Botswana's culture.

The National Museum has been very supportive of the arts and has maintained several exhibit spaces for local and international exhibitions for almost 40 years. Recently, the museum began a new initiative called the Princess Marina Hospital Public Art Program, which is designed to expand visual arts beyond the walls of the museum gallery by displaying it at the hospital buildings and grounds. The idea is to take art to the people, especially those who may never visit art galleries. Many think that the hospital buildings and environment have been transformed to the benefit of staff, patients, and visitors.

The National Museum has also allocated the old colonial fort and post office complex in the "Village" in Gaborone to the Thapong Visual Art Centre, which has restored the building in exchange for its use. The center provides space and training for artists involved in painting, sculpture, printing, and traditional pottery. It also sponsors annual workshops in the fine and applied arts.

The Thapong International Artist's Workshop

The Thapong International Artist's Workshop represents another facet of the Museum and Art Gallery's support for the arts in Botswana. The intent of the workshop is to expose local artists to artists and their work from a variety of countries, fostering cooperation and dialogue. The basic premise of the workshop is that intense interaction and concentration leads to an expansion of creativity. At the same time, while public attitudes toward professional artists are gradually changing for the better, Neo Matome, one of Botswana's most renowned women artists, argues that artists in Botswana are often viewed with skepticism because art is not seen as a "real" profession that contributes to society despite the fact that art can promote and encourage such goals as independent thinking, innovation, and resourcefulness. Botswana artists also experience practical problems, especially a lack of studio space where artists can work. In rural areas, it is even more difficult, as artists often have problems acquiring the materials they need to produce their work and to transport it to major cities for exhibitions and sale.

The Bank of Botswana has built up a collection to encourage the growth of contemporary art in the country that complements that of the National Museum. While corporate efforts toward the promotion of visual arts is important, the ultimate future of the arts in the country rests with the artists. A recently revived Artist Association is an important step toward reviving interest in the arts. In addition, the Department of Education and Arts at the University of Botswana has created a Visual and Performing Arts program that combines both theoretical and practical components, including a section on how the arts can contribute to national development through multimedia communication.

The Kuru Art Project

The Kuru Art Project, a Sarwa-owned organization on the D'kar farm in northwestern Botswana, provides clear testimony of how history, folklore, and nature can influence art. The art center provides facilities, materials, and encouragement to Sarwa artists who are invited to experiment with art while being provided with personal instruction on the handling of unfamiliar paints and other materials. Through a series of workshops, Sarwa artists have produced lithographs, black-and-white and color prints, etchings, and monoprints. Men and women artists tend to paint different subject matter and use different materials, with women generally producing more depictions of wild plant foods and birds along with beadwork, items of clothing, and jewelry. Men, on the other hand, tend to paint animals, mythical creatures, and people.

While there is an occasional overlap in subject matter, the artists seem to let their art follow such traditional and engendered divisions of labor and experience. If these divisions were also true in the distant past, it would suggest that most of the thousands of rock paintings and engravings that depict mostly animals and humans in the Tsodilo Hills, at the Savuti game reserve, and at Matsieng and Mamunowere were the work of male artists.

International organizations have worked with the Sarwa artists of the Kuru Project to market their art. One woman's painting, for instance, was chosen as one of the tail-art designs used on British Airways planes. By 1999, Kuru artists had mounted more than 25 exhibitions and shows throughout southern Africa, Europe, Australia, and the United States. They have won many awards, both collectively and individually, in venues such as the Artists in Botswana Competition held at the National Museum and Art Gallery and the Graphic Creative Printing Awards in Finland. In 1994, Qwaa, Thamae Sethogo, Qoma, and X'were exhibited at the International Prize Winners' Exhibition in Poland, and their works are now found in private collections throughout the world.

CONTEMPORARY CRAFTS

Thusano Silversmith Corporation produces sterling silver jewelry that incorporates traditional basket designs and San paintings from the Tsodilo Hills. Other artists produce bracelets, rings, and necklaces made from materials such as palm fiber, *mopane* wood, glass beads, animal horn and hair, and clay. Hollowed-out gourds and calabashes, with a variety of designs burned into them, recall those illustrated in nineteenth-century travelers' journals. Such items are still common sights in curio shops and vendor's stalls across the country.

These informal markets also sell a variety of other arts and crafts, especially sculpture, from the neighboring countries of South Africa, Zimbabwe, and Zambia as well as from as far away as the Democratic Republic of Congo. The Batswana who operate these curio stands usually enjoy an exchange rate advantage and buy curios in large numbers for resale to tourists. Ordinary citizens, on the other hand, seem to take their own arts and crafts for granted and seldom decorate their homes with the products of local artisans, perhaps because these items project a rustic aura that they do not wish to introduce to their urban homes. Instead, they import more "Western" works of fine art from South Africa.

While Batswana work in wood and clay, most are not trained in the techniques of modern monumental sculpture. Recently, this sparked a controversy when local artists failed to win the tender to produce a public bronze statue of the three nineteenth-century Tswana chiefs who went to Britain to seek protection for Bechuanaland from Cecil Rhodes's attempts at empire building. After the competing models were displayed, the tender was awarded to a Korean company. This did not sit well with some artists, who saw it as a gloomy sign for the future of indigenous sculptors. In response, the Korean company that won the tender put on a short course on bronze sculpture for Batswana artists at the Thapong Visual Arts Centre. Finally, the Phuthadikobo Museum in Mochudi has a popular and active screen-printing business, producing T-shirts, curtains, tablecloths, aprons, and other household items with traditional designs that include Tswana house art and even rock art paintings.

ARCHITECTURE

The Architecture of Landscapes

More than 1,000 years ago, Iron Age villages in eastern Botswana were constructed using spatial layouts that are still familiar in most Tswana villages and towns today.[6] At the center of the village was a large animal corral (kraal, *lesaka*) where family members kept their cattle and small stock for protection from predators such as lions, leopards, and hyena. The circular corral was usually made of closely spaced logs set vertically into the ground or of thorn brush dragged into an impenetrable circle. Sometimes clay-lined grain storage pits were dug into the center of the corral to provide food reserves in case of raids or other emergencies. Male ancestors were also buried in the kraal, in part so that they could remain associated with the animals that represented their wealth and the reserves they drew on for bride-price payments at marriage. As one proverb put it, "Chiefs were buried in the kraal so that they could continue to hear the hooves of their cattle as they passed overhead." Another reason was to protect the burial from people who might desire to exhume the body for evil purposes or witchcraft, as the trampling of the cattle hooves hid the exact burial location.

Homesteads were arranged in a semicircle around the corral, and in some communities the headman's homestead was supposed to be built to the east of the corral and, if possible, on higher ground. Between the headman's compound and the corral, a men's meeting area *(kgotla)*—a semicircle of upright logs set into the ground facing the corral—was erected. A hearth was then situated inside the log semicircle, and medicines were buried at the entrances to "cool the blood" and prevent people from bringing their jealousy and anger into the *kgotla*. In the past, only initiated, circumcised men could attend *kgotla* meetings. In theory, all men were free to express themselves inside the *kgotla*, but in practice, outsiders and men from subservient groups were cautious about this. Younger men sat on the ground or on small stools, while elders, family heads, and important visitors seated themselves on folding hardwood chairs with rawhide thong seats. Most households possessed at least one of these sturdy *setilo sa dikgole,* or "*kgotla* chairs" as they are now known, which were decorated with delicately carved geometric designs on their wooden backs. As with many other traditional crafts, these chairs are now something of a rarity, as mass-produced products have replaced them.

Women were generally excluded from *kgotla* meetings, except for general celebrations such as the harvest ceremony, or *dikgafela,* when the first fruits of the harvest were presented to the *Kgosi* in his position as a priest representing God.[7] Even today, while women may go to the *kgotla* when they are involved in hearings on matters such as marriage and divorce, they must be accompanied by a man who will speak on their behalf. Furthermore, even during the national celebrations like *dikgafela,* at least in traditional circles, women do not attend meetings on political issues.

At the beginning of the nineteenth century, the Tswana lived in some of the largest traditional villages in Africa, some with as many as 15,000 to 20,000 inhabitants. The organizing principle of the towns was the same as smaller villages, however, as the semicircular homestead–corral units were simply multiplied over and over again as the population grew. According to custom, towns were planned and laid out around the chief's or elder's kraal in a specific order of seniority, beginning with the chief's house, followed by the senior son's homestead to the right of the chief, the next senior to the left, and so on, as Mackenzie described in the nineteenth century:

> In laying out a Bechuana town, the first thing is, to ascertain where the Chief's courtyard with the public cattle pen is to be placed. As soon as this is settled the remainder is simple ... as soon as the Chief's position is ascertained, one says, "My place is always next to the chief on this side"; another adds, "And mine is always next on that side" and so on till the whole town is laid out. The chief is umpire in such matters and settles all disputes.[8]

Vestiges of this layout can still be seen in the older sections of Molepolole and Mochudi, where homesteads and wards are laid out in a horseshoe shape around family animal corrals. Separating the homestead units were pathways and open spaces that were left untended. Indeed, Burchell's description of his first view of a Tswana town in 1812 resonates in many respects with what can still be seen in the older neighborhoods of the district capitals:

> As we advanced nearer, and gained higher ground, the multitude of houses which continued rising into view as far as I could see excited astonishment; while their novel form and character seized my whole attention, as my eyes

surveyed and examined their outline though yet at a distance. They occupied, in detached groups, a portion of the plain, not less than a mile and a half in diameter.... In our way we passed through many clusters of houses; between which there were most frequently large spaces of unoccupied ground ... the intervening ground remained in a state of nature, scattered over with bushes and here and there with a tuft of smaller plants or a patch of herbage.... The houses were all built in the neatest manner imaginable; but beyond the fence which encircled them, not the least labor had ever been bestowed.[9]

Many smaller villages throughout the country still preserve the remnants of this household–corral pattern that has a history of more than 1,000 years in southern Africa. The remains of stone-walled villages dating to the seventeenth, eighteenth, and nineteenth centuries also preserve this structure. While the use of stone for a building material may partly be due to scarcity of wood poles for building materials around larger settlements, in some cases stone was also used for defense, as the early nineteenth-century hunter Roualeyn Gordon Cumming found at the Kwena capital:

A short time previous to my arrival a rumour having reached Sichely [Sechele] that he was likely to be attacked by the emigrant Boers, he suddenly resolved to surround his city with a wall of stones. It was now completed, with loopholes at intervals, through which to fire upon the advancing enemy with the muskets which he had resolved to purchase from hunters and traders like myself.[10]

Generally, smaller villages surrounded a large town, and the inhabitants divided their time between the two as they moved seasonally from town to their village farmlands (mashimo) and, at a much greater distance, their cattle posts (meraka), where they kept most of their livestock.

In the past, people who lived next to one another were for the most part patrilateral kin or other relations. In some of the larger towns, such as Serowe, Mahalapye, and Maun, one can still navigate through neighborhoods or wards where people share kinship, both fictive and real, while at the same time maintaining family connections to smaller surrounding villages in the lands and grazing areas. But in rapidly growing cities like Gaborone, Francistown, and Lobatse, a grid of streets has replaced the cattle corrals as the organizing principle, and neighbors, no longer relatives, are a more disparate collection of strangers and friends who usually consider their "real homes" to be the district capitals and rural villages from whence they came and where they still retain land and grazing rights.

Nonetheless, traditional values are still often exemplified in housing styles. In rural areas and villages, many people still live in round houses constructed of earth and cow dung, with grass-thatched roofs; in larger villages, round

An aerial view of Paje in the 1970s illustrates many of the characteristics of early Tswana towns. Each family compound has its own fence of posts or thornbushes that sets it off from its neighbors. Many of the round, thatched houses in this photo have now been replaced by concrete block houses with metal roofs.

mud houses known in Afrikaans as rondavels now usually sport Boer-style "improved" thatched roofs with more even thatching and metal "caps" on their peaks to prevent them from leaking. In towns, square, concrete-plastered brick houses with glass windows and corrugated metal roofs have almost completely replaced earthen structures, but the layout of the yards and courtyards still reflect earlier designs. In the nineteenth century, homesteads were usually surrounded by reed fences five feet or more high. Today, chain-link fences, sometimes planted with euphorbia bushes for privacy, have mostly replaced these yard walls except in some parts of northern Botswana. Inside the yard and connecting the multiple houses that generally go together to make up the housing for a household are molded clay walls that join these structures together to form an open courtyard, or *lolwapa*. Modern *lolwapa* walls, which are usually only two to three feet high, can be a site for expressive art, and some women mold them into personalized shapes and decorate them in designs executed in a variety of natural earth pigments.

The Architecture of Housing and Family Life

The Tswana term *lolwapa (lelapa; lelwapa)* is synonymous with family, home, and household. The term itself means a walled public courtyard that connects the area in front of the principal houses of a family homestead. This is the place

Traditional Kalanga homestead at the lands. The courtyard, or
lolwapa, wall bears a molded shape, while simple designs in red
ocher outline the door and decorate the walls. Two styles of
thatching can be seen—traditional on the right with a woven
centerpiece and modern on the left with a metal cap. The separate buildings that make up a compound function more like
"rooms" connected by the *lolwapa* rather than as separate
"houses."

where visitors are received, and in many respects it plays the same role as a "living
room" in Western houses. Just as the animal corral is considered the domain of
men and the ancestors, the home is the domain of women, and Batswana traditionally identify a home by the name of the wife, not her husband.[11]

Traditionally, it was women who played the largest role in home construction. Men contributed their labor by cutting the poles needed for the wall
and roof supports, but women were responsible for cutting, laying down, and
tying the grass onto the roof; collecting and mixing in the proper proportions
water, earth, sand, and fresh cattle dung; and plastering this mixture onto the
house walls and floors and the outdoor *lolwapa.* The involvement of women
in house construction has a long history, an activity that some early missionaries such as Robert Moffat found hard to understand from European perspectives on gender and work:

> While standing near the wife . . . who, with some female companions was building
> a house, and making preparations to scramble, by means of a branch, to the roof,
> I remarked that they ought to get their husbands to do that part of the work. This
> set them all into a roar of laughter. Mahuto, the Queen, and several of the men
> drawing near to ascertain the cause of the merriment, the wives repeated my
> strange and, to them, ludicrous proposal, when another peal of mirth ensued.[12]

Women also obtained the ocher and other oxide pigments used to decorate the house and *lolwapa* walls and floors with a varied array of painted, textured, and molded designs. The natural colors used range from reds and browns to ocher and yellow and from gray-blue to white. The choice often depends on the minerals and soils that are available locally, although some colors are traded hundreds of miles across the county.

An engendered distinction can be made between traditional earth and cow dung houses built by women with few tools other than their own hands and newer cement block houses plastered with concrete that are built by men using tools that include cement mixers and trowels. The older, more traditional style of house with its walls and courtyards of kneaded earth can last for many decades if their materials are periodically renewed by rethatching and mudding. But because rain and weather take an annual toll, they are generally renewed every year or so as new layers of mud placed on top of old. Sand and small stones are added to the clay to make it more resistant to the rain, particularly near the base of the wall where the roof overhang provides less protection from the elements. During remudding, women may choose to renew old designs or paint new ones on the outsides of their houses and courtyards. Over time, the annual remudding and decoration has increased the thickness of some house and *lolwapa* walls to two feet or more. The insulating properties of traditional houses, with their thick earthen walls and thatched roofs, are particularly advantageous in the hot Kalahari climate, where summer temperatures often exceed 100 degrees Fahrenheit for many days. Inside these earthen homes, temperatures are usually 20 degrees or more cooler. The same cannot be said for more modern concrete block homes with metal roofs. Without air conditioning or electric fans, these homes can become almost unbearable in summer; their major benefit is the durability of their materials and their resistance to termites and rot.

Painted designs on houses have a long history in Botswana. An illustration by the Reverend John Campbell in his work *Travels in South Africa* published in 1822, for instance, shows the interior of a double-walled house that was decorated with outline paintings of elephants and giraffes.[13] Today, human and animal motifs are found mostly on commercial brick and cement structures such as bars, bottle stores, and hotels—in other words, structures built by men rather than women. They are also common on the backs of buses. The variety of motifs painted by women range from playing card designs— hearts, spades, clubs, and diamonds—to more traditional motifs, such as flowers and arcades, and more abstract depictions, such as the *lekgapho* design, which is produced by dragging the fingers through fresh cow dung. The *lekgapho* motif is a square that has been bisected diagonally and then decorated by running the fingers in wavy lines through the wet clay to create a series of grooved parallel lines that meet at right angles along the bisection line; the wavy grooves are known as *ditema,* or plowed fields. Occasionally, *lekgapho* and playing card designs are also painted on the insides of houses. In the past, clay shelves to hold dishes and other materials were sometimes molded into the walls, but few examples remain. While perhaps a passing art, the beautiful designs painted on some house and *lolwapa* walls represent the personal expressions of the women who live there. It has been observed that

> those who continue to beautify their homes in the old manner do so for two reasons. Firstly, in order to satisfy their own creative instincts and secondly, to elicit the admiration of their local communities. The creativity of these women artists is not, therefore, a response to external or foreign interests nor is it dependent on these factors. Their artistry is the product of the society of which they are a part. Botswana's women artists need to satisfy only themselves and their local community. No one else in the wider world even knows that they exist. They sell nothing, have no need to advertise or to adjust to the whims of a commercial market. Governed only by the characteristics of their materials and the limitations of their personal skills their work is always honest and refreshing.[14]

Much like Western living rooms where guests are received in a formal, public setting, the *lolwapa* yards can be quite elaborate, with the enclosure walls sometimes mirroring the painted designs on the house walls. But in other examples, they can be embellished with extravagant moldings of hearts, circles, squares, and other shapes. *Lolwapa* walls are often elaborately painted for weddings, funerals, and other memorial occasions. The floor of the *lolwapa* between the outer wall and the house is also frequently renewed with mud and decorated, sometimes in *lekgapho* squares that leave a textured design that in the past could last for many months. Today, with more people wearing hard-soled shoes, these inscribed floor patterns crumble easily, and few instances of this artwork are now produced. In the nineteenth century, the *lolwapa* also had a formal hearth, often with molded edges, around which family members and visitors would gather in winter. Evening family gatherings around an outside fire are still common today, even in urban areas where the small size of the sitting room inhibits large get-togethers. That is one reason, but one cannot deny the cultural appeal felt by these families as they sit outdoors around the fire, sharing stories and jokes, while turning to avoid fire-burned shins and the smoke that flits in different directions with each change in the wind.

Along the edges of the Okavango Delta in northern Botswana, different building materials are sometimes found. Here many traditional homes have enclosing walls built of reeds, which are more easily obtained than poles. The bottoms of the reeds are dipped in old motor oil to retard attack by termites. Most thatched reed houses are plastered with mud but may also be left unplastered to allow cool breezes to blow through them as an adaptation to the hotter climates of northern Botswana. Because of the fine-grained nature of the Kalahari sands, the gray earthen walls found in Ngamiland are more fragile than their counterparts on the eastern side of the country. The same problem affects more modern concrete buildings. Because there are few places where suitable stone may be quarried to mix with the fine-grained sand, buildings and building materials are weaker and more prone to cracking. The Mbukushu, who live along the west side of the delta, sometimes even weave mats of split reeds to use as walls. These are interlaced between the roof supports to form walls.

URBAN ARCHITECTURE

Housing in urban areas marks a shift from extended family, kin-based residential units to nuclear families housed in Western-style neighborhoods where rows of cement block houses parallel streets rather than encircle cattle corrals. Homes are generally built of durable concrete blocks walls, with metal doors and windows and tin roofs that require special tools for construction. Even in self-help areas where families build their own homes, the use of more durable but specialized materials has meant that the responsibility for building construction has shifted from women to men. Coinciding with this is the disappearance of the personal artistic expression that Tswana women once put into their homes—at least on the outside. If houses are decorated at all, it is usually with commercial paint. Urban buildings are sometimes painted brightly in geometric and naturalistic motifs, but the painted designs often convey advertising or commercial content rather than the personal preferences of the occupants.

Because colonial rule in Botswana was directed from Mafikeng in South Africa, little of Botswana's urban architecture reflects the Victorian architectural styles found in the older sections of towns and cities in South Africa and Zimbabwe. In the older, colonial section of Gaborone known as the "village," there are the remains of a few early buildings, including the remnants of a late nineteenth-century British fort and the first post office and prison. The remainder of the buildings and houses were constructed in an uninspired International Style that spread throughout the developing world during the 1930s, 1940s, and 1950s. These generic, whitewashed buildings are still common, but the increase in wealth brought about by diamonds since the 1990s has led to the construction of more modern multistory buildings and commercial malls. The capital, Gaborone, has more than doubled in size in the past 20 years. In some of the older tribal capitals, such as Palapye, Mahalapye, Molepolole, and Lobatse, a rural version of the generic colonial architecture of flat-roofed, whitewashed concrete block buildings with wide verandas and industrial metal window and door frames is still the norm, although malls filled with fast-food restaurants, discount centers, and clothing stores are springing up even here.

Built from scratch at independence, modern Gaborone was erected after independence on the "neutral" ground of the Imperial Reserve to the west of the colonial "village." A large dam across the Notwane River on the south side of town provides most of the city's water; it is also a spot favored by local fishermen and sailboat and water sports enthusiasts. Gaborone has all the usual features of a modern city—multistory buildings and houses with running water and electricity that are linked by tarmac roads to offices and shopping malls. In addition to government ministries and Parliament, the city is home to international hotels, casinos, the University of Botswana, the National Museum, and the Sir Sereste Khama International Airport, which is able to handle direct international flights from Europe.

Civil service architects are responsible for safety and building standards through the Department of Architecture and Buildings and Engineering Services, the Botswana Bureau of Standards, and the Botswana Technology Centre. These civil servants, many of whom are expatriates, design many government buildings and set technical standards, but they are not charged with the responsibility over design creativity. The private sector includes the Architectural Association of Botswana, which has more than 100 private members representing almost two dozen firms.

One of the tallest buildings in the capital is the Orapa House, where diamonds from Botswana's mines are sorted and packaged for sale. A newer addition to the Gaborone skyline is the 14-story building that houses the Botswana Department of Taxes and the attorney general's chambers. This $42 million building, originally intended to house the Botswana Housing Corporation headquarters, was plagued at the start by controversies over irregular allocation of tenders, corruption, and bribery. This led to a halt in construction and an unfinished eyesore in the middle of the government enclave for some time. The building is now complete and forms a striking contribution to the city's new skyline.

But these relatively modern and wealthy sections of town are interspersed with slums where poverty and poor sanitation reign. Other urban problems are also evident as the multilane highway network, replete with roundabouts and traffic signals, that carries traffic across the town is a virtual parking lot during rush hours when it can take well over an hour to cover just a few miles. As one driver commented, "To drive in Gaborone you cannot just follow the rules of the road, you must learn to 'negotiate' your way with other drivers using hand signals, smiles, stares and prayers through the windscreen."[15]

Government and private housing built during the colonial era and in the first two decades after independence usually had "servant's quarters" in the backyards. Even though the primary residence had electricity and hot and cold running water, the servant's quarters housing usually lacked these amenities, reflecting the social and class divisions enforced at the time. With the rise in the financial importance of the private sector, the emergence of an educated Botswana middle class, and the greater availability of labor-saving devices such as washing machines and dishwashers, these features of urban housing are becoming less prominent as existing servant's quarters are put to use as store rooms or as temporary rented housing for students and middle-income workers, as housing is expensive in the major cities and towns.

The migration of large numbers of people from rural to urban areas has made it difficult for people to cope with job and housing scarcity. Salaries are generally low, and most people have difficulty dealing with the high cost of urban living. The government's recommended minimum wage in 2004 was about P675 ($150) a month, and most private companies pay less than this. The Botswana Housing Corporation, a parastatal organization, has been charged with the responsibility of providing housing for some government workers, but the supply is short, and the market-driven rents are often too high for most workers and civil servants to pay. The District Councils provide for other government employees, such as council officials, nurses, and teachers. A few government departments, including the police, prisons, the Botswana Defense Force, and the Botswana Housing Corporation, also build or lease housing that they sublease to lower costs for their employees because privately owned housing is so expensive in Gaborone and other cities. Because of the high costs and limited availability, many people resort to a "communal style" of living with several individuals or families coming together to share small, single-family dwellings, especially in the low-income neighborhoods of Bontleng, White City, Maruapula, Old and New Naledi (Botswana's famous ghettos), Ditakaneng, and New Stense. Other people manage by commuting distances of 30 miles or more from outlying "home" villages, such as Ramotswa, Kanye, Molepolole, and Mochudi, where housing is less expensive or sometimes even free. This enables them to keep in contact with their friends and relatives while using their salaries and housing allowances to construct their own homes rather than pay rent to the government or a landlord. While this is advantageous for those whose homes are in villages surrounding Gaborone, difficulties with acquiring land by outsiders puts those from more distant villages, such as Maun, Serowe, and Mahalapye, at a disadvantage when it comes to working in Gaborone and buying their own homes.

The capital city of Gaborone has grown rapidly since independence. Many newer buildings, such as the building in the background that houses the Department of Taxes and the attorney general's chambers, reflect a more modernist, less colonial atmosphere. Photo courtesy of Mike Main.

Increases in population, combined with immigration from neighboring countries by workers seeking jobs or political asylum, have contributed to rampant crime in the urban centers of Botswana.[16] While little of this crime so far involves violence, it has had an impact on architecture.[17] In the wealthier urban neighborhoods, most houses cannot be seen from the street because they are surrounded by high brick or stone walls. These walls are topped by shards of sharp broken glass in older subdivisions to deter thieves from climbing over. In newer areas, broken glass has been replaced by iron spikes or, in some cases, strands of high-voltage electric wire. Apartments or condominiums supplement these passive protections with guards and watchmen who occupy guardhouses built into the protective walls. In all but the poorest areas, all houses have burglar bars on the windows. In the wealthier parts of town, these are supplemented by automated burglar alarm systems that are answered by private companies that maintain teams of security guards armed with clubs who promise to arrive "within minutes" of an alarm. Burglary is so prevalent that city police cannot hope to keep up. They usually take hours, if not days, to answer the call of a citizen reporting a burglary in progress. "We have no transport," is the usual response over the phone. In response, "mob justice" sometimes prevails when the public catches criminals in the act. On some occasions, the mobs have prevented the police from getting to the suspects until such time as they feel justice has been done. While most crime is petty theft and not violent, its prevalence has left its distinctive mark on the urban culture and architecture of Botswana—as it has on all countries in Africa.

Lack of land in urban areas has also led to contradictions between the more communal traditional system of residential land allocation in villages and the privatization of property in urban centers. In urban areas and smaller villages, it is becoming difficult to be allocated a plot of land on which to build a house, and bureaucratic delays of up to 10 years are not unusual. In more rural locations where they are fewer applicants, land can still be obtained fairly quickly at little to no cost. Because most people are related and land is communally owned and plentiful, infringements are generally overlooked unless neighbors complain. Many of the villages surrounding Botswana's urban areas appear on the surface to operate in a similar manner, but in the past several years, the government has begun to crack down on what it terms illegal "self-allocated" housing put up in what appeared to be "empty" spaces. Because formal applications were not made to land and housing authorities (a system conducive to bribery and graft), the government demolished dozens of self-allocated houses, leaving the occupants homeless. The then minister of Lands and Housing argued for an extension of this program, recommending the demolishing of illegal allocations across the country. The demolitions are very unpopular, but they have slowed the problem of illegal land allocation around Gaborone and suburbs such as Mogoditshane and Tsolamosese; people continue to build ghettos on self-allocated land in Jwaneng, Francistown, and other urban areas.

PUBLIC WATER SUPPLIES AND SANITATION

Botswana boasts of one of the best sewage systems in Africa, with water-based systems in place in all urban areas and pit latrines in most villages. This can be attributed to its good economy. Gaborone and Francistown derive most of their drinking water from the Gaborone and Shashe Dams. New dams in the Tati and Shashe Rivers in the North-East district will provide water to villages in that area, and other dams are proposed for the Lower

Shashe and Thuni Rivers. Towns, villages, and cattle posts, on the other hand, are usually supplied by boreholes drilled hundreds of feet into the ground. In some cases, these wells are so deep that there is concern that they are tapping nonrenewable fossil water reserves rather than rechargeable underground reservoirs, thus depleting a scarce resource in this drought-prone, desert land.

While some rural areas do not have running water because they are "outside the planning area," most homesteads now have access to safe water supplies from communal taps placed at strategic locations in the village. Such communal water systems are expensive for the government to maintain, however, because some people waste water knowing that they do not have to pay water bills. As a result, prepaid taps, for which people have to buy cards to get water, are now replacing public standpipes. While still experimental, it is likely this program will be expanded to villages throughout the country. The government will continue to pay the water bills for those who cannot afford it. The main responsibility for public water supplies lies with the Botswana Water Utilities Corporation for towns and the Water Affairs Department in rural areas. Because of the escalating cost of water, private lawns and gardens are often considered a Western luxury—especially in drought years when watering restrictions are enforced. Traditional yards did not have grass but were simply bare earth that was swept clean on a daily basis.[18]

At independence, there were a few water-system toilets in the country, and many people, even in urban areas, used pit latrines. In smaller towns and villages, even pit latrines were uncommon 20 or 30 years ago. Today, Botswana generally has a very good sewage system in towns. Pit latrines, however, are still common in rural areas. They are cheap to construct, and, importantly, they do not require water—a scarce commodity in a country whose national cry is "Pula" (rain). But they also have serious environmental drawbacks because they contaminate the local water table. As a result, in many villages and towns the government is encouraging people to change to water-based sewage systems even though there is shortage of water in the country. This, in turn, introduces additional problems because the dispersed settlement layout of most villages makes it difficult to provide centralized wastewater systems. At the cattle posts and farmlands, there are few latrines, and unimproved "natural areas" are designated for this purpose instead.

ELECTRICITY

Electricity, once available only in cities and larger towns, is also being extended on a prepaid basis to more and more villages in the countryside. Botswana's electricity is expensive, however, because it is produced from a coal-burning plant placed directly over a coal mine at Morupule between

Serowe and Palapye. A national power grid carries the electricity to Gaborone and Francistown. For towns and villages nearer the borders of South Africa and Zimbabwe, it is sometimes cheaper to get their electricity from those grids. Botswana, in turn, sells electricity to parts of South Africa that are close to Morupule and its national grid. Towns in more isolated parts of the country, such as Maun and Ghanzi, once had to use expensive, diesel-powered generators, but these have now also been connected to the national grid.

NOTES

1. From J. Comaroff and J. L. Comaroff, *Of Revelation and Revolution: The Dialectics of Modernity on a South African Frontier,* vol. 2 (Chicago: University of Chicago Press, 1997), pp. 277–78. Copyright vol. 2, 1997 by the University of Chicago Press. Reprinted with permission from the University of Chicago Press and the authors John and Jean Comaroff.

2. According to David Livingstone, "the rude footprints" carved around the margin of the spring are "apparently the work of children. The 'spoor' with one exception goes into the pit. The exception is that of Matsieñ, the former of the Bechuanas. As the story goes he returned to it as the men left it, but the spoor if intended to represent anything shews the opposite. . . . The tradition seems to refer to the splitting up of the people into different tribes from Loe as the central population." David Livingstone and I. Schapera, *Family Letters, 1841–1856,* vol. 1 (Westport, Conn.: Greenwood Press, 1975), pp. 253–54.

3. A. Campbell, J. Denbow, and E. Wilmsen, "Paintings Like Engravings: Rock Art at Tsodilo," in *Contested Images: Diversity in Southern African Rock Art Research,* ed. T. Dowson and D. Lewis-Williams (Johannesburg: Witwatersrand University Press, 1994), pp. 131–58.

4. In the mid-nineteenth century, these skillfully made karosses were much in demand by European customers, and missionaries were constantly asked to procure them as gifts or rewards, sometimes in exchange for goods sent to them. In drought years, the supply was not always good, however, and Livingstone remarked that "Mrs. M. [Moffat] mentioned a wish to have a karross from this side. The drought in the Kalahari side has been so great very few have been able to go thither in search of skins, so they are scarcer this year then we ever knew. Only those who have Gakalahari near them have been able to procure any." Livingstone and Schapera, *Family Letters,* vol. 2, p. 15.

5. These are not worms but caterpillars of the species *Imbrasia belina.*

6. J. Denbow and J. S. Denbow, *Uncovering Botswana's Past* (Gaborone: National Museum Monuments and Art Gallery, 1985).

7. Some Christian denominations in Botswana have also adopted this ceremony, which finds precedents in the Bible. See chapter 2.

8. John Mackenzie, *Ten Years North of the Orange River 1859–69* (London: Frank Cass, 1871).

9. John Burchell, *Travels in the Interior of Southern Africa* (London: Batchworth Press, 1822).

10. R. Gordon Cumming, *The Lion Hunter of South Africa: Five Years' Adventures in the Far Interior of South Africa, with Notices of the Native Tribes and Savage Animals* (London: John Murray, 1911), p. 336. In 1852, the Boers, convinced that David Livingstone was a major supplier of the muskets used against them, burned his nearby mission station at Kolobeng to the ground.

11. Sandy Grant and Elihah Grant, *Decorated Homes in Botswana* (Cape Town: Creda Press, 1995), p. 118.

12. Robert Moffat, *Missionary Labours and Scenes in Southern Africa* (London: J. Snow, 1842), p. 252.

13. J. Campbell, *Travels in Southern Africa, Undertaken at the Request of the London Missionary Society* (London: Francis Westley, 1822).

14. Grant and Grant, *Decorated Homes in Botswana,* pp. 118–19.

15. Comment made to Denbow by a pedestrian while standing on the sidewalk watching a traffic jam in May 2003.

16. While theft also occurs in rural areas, it is less easily distinguished from "borrowing" among neighbors who are often related. Respect for traditional beliefs and customs may also be a greater deterrent. Children, for instance, are told that if they steal a calf or goat, their stomach will betray them by mooing or bleating if they happen to encounter the animal's owner on a path.

17. Violent, armed bank robberies carried out by South Africans criminals working in conjunction with less experienced Batswana are becoming more frequent.

18. Sometimes the daily sweeping was even done in patterns or swirls, mirroring the more permanent designs etched into the mud of *lolwapa* floors. In the American South, some early twentieth-century African American households continued this generalized African tradition of having swept yards rather than grass lawns.

5

Cuisine and Traditional Dress

Our lives depend mostly on meat, and the laws have kept us from eating.
I believe that when God created man, he provided wild animals to be the food
of the Masarwa. The Bangwato depend on their cattle to provide their food.
The Kalanga depend on their crops. White people live on money, bread, and
sugar. These are the traditional foods of these groups of people, so it can be
seen that the law is against us, the Masarwa, because it has prevented us from
eating.[1]

The Bechuanas are extremely fond of flesh, which they consider the only
food befitting men; corn and milk the food of women.[2]

Among the Tswana . . . females, royal and commoner alike, built houses and
cultivated crops; their husbands "ma[d]e the dresses" for everyone. That women
should sow while men sewed struck the evangelists as decidedly peculiar.[3]

INTRODUCTION

Few things are closer to the heart of cultural and personal identity than food
and clothing. In Botswana, most meals reflect long-standing tradition and
taste, and the "typical" cuisine still includes many ingredients hunted and
harvested from the wild or grown in home gardens and fields. Modern clothing, on the other hand, is hardly traditional, and almost everyone wears mass-
produced, Western fashions that include T-shirts, jeans, blouses, dresses,
skirts, and suits. Contrary to what many visitors think, however, this is not a
sign that the peoples of Botswana have lost their traditions. Their cuisine is
one indication among many that this is not true.

CUISINE

Wild Foods

To a great extent, Botswana cuisine centers around meat. While the amount of meat eaten varies according to family circumstance, there is little doubt that meat, whether domestic or wild, is expected to be the centerpiece of the meal. Especially in rural areas, the consumption of wild game and birds is an important contribution to the diet, along with a wide assortment of wild fruits and vegetables.

According to one study, wild plants contribute almost 40 percent of the food intake of contemporary Batswana, who commonly use more than 100 different wild tubers, greens, beans, fruits, and nuts in their traditional cuisine.[4] Among the most important are high-protein beans such as Morama *(Tylosema esculenta)*, Mongongo nuts *(Ricinodendron rautenenii)*, Morula fruits and nuts *(Sclerocarya birrea)*, Motsintsila berries *(Berchemia discolor)*, Motsotsojane and Moretlwa or raisin berries *(Grewia retinervis* and *Grewia flavenscens)*, Motlopi roots *(Boscia albitrunca)* that are pounded to make a porridge, sour plums such as Moretologa *(Ximenia* sp.), wild mushrooms and truffles known as Mabowa *(Amanita* sp., *Psalliota* sp.), and wild figs from the huge Mukuchomo trees in the Okavango Delta *(Ficus sycomorous)*. Boiled leaves called Longana, Mosokot-shwane, and Kgomodimetsi are made into teas *(Artemisia afra; Lippia javanica)*. Alcoholic drinks include the much-maligned *Khadi*, which is traditionally made from honey and Grewia berries, and cream of tartar from the seeds of the baobab *(mowana)*. The traditional ingredients for Khadi, however, differ from place to place, depending on what the environment has to offer. In southern Botswana, for instance, there are no baobab trees. Another delicious and highly alcoholic drink is made from fermented Morula fruit. Wild plants that are smoked or added to tobacco as a supplement include Monnamontsho and Serepe *(Cadaba* sp., *Portulaca oleracea,* and so on).

Wild animal and plant foods are not restricted to the diets of pastro-foragers such as the Khoisan or Sarwa but are important dietary items for almost all Batswana, whether they live on farms and cattle posts or even, to a lesser extent, in towns and cities. Wild greens *(Merogo)* such as rothwe (pronounced ROW-tway; *Gynandropsis gynandra)* and thepe (pronounced TAY-pay;[5] *Amaranthus thunbergii)*, for instance, are picked in the rainy season and boiled and dried to preserve them for sale by street vendors in local markets year-round.[6] Ground watermelon seeds are sometimes mixed with merogo for added flavor. Another popular wild food sold in markets and exported to other countries is dried caterpillars, known as mopane worms in English and *Phane* (pronounced PA-nay) in Tswana. These are not really worms but spiny-backed caterpillars of the genus *Imbrasia belina,* whose adult stage is a large emperor moth. They consume the leaves of the mopane *(mophane)* trees that grow in northern and northeastern Botswana. The caterpillars are harvested by hand, and the trees are sometimes cut down to reach those at the top.[7] After harvesting, the guts of the caterpillars are squeezed out, and they are then dried and salted for sale, usually by street vendors.[8] They are a seasonal delicacy and can be eaten in a variety of ways. The late president Sir Seretse Khama, for instance, was well known to carry dried mopane worms in his pockets for snacking. They can also be rehydrated and cooked in water before being fried in oil; today some also add onion and tomato and serve them with a side dish of *bogobe* (bo-HOE-bay), a porridge made of sorghum flour and water, or *paletshe* (pa-LAY-chay), which is made from maize flour.[9]

Hunting and snaring also provide important additions to most diets in Botswana. While hunting is regulated by the Botswana government and permits are required to purchase rifle cartridges and shotgun shells, a large number of unregulated nineteenth-century Tower muskets that use gunpowder and scrap metal for shot remain operational in rural areas. Currently, Botswana is the only African country with national-level legislation allowing subsistence hunting rights to all citizens, although hunting in some areas, such as the Central Kalahari Game Reserve, requires a special permit.[10] This requirement has led to complaints on the part of some Khoisan who view hunting as part of their traditional heritage. They believe that the numbers of animals specified on game licenses are not sufficient for their subsistence needs.

Domestic Foods

Agricultural Crops and Production Systems

The arid and unpredictable climate of Botswana, while excellent for animal husbandry, sets limits on the crops that can be grown. While much of the maize meal eaten in Botswana today is produced in the country, in drought years maize is imported from Zimbabwe and South Africa and processed locally. Almost all the vegetables available in grocery stores are imported from South Africa. The most productive farmers use tractors or oxen to till their fields—no farms, apart from small household gardens, are tilled by hand. Draft animals and machinery are now universally seen as essential equipment for agricultural production, and few people without access to them bother to plant. Instead, they rely on wage labor or other jobs to provide cash to purchase maize meal and other food in local markets and stores.

The adoption of the plow and its transformation of the economics and engendering of agricultural production is an interesting story. While most people today think it is nearly impossible to feed a family using hoe agriculture, in 1854 Robert Moffat found that the hand-hoed fields in Shoshong were so extensive that people "are not in want of food. You would be astonished to see the extent of their gardens . . . a plain between two ranges of hills with millions of acres as far as the eye can reach in west and east. We . . . passed through extensive fields of native corn, some of which was unreaped from the abundance of the season."[11]

This was undoubtedly a good year, and while the total area of land between the two ranges of hills he mentions is on the order of 50,000 rather than millions of acres, the observation that grain was left unharvested suggests that at least in good years Tswana families were self-sufficient in grain, even using hoe agriculture. Of course, it is doubtful that grain was ever left "unharvested" no matter how good the season, and it is likely that such grain eventually found its way into granaries where it was held in reserve for drought years. In the 1850s, it is also likely that there was not much of a market for surplus grain in good years—perhaps because almost everyone was a farmer and had benefited equally from the good rains. In the absence of wagons, inadequate transport systems would have made it costly to move grain to more distant markets where rains may have been less favorable.

It was thus possible, at least in years with good rains, to feed a family using hoe agriculture in Botswana. But the risks and uncertainty of crop production on the fringes of the Kalahari favored the early adoption of new technologies, such as the plow, by Batswana farmers. Even as recently as the 1970s, Botswana was one of the few countries in sub-Saharan Africa to put ox-drawn plows to almost universal daily use in agricultural practice.[12] Other factors were also important in the nineteenth-century transition from hoe to plow agriculture in Botswana. One was undoubtedly the widespread availability of oxen in Tswana society that could be used to pull plows. In the more forested parts of Africa where tsetse-borne illnesses severely limit animal husbandry, there was no choice but to use human labor to till fields. A second was that cattle not only could pull the plows but also could be used to pay for them and for the harnesses and other equipment needed. A third factor was that by the middle of the nineteenth century, Boer farmers and European missionaries in the Transvaal were manufacturing and using plows to increase production in their own fields. Batswana had the opportunity to see how plows could be used to increase production, and they soon learned how to incorporate draft oxen and plows into their own agricultural practices. Finally, those wealthy enough to afford plows could even profit in years of poor rainfall by exchanging surplus grain for livestock or by distributing it out to those less fortunate in return for subservience or political advantage. It is thus no accident that the earliest adopters of plows were kings and other wealthy Tswana who had the cattle to both purchase and pull them. The introduction of barbwire fences also helped to increase productivity by solving the age-old problem of keeping animals (both domestic and wild) from eating or destroying the crops.

In addition to enabling already-wealthy farmers to increase their production, the ox-drawn plow introduced men into an agricultural sector (to lead the oxen) that had formerly been the responsibility of women. Men did not replace women in the fields but rather led the oxen while women held the handles of the plow, much as they had held the handles of their hoes in earlier times. The adoption of the plow and the resulting changes in agricultural productivity in turn affected the marital economics of polygynous marriages. While one explanation for the abandonment of polygyny in Botswana has been the impact of missionary teaching against it, with plows wealthy farmers were able to increase their harvests without adding extra wives to till the soil. They could thus more easily choose to follow missionary admonitions while not necessarily suffering adverse economic effects. Of course, in earlier times, polygyny also served to cement political power by creating multiple relations between lineages. But with changes in the calculus of political power resulting from missionary activity, white traders, Boer farmers, and, finally, colonial overrule, polygynous marriage "no longer provided the returns it once did ... [and] women were increasingly banned from plural unions with a smaller pool of men [due to labor migration]. Under these circumstances, both men and women tended to engage in a series of relationships, investigating the potential of various marriage partners and testing the benefits of such associations before committing themselves to one partner."[13]

Greater agricultural productivity also meant greater participation in emerging colonial markets where European clothing, cooking wares, utensils, and tools were purchased as new symbols of status. Quantities of soap and detergent to keep these new goods and clothes clean (and Christian) contributed to the integration of Tswana foodways and dress with regional commodity markets. The greater productivity per person per hour permitted by plow agriculture may also have enabled maize, a drought-sensitive crop, to gradually replace the more drought-resistant sorghum as the staple grain in the higher-rainfall areas of Botswana, such as Francistown, where maize and millet (lebelebele) are the principal staple crops today. In the dryer parts of Botswana, sorghum and millet continue to be planted, although most households prefer to buy already-prepared mealie meal in the grocery store if they can afford to do so.

The climate and economies of scale have encouraged the development of more capitalized commercial farms, such as Talana Farms in the Tuli Block, which produce much of the maize that is refined at mills in Lobatse and Ramotswa. These large-scale farms are gradually replacing small-scale subsistence production in many areas. In drought years, grain is imported from

Zimbabwe and South Africa for local processing. The country relies on South African farms for vegetables such as cabbage, onions, and squash that are grown at lower costs by commercial farmers, replacing homegrown products and in some cases even wild greens.

BATSWANA CUISINE

Meat Dishes

Beef is the most popular meat and is consumed in large quantities at weddings and funerals, but goats are more common everyday fare because the amount of meat they produce is better tailored to the needs of an average household without refrigeration. When cattle are slaughtered, the meat is traditionally divided so that a man's maternal uncle receives the head, his paternal uncles the forelegs, and so on. The chest and stomach are reserved for the family.[14] "Meat with bones" that can be chewed are the most favored cuts.[15] Chickens are also popular. Fish, while eaten by the Yeyi and some other peoples in the Okavango, are avoided by most Tswana.[16] This is ironic, as the name for a commonly farmed fish in the United States, tilapia, is a Latinized form of the Tswana word for this fish, *tlhapi,* which was first described by David Livingstone in the middle of the nineteenth century. The Yeyi use both baskets and reed weirs, some stretching 50 meters from shore to shore, to catch fish. Tilapia, known locally as "bream," along with a type of catfish known as a barbel, are also harvested from the Gaborone Dam and sold in roadside markets. Only a few Tswana, such as the Lete, Tlokwa, and to a lesser extent the Kgatla, eat pork; most consider pigs to be unclean animals. Donkeys and horses are also not generally eaten, although some find them tasty.[17] Apart from the python, snakes are not eaten, nor are animals belonging to a person's totem. Within each ethnic group, there are a variety of totems, but some of the most common "respected" animals include the *phuti* or duiker among the Ngwato, the crocodile among the Kwena, and the elephant among the Ngwaketse.

The most popular meat dishes are *seswaa, serobe, and segwapa,* made of chicken, oxtail, and barbecued beef. *Seswaa,* also known as *chotlho,* is made by boiling beef (or sometimes chicken) in water with considerable quantities of salt (other spices are unthinkable) until it is very well done and soft.[18] The meat is then removed from the large three-legged cast-iron pot it is cooked in and beaten with a wooden spoon until it takes on the texture of shredded beef. This pounded meat is the most popular meat dish and is enjoyed at weddings, funerals, and other ceremonies. *Serobe* is another much-sought-after delicacy. To make it, the intestines and selected internal parts of a goat, sheep, or cow are first cleaned (although many insist this not be overdone, or it will remove much of the "flavor"). They are then boiled along with peeled goat or sheep hooves before being finely chopped. The meal is normally served with porridge or with samp—coarsely stamped maize, often mixed with beans to form a casserole-like dish known as *dikgobe.* Custom dictates that elders in the *kgotla* should be served the head, while children are forbidden to eat the tongue lest they become "talkative" or "liars." Chicken intestines *(mala),* on the other hand, are a delicacy reserved for children. While traditional free-range village chickens are thought to be much better tasting than commercially grown ones, their "traditional price" of $1.00 each is often more than the cost of a frozen chicken in the store; they may also be difficult for foreigners to chew unless they are boiled for a considerable time.[19] At home, chicken is usually boiled in salted water, with a chili pepper sometimes added for flavor. The gift of a live chicken, an invitation to a home-cooked meal, or a cup of tea (even on a hot December day with temperatures hovering over 100 degrees Fahrenheit) are traditional symbols of hospitality accorded to special visitors as a sign of respect and friendship. In addition, because of their small size and low price, chickens are often held to be the ideal creature for the animal sacrifices required for certain traditional rites.

Most animals, apart from baboons, hyenas, and a few other species, are consumed by Batswana, both Khoisan and Bantu speakers alike. The liver, kidneys, and other perishable organs are usually roasted over the coals and consumed, with some celebration, by hunters at the kill site.[20] Almost all the animal, including the head, skin, and hooves, is used in one form or another; little is wasted. After the animal is butchered, the meat is cut into long, thin strips; coated with salt and sometimes additional spices; and hung from the trees for several days to sun-dry into a type of jerky known in southern Africa as *biltong* in Afrikaans or *segwapa* in Tswana.[21] *Biltong* can last for many months without spoiling. It is consumed both dry, as a snack, or rehydrated in stews and other dishes. Even domestic meat is made into *biltong* to preserve it because few rural people have access to refrigerators or freezers, and even city dwellers may lack sufficient freezer space to keep the meat of a large animal because of the high cost of appliances and electricity. Of all the animals, including cattle, the cape buffalo are believed to produce the best *biltong.* Other animals that produce fine *biltong* are kudu, gemsbok, eland, and ostrich. Wildebeest and hartebeest *biltong,* on the other hand, are not considered delicacies. One can see rows of *biltong* hanging from strings in almost every local butchery.

Almost nothing is wasted when an animal is slaughtered. And if it is a large animal, such as a cow, there is a traditional way of distributing the meat (*go gasa kgomo:* the oldest brother should get a shoulder and front leg, the younger

Rural cooking at the cattle post. Cast-iron, three-legged pots are still the most suitable to prepare food for large family gatherings.

brother a thigh, the mother's brother the head, and the *kgosi* or *kgosana* [headman] the chest). Women eat the filets and T-bones, while the old men get the liver and kidneys. Those who assisted with the skinning of the cow take the ribs and other small pieces, such as intestines, to their homes. If the cow was slaughtered at an advanced stage of pregnancy, the unborn calf will also belong to the old men. The institutionalized distribution of specific body parts to a wide set of relatives thus follows a Botswana principle that "no man is an island," or, in local terms, "a person is a person because of [the help] of others" *(motho ke motho ka batho)*. No matter how small something is, it is expected that it will be shared among relatives, hence the saying *bana ba motho ba kgaogana tlhogwana ya ntsi* ("children of the same family have to share even the head of a fly"). Those that refuse to share may be ridiculed as "capitalists," or as people who "like things" *(go rata dilo)*.

All meats may be boiled or fried to make one-pot stews along with beans, cowpeas, peanuts, vegetables, and spices such as curry, chilies, and chakalaka that come prepackaged.[22] For only the most informal of occasions is meat roasted over an open fire. For family eating, a basin of warm water and a towel are usually brought to the table by a wife or child who kneels down and holds them for her husband, elders, and visitors to wash and dry their hands. Presenting people with cold water to wash their hands is considered very impolite and, in the case of visitors, a sign that they are not welcome. Plates served with the stew, *bogobe,* and vegetables are then brought out,

Herero woman churning butter in a large gourd suspended by ropes from a branch. Butter, or *maere,* is one of the foods for which the Herero are especially known.

with visitors and the head of the family being served first. In very traditional families, there may be special cutlery reserved for the family head, and it is considered polite for everyone to wait until the visitor has taken the first bite before beginning to eat. In urban settings, ginger drinks, bottled soft drinks, wine, or beer may be served with the meal unless the family has religious objections to alcohol.

Staple Grains and Porridges

Stews and meat dishes are always accompanied by *phaleshe* made from maize (mealie meal) or *bogobe* made from sorghum or millet. It is made by slowly adding finely ground maize, sorghum, or millet flour to a container of rapidly boiling water while stirring rapidly to produce a paste. The mixture is then left to cook slowly until it achieves a texture similar to mashed potatoes. There are many ways that this basic mixture can be modified to produce different dishes, all of which are accompanied by meat and vegetables if eaten for dinner.[23] Among the Kgatla and Tlokwa, sorghum meal mixed with a little water may be left to ferment overnight to make a dish called *ting,* which is often associated with these two groups. Milk and sugar are then added for breakfast, or boiled milk may be used to produce a rich, soft porridge known as *logala* or, if mixed with sour milk, *sebube.* A thicker version made with less milk may be served for lunch or dinner, accompanied by meat and vegetables. In this case, the sour milk may be eaten as dessert. Sorghum flour mixed with melon *(bogobe jwa lerotse)* is considered a delicacy, but it is time consuming to make at home and expensive to purchase in a restaurant. Another dish in which sorghum is mixed with melon *(lekatane)* is known as *legodu.* It has a tendency to stay hot for a long time, and greedy children are often known to grab for it before it cools down, leading to the proverb *"Fa a lelela legodu le monnele,"* which translates as "If they cry for *legodu,* let them have it [so that they will learn by experience that it is hot.]" The proverb is also applied to anyone too stubborn to heed a warning. The Kalanga cook *bogobe* and squash in sour milk *(madila)* to produce a dish known as *tophi.*[24] Another favorite dish is a mixture of a tree gum known as *delele* with peanuts and spices to make peanut soup.

Today the vast majority of Batswana purchase their mealie meal and sorghum meal already prepared and packaged. This saves them the trouble of processing it: pounding it with a heavy wooden pestle in a wooden mortar hollowed out from a large log, then winnowing out the chafe in a winnowing basket and storing it in the cooking hut before cooking. Sometimes the grain may also be ground to a fine flour using a grinding stone rather than a mortar and pestle. Both the economics of production and the labor costs of refining the grain to flour make it more economical for most families to simply buy their mealie meal from stores and shops, even in rural areas. As mealie meal is quite bland, it is never eaten by itself but always in combination with meat or vegetable sauces.

Beverages

Economies of scale have also affected the brewing of traditional beer known as *bojalwa jwa setso/setswana.* Traditional sorghum beer is still sometimes brewed for special occasions or as a historical demonstration, but few people have the time (several days), the equipment (large ceramic pots of a capacity of 10 to 15 gallons or 44-gallon galvanized drums), or the raw materials (quantities of ground sorghum, yeast, and so on), to produce it. It is considered polite for people to have a sip of *bojalwa,* even if they do not drink, during special occasions; a little is also customarily spilled on the ground as an offering to the ancestors.[25] Sometimes traditional beer may be brewed as a reward for members of the community who come to work on communal projects, such as constructing a traditional house, weeding fields, or branding cattle. The traditional beer consumed as a reward is considered not a payment but rather a token of appreciation for the assistance given.

A commercially produced traditional beer known as *Chibuku* is now ubiquitous and has almost completely replaced home-brewed *bojalwa*. *Chibuku*'s nickname is "shake-shake" because the liter-sized, red and blue, waxed containers it comes in must be shaken vigorously before drinking to remix the sorghum sediment that falls to the bottom. It is available almost everywhere, including from unlicensed outlets. A fast-fermenting *Chibuku* brewing "kit" known as Power Shake is now marketed for those wanting a shortcut to making home brew.

Khadi, which tastes something like apple cider, is made from *Grewia* berries and honey and requires less effort; it is readily available in most rural homesteads. In urban areas, *Khadi* is made into a more lethal brew that sometimes incorporates such toxic substances as battery acid, pool chemicals, tobacco, and even old shoes.[26] This has contributed to its poor reputation. Home brews (apart from *bojalwa jwa setswana*) are often stigmatized because they tend to be associated in people's minds with rural life and the lower classes. But even members of the upper classes are known to occasionally drink them (especially *khadi*) in private.

A different traditional alcoholic drink is made from the fermented fruit of the *morula* tree.[27] These are small, round fruit with a light green skin that must be peeled before eating; the large seed in the center produces a small, delicious nut that is collected from the ground around the trees in the fall. In the rainy season, elephants and monkeys are known to get drunk when eating naturally-fermented *morula* fruit that has fallen to the ground, and it is now also made into a liquor, known as Amarula, that is exported throughout the world.[28,29]

A watermelon brew known as *sepopoti* can be extremely high in alcohol content, although the percentage is inconsistent and varies with the brewer and with weather conditions. In both rural areas and cities, home brews are sold at neighborhood bars (shabeens), some of which attain reputations for producing better and stronger brews than others. Shabeens operate something like clubs and normally have a number of loyal customers. They also operate without licensees, but their popularity has frustrated government efforts to close them down. One thing that makes traditional beers popular is their price—a 1.5-liter cup often sells for as little as 25 thebe (five cents).

A popular nonalcoholic drink, *gemere,* is made from ground ginger, cream of tartar, and sugar. It is a favorite drink consumed at weddings and funerals.

In the past, cream of tartar was obtained by scraping the white coating from the seeds of baobab fruit—yet another instance of the use of wild products in Tswana cuisine.

Next to *bojalwa,* milk *(mashi)* is probably the most favored drink in Botswana, and children's memories of visits to the cattle post during school holidays are replete with tales of how much milk they drank warm and foaming from the milk bucket. Unpasteurized milk spoils quickly, so to conserve milk for a longer time, *madila,* or sour milk, is made at practically every cattle post. In the traditional method, cow's or goat's milk is placed inside leather bags where, after several days, the lactose in the milk is converted to lactic acid by natural fermentation. By increasing the acidity, the growth of bacteria and other enzymes that cause spoilage is retarded. *Madila* is extremely popular and is available both in the streets from vendors and in commercial varieties sold in supermarkets.

Butter is another method for preserving milk for longer periods. The Herero, in particular, are known for their butter *(maere),* which they make by agitating milk in leather bags hung by rawhide strips from a wooden tripod. The shaking separates the fat globules from the milk and causes them to join together to form a semisolid mass that is typically about 80 percent fat and 20 percent water. In this form, it can be kept for many days, especially in the winter months. Among the Herero, who often carry *maere* with them in calabashes while on long trips, butter also serves as a metaphor of identity, much as *ting* does for the Kgatla and Tlokwa.

RESTAURANTS AND COMMERCIAL FOOD

Fried chicken from the hundreds of fast-food restaurants found in most towns and cities is among the most favored foods for Batswana on the road or on a lunch break at work. One of the more popular local restaurants in the country that supplies "Tswana chicken" (boiled for a long time and then fried) is Katis in Mahalapye, a "halfway" station along the national road between Francistown and Gaborone. Foreign-based franchises such as the American Chicken Licken and KFC (Kentucky Fried Chicken), with billboards advertising "finger licking good," have appeared in most towns. Their Portuguese competitors, Nandos, have also penetrated the local market, challenging that "oil is meant for your car, not your body."

Batswana prefer beef to almost all other meats, and many cafés and bars sell barbecued beef to their customers.

All cities, towns, and larger villages have at least one bakery that produces bread along with deep-fried-fat cakes known as *magwinya.* Commercially prepared food is also sold in small tuck shops *(semausu)* that are usually located in front of the owner's house. Although small, they function much like American "convenience stores," selling small items such as matches, cooking oil, toilet paper, soap, and cigarettes. Some also sell illegal beer secretly to regular and trusted customers despite raids by licensing authorities.

DRESS

One of the biggest disappointments for foreign visitors coming to Botswana for the first time is the lack of colorful tie-dyed dresses, embroidered shirts, and other garments and robes that constitute the "folk" or "traditional" dress found in other parts of Africa. The usual conclusion drawn is that people in Botswana have lost more of their cultural traditions because, almost without exception, they dress in blue jeans, T-shirts, dresses, suits, ties, and other Western clothing. As a result, in the days of apartheid, white visitors from South Africa were often heard to remark how people in South Africa had "retained" their cultural traditions, while those in Botswana had lost them. Such observations are curious given the fact that in comparison with South Africa, people in the Bechuanaland Protectorate and Botswana experienced far less intrusion on their daily lives from apartheid regulation and oppression or even colonial rule. But by the measure of clothing, most Batswana appear completely westernized. Using this standard, the only people in the country to have retained their "traditions" are Herero women who continue to dress in a style adopted from nineteenth-century German missionaries in Namibia. As will be developed later, this is a misleading and erroneous impression because the relationship between styles of dress and cultural "retention" or "tradition" is not as simple or straightforward as it seems. As one anthropologist put it, clothes are "social skin."[30]

So when did the tradition of wearing brightly colored cotton prints, mud cloth, and tie-dyed fabrics become "traditional" for Africa? And why, for the most part, are these traditions not in evidence in Botswana? In part, the answer lies in the historical context within which southern African communities constructed their relationships to the outside world and to one another. Before the European trade in slaves that began in the fifteenth century, almost everyone in sub-Saharan Africa fashioned their clothing from the skins of animals, cloth made from pounded tree bark, or woven palm frond fibers. The few exceptions were the elite living in the Sahel of West Africa and the Swahili on the East African coast, who wore cotton clothing that was influenced by frequent contact with Islamic travelers and traders after 800 C.E. During the sixteenth to eighteenth centuries, bundles of cloth were among the most highly prized imports to the shores of western and central Africa, where they were exchanged for slaves at ports such as Loango and Luanda.

The African elite, in turn, creatively used the imported cloth and clothing to legitimize new positions of status and power they achieved through the trade and to reinforce preexisting social hierarchies.

> Wealthy princes bedecked themselves and their retainers in the finest and most stylish fabrics obtainable, with scarlet silks occupying a favored position... lesser dignitaries wrapped themselves in lengths of imported cottons in all their lively colors and patterns, competing with one another to set the fashions that others might follow. Ordinary people made do with whatever coarse woolens or flimsy cottons they could acquire... imported textiles covered common folk with quantities of stuffs that only the wealthiest and most powerful had once worn, and the wealthy kept ahead of the generally rising standards of sartorial display by adding length upon length of foreign fabric to their costume until they could hardly move about.[31]

Thus, in West and East Africa, centuries of interaction with Islamic and Christian traders and raiders led to the development of new cultural identities in which distinctive styles of elite clothing and bodily adornment "gestured not only to Christian Europe but also to the Muslim north and east."[32] Through the development of new distinctive attire, relations of inequality and difference were reworked symbolically and then reinvented as "tradition." The wearing of foreign items not only became embodiments of wealth and social position but also, in many instances, associated the wearer with spiritual power, as evidenced by the nineteenth-century Mboma of the lower Congo, who

> believed that foreign-manufactured goods had a magical quality. According to one account of this belief, foreigners did not weave the cloth that they brought to Mboma's port. This was the work of *simbi* spirits who lived beneath the ocean, which the trade vessels crossed on their way to the African coasts. The foreigners, who had found the hole leading to the aquatic *simbi* factory, simply steered to the *simbi* hole and rang a bell whenever they needed cloth. The *bisimbi* responded by pushing up the end of a piece of cloth through the hole. Ships' crews pulled on the cloth for several days until they had all they wanted. As payment to the *bisimbi*, the captains threw into the hole the bodies of BaMboma and other Africans who had been sold to them through witchcraft.[33]

In southern Africa during the nineteenth century, many Tswana also cooperated with missionary wishes that they purchase and wear clothes. Like the Mboma, they did this not so much for purposes of modesty or to show compliance with Christian practices but because there were suspicions that European clothing and other commodities were similarly imbued with supernatural qualities. These beliefs may have been reinforced as nonconformist missionaries such as Robert and Mary Moffat, David and Mary Moffat Livingstone, and others began to use clothing made from imported cloth, along with cleanliness and good housekeeping, as the first visible steps in a conversion process designed to transform unclothed and heathen Tswana bodies into clothed, righteous ones. By combining the spiritual benefits of Christianity with the material benefits they believed to be inherent in consumerism, the "market economy," and the "mundane benefits of clothing and cleanliness [soap]," missionaries hoped to open up "numberless channels for British commerce which but for the Gospel might have remained forever closed."[34]

Batswana were not simply receivers of foreign fashions; they used them to construct their own statements of identity and social position. Initially, the result was a patchwork of traditional garb and imported goods that confounded the engendered distinctions about clothing and its manufacture held by Victorian missionaries. Moffat, for instance, found it bizarre that women were the builders and architects in Tswana society, while it was men who sewed the karosses and much of the other clothing worn by themselves and their wives. Clearly, Mary Moffat had her work cut out for her if she wanted to create Christian women's "sewing circles" in Africa to parallel those she was writing to in England when she requested gowns "made with bodies to fit very stout women . . . I like them best as Gowns were made 20 or 30 years ago, or as I should say *as the fashion is now,* except the tight sleeve, which would be a great misery in a warm climate . . . the materials may be coarse, and strong, the stronger the better. Dark blue prints, or Ginghams . . . or in fact, any kind of dark Cottons, which will wash well—Nothing light-coloured should be worn outside."[35]

Early Dress

In spite of Mary Moffat's efforts to construct a sturdy, not-too-stylish, peasant "uniform" for Tswana women in the mid-nineteenth century, in the 1920s "traditional" Tswana garb sewn from furs and skins was still the norm in the rural areas of Botswana. Indeed, some Europeans thought that this more traditional costume of skins and furs contrasted favorably with the "unpicturesque" combinations of traditional and Western clothing being put on in more urban contexts:

The clothing of most of the Bechuana at present shows most of the unpicturesque leveling effect of European contact, but in the parts further removed from such influence the old dress still holds sway—the *tshega* (loin-skin) for the men, with the addition of a skin cap, sandals, and a kaross, and for the warriors belts of tails; to these items of dress were added various ornaments such as bead strings around the neck, armlets of woven grass or of copper wire, etc., and the inevitable snuff-box and leather pouch for odds and ends; for women, the dress consists of an apron *(khiba)* in front, and a skirt *(mosèsè)* behind, with various ornaments, with a kaross or skin covering the upper part of the body. Women with very young children also had the *thari,* or skin for carrying babies, suspended on their backs. Boys wore a small flap of skin in front, and girls a fringe of strings made of bast or skin, up to the age when they adopted the *tshega* or *khiba* and *mosèsè* respectively, while very little children usually went absolutely naked. But everyone, from the youngest to the oldest, and from the inferior to the superior, wore at least one of the various ornaments so dear to the Chuana heart—beads, and bangles, and anklets, and armlets, some or all of which acted at the same time as charms of various kinds.[36]

This description of dress in Botswana varies little from descriptions made in South Africa at the end of the eighteenth century. And even though the

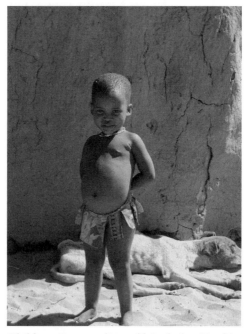

Child wearing a traditional loincloth at Tsodilo. It is still not uncommon for very young children to wear such garb, especially in small villages and rural areas. Photo courtesy of Jennifer Denbow.

clothing was manufactured exclusively from tanned hides, it still encoded distinctions of age, gender, and social status. For instance, at the end of the eighteenth century, only the elite could wear "coats . . . of 15 to 18 neatly sewn together furs of genets, jackals, wild cats [bat-eared foxes], or jumping hares [spring hares] . . . poorer Beetjuanas cannot afford such a sewn-together coat as it costs between one or two oxen. They wear tanned skins of hartebeest or other large antelope."[37] The warm fur blankets (karosses, or *dikobo*) that were the exclusive work of male tailors were still commonly seen as recently as the 1970s in Ngamiland; loincloths of leather for young boys and leather fringe skirts for girls were also common at that time in some large villages, such as Maun.

Some of the ornaments described at the end of the eighteenth century were likely of indigenous bronze.[38] These and other items that included leather bands of rhinoceros hide and bracelets of "elephants teeth" indexed status while, in some cases, also providing protective medicines against jealousy, sickness, and harm. Bodies were adorned with mixtures of red ocher and animal fat. Fat, combined with silvery specularite (hematite), was used to create sparkling, helmet-like coiffures.[39] Specularite and ocher mines were a well-known source of wealth for Tswana in the Kweneng at the time of European contact, and radiocarbon dates from specularite mines in the Tsodilo Hills of northern Botswana indicate that this valued commodity was widely traded as early as 800 C.E. Like their later counterparts in the Kweneng to the south, trade in specularite enabled Early Iron Age communities at Tsodilo to acquire imported glass beads and marine shells from the Indian Ocean to wear as testaments to their status and wealth.[40]

Thus, far from being static before the arrival of European traders and missionaries in the nineteenth century, "traditional" dress in eastern and northern Botswana had began to incorporate foreign items such as glass beads, cowry, and conus shells more than 1,000 years ago. The cowry shells were cut smooth along the back and sewed onto leather or cloth. Glass beads were strung on sinew as necklaces, waistbands, and bracelets. Sometimes they were even used as "spacers" on copper and bronze bracelets worn by the elite. Archaeological excavations indicate that glass beads and marine shells were imported into Botswana in considerable numbers to supplement locally produced iron and copper jewelry after about 800 C.E.; it was exchanged for ivory and other valued commodities.[41] After 1100 C.E., spindle whorls made from recycled potsherds are common finds on many sites in northeastern Botswana, indicating that cotton cloth was being locally produced. Given the lateness of their appearance in the archaeological record of southern Africa, one suspects that weaving of cotton cloth may have been a technology introduced into the subcontinent along with glass beads, cowry and conus shells, chickens, and perhaps even xylophones and other commodities from a trade network that reached far across the Indian Ocean to India, Indonesia, China, the Persian Gulf, and Egypt.[42] Clay figurines of women dating to the thirteenth to sixteenth centuries in the Toutswe area of east-central Botswana suggest that the cloth was wrapped around the waist and then brought forward between the legs, where it was tied in a knot in front. In Zimbabwe, remnants of actual cloth have been found in burials where it was preserved through contact with copper bangles. No mention of such indigenous cloth is found in nineteenth-century journals describing Tswana dress, so it is possible that locally woven cloth had either fallen out of favor as a commodity that marked elite status or was already in the process of being replaced in elite circles by goods of European manufacture by the time the first white observers arrived.

Missionaries and "Folk Costumes"

Extensive use of ocher, specularite, and fat as items of bodily adornment led to difficulties for the Moffats and other early missionaries who often complained that their clothes were ruined because "all the heathen population besmear themselves with red ochre and grease, and as the Christians must necessarily come in contact with their friends among the heathen, they soon look miserable enough, if clothed in light-colored things."[43] Similar sentiments were mirrored by her husband, Robert, who remarked that "as many men and women as pleased might come into our hut, leaving us not room even to turn ourselves, and making every thing they touched the colour of their greasy red attire."[44] What some missionaries failed to recognize, however, was that generous applications of ocher and fat provide excellent protection against the harsh effects of the intense Kalahari sun and drying winds. Livingstone at least recognized the benefits of skin creams, writing that "to assist in protecting the pores of the skin from the influence of the sun by day and of the cold by night, all smeared themselves with a mixture of fat and ochre; the head was anointed with pounded blue mica schist mixed with fat; and the fine particles of shining mica falling on the body and on the strings of beads and brass rings were considered as highly ornamental and fit for the most fastidious dandy."[45] Even today, Batswana are fastidious about applying lotion to their bodies—the products they use today just happen to be available for purchase in enormous variety in stores rather than having to be manufactured at home from local ingredients. Clothing and bodily adornment were thus two fronts along which early missionaries measured the success of their attempts to convert the Tswana to godliness and cleanliness, contrasting the "lubricated wild man of the desert" with the "clean, comfortable and well-dressed believer."[46] In addition to godliness and salvation, "decent dress," according to Livingstone in the 1840s, led to a decline in "conditions like inflammation of the bowels, rheumatism, and heart disease."[47]

Mary Moffat and other missionary wives were in part responsible for the development of a traditional, "folk" style of clothing that would form the foundation for women's attire for generations to come. While some wealthy and important Tswana donned Western clothing as a sign of status and modernity or as evidence of conversion to Christianity, others just as passionately rejected it—usually as a political statement. As late as 1885, for instance, Khamane, in an attempt to wrest the chieftainship of the Ngwato in Serowe from Khama III, pledged to the more conservative elements of the community that he would reinstate circumcision and rainmaking rites, and, in addition, he "gave orders to the young regiment to strip off all European clothing [and] to meet naked in the court."[48] A locally constructed middle ground also developed, as was observed in 1828:

> Mateebe was dressed in a pair of pantaloons, a shirt and waistcoat, with a cat-skin caross over his shoulders.... The young women were dressed in gowns...and above these, each of them wore a jackal-skin caross, which served as a covering by day, and a blanket by night. They were covered with a profusion of ornaments.[49]

In the early twentieth century, such locally contrived "mixtures" of African and Western attire confounded European traders and travelers who saw them as debased and "unpicturesque" because they violated their Western sense of fashion and style. By the 1930s and 1940s, the sturdy indigo and brown garments first proposed by Mary Moffat had evolved into an ethnicized style that included ankle-length dresses with a tight bodice that billowed out at the waist over layers of petticoats. The dresses were made of a starched type of patterned cloth now known as German or "Geremani" cloth *(leteitshe, chiba),* which still comes mainly in patterned dark blue or brown. In place of jackal fur karosses, brightly colored woolen or polyester blankets are draped over the shoulders or pulled around the body and tied under the arms. A cloth scarf called a *tukwi,* or *"doeke"* in Afrikaans, is tied around the head. The blanket serves the same purpose as the skin *thari* and is used not only for warmth but also to tie babies securely onto their mothers' backs. Soft leather sandals complete the outfit. This subtle mixture of Western materials and African practicality, generically known as *mateitshe,* is now mostly worn only on special occasions, such as weddings, funerals, or cultural gatherings.

In South Africa, where the direct effects of European colonization culminated in the racially and economically divisive system of apartheid, the "folk

An illustration of the components that make up the Tswana
traditional dress. The blanket
is a direct adaptation of the
nineteenth-century skin kaross,
or *kobo*. Photo courtesy of
Morongwa Mosothwane.

costume" of blanket (kaross) and long Western gown became a symbol of
both marginalization and resistance, a style that was

> neither straightforwardly European nor "authentically" vernacular... [but]
> combined elements of both to signify a novel sense of anachronism: that of
> being citizens of a marginalized, "ethnic" culture. Like other peoples... these
> Tswana found themselves refigured as quaint premoderns, as "natives" at the
> exploitable fringes of empire. In conjuring up their costumes, they opted for a
> form of dress that reworked imperial designs... the "folk costume" of those
> peoples who have been socially and spatially peripheralized... by a largely
> Eurocentric cosmopolitanism.[50]

The South African woman's "folk costume" that evolved through the interaction of African and European under colonial rule in the nineteenth century

was refined but not radically transformed in the first half of the twentieth century. While in the towns and homelands of South Africa, the conservative "German cloth" long dresses, petticoats, bright blankets, and head scarves worn by Tswana women became iconic of "a 'tribal' center far from the reaches of modern economy, society, and history," in Botswana the legal and social lines of division imposed by apartheid in South Africa were less clearly drawn— and after independence in 1966 they were purposefully confounded and disrupted.[51] Racially segregated trains from South Africa, for instance, were stopped and intentionally "mixed" at the border while en route to white-ruled Rhodesia, and political refugees from both countries found sanctuary in Botswana. The socially constructed "messages" transmitted by "traditional," mission-inspired clothing were also different. And after independence in 1966, the "Geremani" costume became increasingly reserved in Botswana, at least by the younger generation, for use on special occasions such as parties, weddings, and funerals, where it reinforced values of cultural heritage, tradition, and pride. Thus, the same women's costume that became a daily symbol of tribalized homelands in apartheid South Africa was transformed in Botswana into a modern "cultural costume," worn mainly on special occasions as a symbol of cultural solidarity and respect for the past. In this sense, the style plays a cultural role similar to the feelings of heritage and pride evoked by the wearing of replica skin clothing by modern traditional dancers as they perform for audiences on Independence Day or on Botswana Television.

For Botswana men in the 1930s and 1940s, going to work in the South African mines became almost a form of initiation—an initiation that provided workers with not only much-needed family income but also a more urbane, "worldly" status on returning home.[52] Their work clothing of coveralls and rubber boots reflected their status as undifferentiated laborers. Formal wear worn on social occasions, however, tended to follow fashion styles of their white and black male counterparts in South Africa.

So where does this leave the traditional nineteenth-century dress of Herero women? The Herero sometimes view themselves as an "encapsulated minority," living in exile in Botswana since the German-Herero war of 1904. Their distinctive high-bodiced, neck-to-ankle dresses, fashioned from brightly colored patchworks of cloth, are worn over numerous petticoats—even in temperatures that rise above 100 degrees Fahrenheit in summer. Triangular, cloth head scarves *(otjikayiva)* folded to resemble cattle horns and shawls of crocheted yarn complete the attire. Nineteenth-century Rhenish missionaries inspired their colorful dress, but other traditions of respect for their ancestors are also continued through, for instance, the tending of a sacred fire known as *Okuruo,* through which headmen address their ancestors, seek advice, and confess their sins. Like the Tswana folk costume, the colorful Herero dresses

Herero woman in traditional clothing along with her butter churn and wooden pots. In the past, the Herero more commonly used wooden rather than clay bowls and pots as containers.

and scarves are constructions of identity that reinforce their memories of an earlier period in their history. But at the same time, Herero women also use their distinctive dress to create cultural difference and distance under conditions of social and political marginality in contemporary Botswana. By visually emphasizing their distinctiveness in a country dominated by Tswana and Kalanga speakers, their position as a marginalized polity is crystallized and acts to mobilize Herero identity not only as a form of resistance but also as a positive political force in the context of a modern, democratic Botswana.[53]

But the traditional dress of Herero women also presents a much more layered set of contradictions in the context of contemporary Botswana. While the heavy dress is indeed an advertisement of ethnic identity (and even of gender relations, as it carries with it a sense of domesticity and subordination), wearing it also embodies cultural concepts of grace and beauty. Herero women are expected not to rush about but to walk regally *(osemba)*—slowly and with dignity—while enjoying a freedom of movement they contrast with that permitted by the tighter, more constraining Western styles worn by Tswana women. Nonetheless, "ethnic dress, like ethnic language, disrupts the image of an undifferentiated citizenry. Layered together—like the underskirts that support the dress—images of domesticity and ethnicity, and of wives' constraint by husbands' desires, sustain a perception that the heavy skirts of the Herero women's dress are restrictive, a drag on both physical activity and the socioeconomic mobility desired in the context of Botswana's liberal democratic society."[54] This is perhaps why, at least in eastern Botswana, many younger women wear the dress only on important social occasions, such as weddings and funerals. Finally, the stylish Western attire worn daily by most contemporary women in Botswana, regardless of ethnicity, makes another form of cultural statement—one that refutes the apartheid-generated notion of cultural marginality attached to African "folk dress" in southern Africa.

NOTES

1. Comment of a Sarwa man arguing against recent laws against subsistence hunting by indigenous peoples in the Central Kalahari Game Reserve. In Robert Hitchcock, "'Hunting Is Our Heritage': The Struggle for Hunting and Gathering Rights among the San of Southern Africa," http://www.kalaharipeoples.org/documents/Hunt-iwg.htm.

2. R. Gordon Cumming, *The Lion Hunter of South Africa: Five Years' Adventures in the Far Interior of South Africa, with Notices of the Native Tribes and Savage Animals* (London: John Murray, 1911), p. 189.

3. J. Comaroff and J. L. Comaroff, *Of Revelation and Revolution: The Dialectics of Modernity on a South African Frontier,* vol. 2 (Chicago: University of Chicago Press, 1997), p. 228. Reprinted with permission from the University of Chicago Press and the authors, John and Jean Comaroff. They quote J. Campbell in "Kuirreechane," *Missionary Sketches,* no. 25 (April 1824).

4. Frank Taylor and H. Moss, *Final Report on the Potential for Commercial Utilization of Veld Products* (Gaborone: Ministry of Commerce and Industry, 1982).

5. In the Tswana language, a distinction is made between aspirated and nonaspirated sounds that is almost impossible for native English speakers to hear or reproduce. As a result, most English spellings leave out the aspirated "h," to the frustration of many Tswana speakers.

6. These are only two of a wide variety of wild greens eaten. Other common varieties include Leshwe *(Pentarrhinum insipidum* and *Pergularia extensa)* and Serepe *(Portulaca oleracea).*

7. Overharvesting of mopane worms in recent years has led to erratic harvests and localized extinction in some areas. To control this problem, the Botswana government recently introduced legislation that would require commercial harvesters to obtain permits for *Phane* collection or face prosecution in customary court. Many are suspicious of this and are afraid that it is a first step in government regulation of other wild foods that people have relied on for generations.

8. On the export market, mainly to South Africa, mopane worms bring up to $5.00 per pound.

9. In Botswana, a very clear distinction is made between these two types of porridges. In South Africa, the terms are interchangeable.

10. Robert Hitchcock, "Subsistence Hunting and Special Game Licenses in Botswana," *Botswana Notes and Records* 28 (1996): 55–64.

11. Robert Moffat, *The Matabele Journals of Robert Moffat, 1829–1860* (Salisbury: National Archives of Rhodesia, 1976).

12. The two major exceptions to this were the Nile valley of Egypt and highland Ethiopia, where ox-drawn plows have been in use for more than 5,000 years. In North Africa, plow agriculture was also practiced from at least 800 c.e., when the Phoenicians introduced it to Carthage and other areas.

13. Anne Griffiths, *In the Shadow of Marriage: Gender and Justice in an African Community* (Chicago: University of Chicago Press, 1997), p. 220.

14. Isaac Schapera, *A Handbook of Tswana Law and Custom* (London: F. Cass, 1970), p. 226.

15. J. Denbow was forcefully reminded of this preference while buying meat for an archaeological camp of University of Botswana students in 2001 and 2002. For several weeks, he went to town and bought filet mignon for the camp because it was readily available at a good price. After three weeks, the camp rebelled and demanded in unison, "We want meat with bones!"

16. It is possible that most prehistoric Tswana societies did not eat fish, hence the song, *nna ga ke je tlhapi, tlhapi ke noga, noga ya mesti,* literally, "I do not eat fish because it is a snake that lives in water." Excavations in the Tsodilo Hills of northern Botswana, however, have found that Early Iron Age settlers, as well as foragers, ate fish regularly.

17. As one man in Rakops remarked, "I can't eat animals that people have been sitting on and farting." Conversation between J. Denbow and Brai Orzo, July 1984.

18. All Batswana like their meat well cooked and will not gladly eat rare or medium cooked meat or any with even a tinge of red remaining.

19. This traditional price of P5.00 ($1.00) for a village hen seems to have remained constant for at least a decade. Many Batswana find the meat of commercially raised broilers "too soft."

20. In the absence of salt, hunters sometimes spice their food with gall. And when there is insufficient water at the kill site to wash their hands, they use the partially digested grass from the rumen of the killed animal *(moswang),* which has a high water content. Hunters may also use liquid from wild *tsama* melons to wash with and drink.

21. The Afrikaans word *biltong* is now used almost universally, although Tswana terms such as *digopa* and *segwapa* exist. For many white South Africans, *biltong* is the quintessential food that evokes memories of their homeland, especially when traveling overseas.

22. *Chakalaka* is a spicy blend of herbs and chilies.

23. The Kgatla cook a thick version of sorghum called *bogobe jwa ting.* This is usually made from fermented sorghum and is served with vegetables. The Kwena and

Ngwaketse make a plainer version called *mosokwane,* which is also accompanied by meat and vegetables. Common traditional vegetables include *thepe* and *rothi.*

24. *Madila,* or sour milk, is very abundant at cattle posts at the end of the rainy season. If some of the liquid is drained off, it is very similar to the sour cream familiar to Western cooks.

25. Gabriel Setiloane, whose mother always left a little food in the cooking pots for the "*badimo*" when she dished up the food, remembers that "our lively juvenile minds used to picture '*badimo*' emerging from the corners of the room after dark when we were all asleep and opening up the pots to have their meal." G. Setiloane, *The Image of God among the Sotho-Tswana* (Rotterdam: A. A. Balkema, 1976), p. 175.

26. An article by Chrispin Inambao in the *Namibian* for March 20, 2000, discussed the deaths of seven workers at the Omuramba Hunting Lodge who consumed nontraditional Khadi laced with swimming pool cleaner, battery acid, and other corrosive substances. Discarded batteries, tobacco, fertilizer, and even old shoes are sometimes said to be added to urban Khadi brews to make them more "potent." Several other homemade brews have such a high alcohol content that they can be dangerous to consume, although their consumption is not against the law. One, known as *tho-tho-tho,* is distilled from sorghum and can have an alcohol content of more than 80 percent. Other powerful drinks, with suggestive names such as *o lala fa* (you sleep right here!), *chechisa* (hurry-up!), *laela mmago* (say good-bye to your mother), *monna-tota* (real man), and *motse o teng godimo* (there is home in heaven), are brewed using commercial yeast and sugar.

27. David Livingstone remarked, "We have a tree called morula, the wood of which makes the best bowls. The fruit is about the size of the largest apricots; has a large stone covered with pulp, not easily detached & tasting when ripe exactly like the mango. The kernel is like the walnut in taste, but does not equal it in size." David Livingstone and I. Schapera, *Family Letters, 1841–1856* (Westport, Conn.: Greenwood Press, 1975), pp. 25–26.

28. An elephant is depicted on the bottle.

29. Other products made from *morula* include jam and personal care products such as shampoos and skin creams, available at some pharmacies.

30. T. S. Turner, "The Social Skin," in *Not Work Alone: A Cross-Cultural View of Activities Superfluous to Survival,* eds. Jeremy Cherfas and Roger Lewin (Beverly Hills, California: Sage, 1980), pp. 112–40.

31. Joseph Miller, *Way of Death: Merchant Capitalism and the Angolan Slave Trade, 1730–1830* (Madison: University of Wisconsin Press, 1988), pp. 80–81.

32. Comaroff and Comaroff, *Of Revelation and Revolution,* vol. 2, pp. 257–58. Reprinted with permission from the University of Chicago Press and the authors, John and Jean Comaroff.

33. Norman Schrag, *Changing Perceptions of Wealth among the Bamboma (Lower Zaire)* (Bloomington: African Studies Program, Indiana University, 1990), p. 5.

34. Comaroff and Comaroff, *Of Revelation and Revolution,* vol. 2, p. 229. Reprinted with permission from the University of Chicago Press and the authors, John and Jean Comaroff.

35. Mary Moffat, "Letter to a Well-Wisher," *Quarterly Bulletin of the South Africa Library* 22 (1967): 18 (emphasis in the original).

36. A. M. Alfred Duggan-Cronin, *The Bantu Tribes of South Africa: Reproductions of Photographic Studies* (Cambridge: Deighton, Bell, 1928), p. 20.

37. Hinrich Lichtenstein and O. H. Spohr, *Foundation of the Cape [and] About the Bechuanas* (Cape Town: A. A. Balkema, 1973), pp. 67–68.

38. Lichtenstein (ibid., p. 67) writes that "light yellow Macquini [Makwena] copper . . . can be recognized as a completely strange metal." Recent archaeological investigations in Botswana have found that the manufacture of bronze jewelry began around 700 years ago. D. Miller, "Smelter and Smith: Iron Age Metal Fabrication Technology in Southern Africa," *Journal of Archaeological Science,* 29 (10, 2002): 1083–1131.

39. D. Livingstone, *Missionary Travels and Researches in South Africa* (New York: Harper and Brothers, 1858), p. 108.

40. Larry Robbins, M. Murphy, and A. Campbell, "Intensive Mining of Specular Hematite in the Kalahari ca. AD 800–1000," *Current Anthropology* 39 (1, 1998): 144–49. See also James Denbow, "Material Culture and the Dialectics of Identity in the Kalahari,: in *Beyond Chiefdoms: Pathways to Complexity in Africa,* ed. S. McIntosh (Cambridge: Cambridge University Press, 1999), pp. 110–23.

41. Importation of glass beads for personal adornment was thus more than 1,000 years old when missionaries such as David Livingstone attached themselves to the trade. Early on, they found that the Tswana had already honed sophisticated preferences for beads, and he commented ruefully in a letter to his parents in 1845 that "the beads [you sent] are nearly useless, because they are not in fashion. The real fashionable sort are . . . not transparent, but bright red, blue or white. But you must not send anything else." Livingstone and Schapera, *Family Letters,* p. 151. Blue, red, and yellow beads are also the most common colors found on archaeological sites in Botswana dating between 1000 and 1500 C.E.

42. Most of these items, apart from xylophones *(marimba, ambira, mbila),* are common finds on archaeological sites in eastern Botswana and adjacent districts of South Africa and Zimbabwe. See Denbow, "Material Culture and the Dialectics of Identity in the Kalahari," pp. 110–23. Wooden xylophones with calabash resonators are unusual but certainly date to precolonial times, as they are first described by the Portuguese friar Joao dos Santos in 1586. One scholar stated that "my firm conviction [is] that the principle involved in the *mbila* [xylophone] . . . of Africa, was discovered in Indonesia and was imitated by Africans who had been in contact with Indonesians." At the same time, he dispelled a common myth that the tuning of these instruments also paralleled that of Indonesia because he found that the difficulty in precisely tuning the instruments makes it "difficult to accept . . . [such] conclusions." P. R. Kirby, *The Musical Instruments of the Native Races of South Africa* (Johannesburg: Witwatersrand University Press, 1968), pp. 272–73.

43. Mary Moffat, "Letter to a Well-Wisher," *Quarterly Bulletin of the South Africa Library* 22 (1967): 16–19, as quoted in Comaroff and Comaroff, *Of Revelation and*

Revolution, vol. 2, p. 237. Reprinted with permission from the University of Chicago Press and the authors, John and Jean Comaroff.

44. Robert Moffat, *Missionary Labours and Scenes in Southern Africa* (London: J. Snow, 1842), p. 287.

45. Livingstone, *Missionary Travels and Researches in South Africa,* p. 108.

46. Comaroff and Comaroff, *Of Revelation and Revolution,* vol. 2, p. 225, quoting I. Hughes, Missionary Labours among the Batlapi," *Evangelical Magazine and Missionary Chronicle* 19 (1841): 522–23. Reprinted with permission from the University of Chicago Press and the authors, John and Jean Comaroff.

47. Comaroff and Comaroff, *Of Revelation and Revolution,* p. 227. Reprinted with permission from the University of Chicago Press and the authors, John and Jean Comaroff.

48. Ibid., p. 244.

49. John Philip, *Researches in South Africa; Illustrating the Civil, Moral, and Religious Condition of the Native Tribes, Including Journals of the Author's Travels in the Interior, Together with Detailed Accounts of the Progress of the Christian Missions, Exhibiting the Influence of Christianity in Promoting Civilization,* vol. 2 (New York: Negro Universities Press, 1969), p. 127.

50. Comaroff and Comaroff, *Of Revelation and Revolution,* vol. 2, pp. 256–57. Reprinted with permission from the University of Chicago Press and the authors, John and Jean Comaroff.

51. Ibid., pp. 258–59. Reprinted with permission from the University of Chicago Press and the authors, John and Jean Comaroff.

52. Isaac Schapera, *Migrant Labour and Tribal Life: A Study of Conditions in the Bechuanaland Protectorate* (London: Oxford University Press, 1947), p. 122.

53. While the Herero experience political marginalization, they are also among the most wealthy Batswana because of their large livestock holdings.

54. D. Durham, "The Predicament of Dress: Polyvalency and the Ironies of Cultural Identity," *American Ethnologist* 26 (2, 1999): 399.

6

Gender Roles, Marriage, and Family

The number of men is relatively small and they have to hunt and go to war, so naturally all the peaceful duties and occupations are done by women. Only such work as can suddenly be dropped and can be interrupted for some length of time, such as the already mentioned sewing of clothes, is done by men. All other work which has to be done continuously such as building, tilling of the soil, the making of pots, baskets, ropes and other household utensils is done by women.... They are quite happy to hoe, dig and build without ever showing any bad mood.[1]

Households form the basis for the political structure of the kgotla and customary law; authority is based on age and status. Children defer to adults, who acquire greater status with marriage and age. But women do not have authority comparable with that of men, and this is underlined by the fact that although they may act as heads of households, they can never qualify for the position of head of a group of households which form a kgotla, the basic unit in the political structure of the *morafe* [tribe]. At each stage of her life a woman falls within the shadow of male authority. When unmarried, it is the authority of her father and her brothers; when married, it is that of her husband; and when widowed or in old age (if never married), it is that of her sons.[2]

This chapter will look at gender in the context of marriage and family relations as well as at some of the ways these relations are being transformed under modern conditions. As one might expect of a country that is home to speakers of the two principal branches of Bantu languages, eastern and western, as well as to speakers of the unrelated Khoisan family of click languages, marriage and family customs vary widely in Botswana. Many of the peoples of northwestern Botswana, for instance, are organized into matrilineages and matriclans in which inheritance and descent give greater emphasis to female or uterine lines than is the case among the patrilineal Tswana and Kalanga of eastern and southern Botswana. Patrilineal cultures generally trace relationships through male or agnatic lines. Matrilineages and patrilineages are known as unilineal descent systems because they emphasize relationships, inheritance, and descent traced through one parent. The Herero of northwestern Botswana, on the other hand, are noted for practicing what is traditionally known as "double descent," a system that traces relationships and inheritance through both male and female lines, usually with specific goods, obligations, and rights passed down either through the mother's or the father's side of the family. A man's cattle, for instance, were supposed to pass to his sister's children (representing the *eanda,* or matriclan), while only a few "sacred" cattle were passed down to his sons (*oruzo,* or patriclan). This mode of inheritance formed a stark contrast with the Tswana custom where all the cattle were meant to be inherited by the eldest son, who would then allocate some to his younger brothers as he desired. Daughters and widows received no cattle at all from their father or husband, although the eldest son and heir was obliged to maintain and support them.[3] In the 1950s, the contrast between Tswana and Herero forms of inheritance tempted at least one Herero family in Ngamiland to challenge "the custom of inheritance by the sister's child in the Batawana tribal courts, with the result that the courts directed the sister's children to turn over their portion of the inheritance to the sons of the deceased."[4] The decision touched off a change in custom, and today the bulk of a Batswana Herero cattle are passed to a man's son, with only enough being given to his sister's children to show "generosity and to engender good will."[5] Finally, the Khoisan trace relationships equally through the father's and mother's family in a system known as bilateral descent. While this system would appear to create the widest possible grouping of relatives on whom one could draw for support in times of need, all the systems create through marriage networks of alliance and support on both sides of the family. Among the patrilineal Tswana, for instance, a mother's brother plays a special role in handling disputes within the family and also in marriage negotiations for his sister's sons.

BRIDE WEALTH

At the beginning of the nineteenth century, a gift of cattle from the groom's to the bride's family was the primary way in which a marriage was recognized as legitimate in the eyes of the public. Cattle were also sacrificed at weddings as well as at other important ceremonies, such as funerals and, in the past, rainmaking rites, to show respect and honor to the families, guests, and ancestors. While giving of bride wealth *(bogadi)* was intended to acknowledge the wife's family for giving away their daughter, it also placed the marriage on firm ground if questions later arose about the position of children within their father's lineage, their rights to inheritance, and the rights to property on the part of the husband or wife if the marriage ended in divorce. Many Europeans oversimplified the complexity of the rights and obligations transferred in the passing of *bogadi* by wrongly interpreting it as a form of commodity payment—the "purchase" of a wife—which it was not:

> As soon as a young man has earned enough by loyalty in the service of his father or another cattle owner, to justify his ability to manage on his own, he uses part of his possessions to buy a wife. A deal is made with the father of the chosen female when in exchange for ten to twelve oxen the father cedes all rights to his daughter and she enters now the service of her husband. The bride... as her first duty... must build a house, for which she has to cut the wood frequently without any help.... She must also see to a good kraal for the cattle and to the cultivation of the land.... Once the herd of cattle grows more numerous after a few years, the husband thinks of enlarging his family and he buys a second wife.[6]

In the past, the "token of appreciation" for the emotional loss of their daughter and her children to their lineage that *bogadi* represents was fairly standardized at between 8 and 10 cattle. Today, however, *bogadi* has become more commercialized, and some families have begun to demand a higher *bogadi* as compensation, especially if they have incurred greater costs in raising and educating their daughters. Another reason that *bogadi* is given is that after marriage the bride's family will have very little say in her life. If she dies, for instance, her funeral would be run according to the customs and wishes of her husband's family. Even strangers, such as Europeans who do not have the custom of giving *bogadi,* are now often expected to do so if they marry Tswana wives. Because many young people now work in cities and do not keep or raise cattle, it is also becoming acceptable to pay in cash, but cattle are still seen as more "acceptable." Depending on their wealth, the number of cattle thought to be acceptable varies from one *morafe* to another. A *bogadi* as high as 10 cattle would now be rare, however.

For most Tswana—and especially for wealthy families—it has long been a custom to marry close relatives.[7] Marriage with a father's brother's daughter was especially favored among the rich not only because the families would then know one another well but also because over generations such marriages kept the *bogadi* within in same lineage, as attested by the Tswana proverb, *"Ngwana wa rrangwane nnyale, kgomo di boelte sakeng"* ("child of my father's younger brother, marry me so that the cattle will remain in the corral").[8] Because of the respect given to elders, it was not considered "polite" to approach a father's older brother in this same fashion.

Among some groups, the custom is for *bogadi* to be paid before the marriage is consummated. In others, an ox or a goat given "to see the teeth" *(podi ya go bona meno)* is slaughtered before a custom known as *"go ralala,"* officially allowed the betrothed couple to live together.[9] Among other groups, the wedding ceremony does not take place until the girl has given birth to a child; other groups may wait until a male child is born before going ahead with the passing of *bogadi* and finalizing the marriage. While a couple were not supposed to have children before the marriage was finalized and *bogadi* given, today it is not unusual for several children to be born before the final *bogadi* is given to the bride's family and the wedding ceremony takes place. In all these cases, however, formal agreements leading to betrothal *(patlo)* must have been completed between the two families before their relationship can be formally recognized. If *bogadi* payments are delayed, in some cases the bride's family may demand a cow (or cash equivalent) for having children before marriage. This cow is known as *kgomo ya tlhagela*—a cow that has "broken into the family's corral." In some cases, the meeting between the two families may become excessively drawn out, particularly if one party to the marriage (bride, groom, or respective families) begins to lose interest. If the dispute cannot be resolved, the *kgotla* may be asked to adjudicate, causing "many a headache because we have to trace back to find out how and when they married."[10]

If a girl gets pregnant without a formal betrothal or consent between the families, the girl's uncle must report it to the man's family within three months of falling pregnant. The man's maternal uncle will then discuss the matter with the girl's family to determine whether they intend to marry. If they decide to marry, the man is expected to support the mother and child until the marriage occurs. If there are no marriage plans, the man must pay "damages" for "spoiling" the girl. Damages can occasionally be as high as eight cows or a cash equivalent for a first pregnancy. This is about the same as a full *bogadi* payment, as it is recognized that it will be hard to get the same *bogadi* from a later suitor. Women with more than one child, especially those with different fathers, are in a much weaker bargaining position. Restriction of damage claims to the first child is usually seen at the *kgotla* to be "necessary to prevent some parents from deliberately encouraging their daughters to lead a loose life, in effect prostituting them, for the sake of cattle which could then be claimed whenever pregnancy ensued."[11]According to contemporary Botswana law, a man must support his child until it reaches the age of 18.

POLYGYNY

In the past, when polygamy was more common, only wealthy individuals could afford to have multiple wives. Each marriage required the payment of *bogadi,* and each wife was expected to be established in her own homestead, with her own fields and houses. To minimize strife between wives, it was often thought to be desirable to marry sisters (sororiate marriage) who "in theory" would get along better than wives from different families or lineages. Tension and jealousy were especially prevalent between half brothers from separate houses and often led to accusations of witchcraft and sorcery as

> men were compelled to construct their own identities, often by "overshadowing" the viability of others. Since property and position depended on it, houses often contested their rank, the interests of "children of one womb" being inimical to those of their half-siblings—and, in the next generation, to those of their paternal uncles and cousins. This is why, for the southern Tswana, the courtly politics of agnatic rivalry, and the effort of men to "eat" [dominate] one another were born in the household.[12]

With colonial overrule, the economic and political conditions that favored polygamous marriages dramatically changed, and by the 1940s it was the rare household that was still polygamous:

> Polygamy, although prohibited by tribal law only among the Ngwaketse, has declined considerably everywhere. In 1850 Livingstone recorded that 43 percent of all the married men among the Kaa had more than one wife; today, according to the 1946 census returns, only 11 percent of married men are polygamists.[13]

If a man wishes to marry more than one wife, it must be done with the consent of the first wife under the traditional system of marriage; polygyny is illegal under the common-law Marriage Act. Polygynous marriages are still sometimes found in the remoter areas of Botswana, particularly among the Mbukushu, but they have become rare in other parts of the country for several reasons. First, polygyny was one of the first targets of Christian missionaries such as David Livingstone. He and his missionary brethren decried such practices as heathen not so much because the Bible prohibited it but because it was contrary to the traditions and laws of their own countries. Not only would they not permit polygamous marriages among their flock, but they demanded that those men who already had more than one wife convert to monogamy before church membership could be confirmed. Needless to say, this caused considerable consternation to all concerned—not only to the husband but also to the second and third wives and their families whose prospects were now uncertain. What were the returned wives' families to do with them? What about the *bogadi* that was given at marriage? Should it now be returned? How were these ex-wives to marry again? Who was now responsible for them and for their children? Whose totem were the children to respect, and to which ancestors should they turn in time of need? Missionaries were aloofly insensitive to these issues.

Furthermore, wealthy men used polygamous marriages not only as an index of their wealth and position but also strategically to cement their relationships with other powerful families, an important part of their power base within the community. Changes in the economics of agricultural production with the introduction of the plow also contributed to the devaluation of the benefits of polygamous marriage, especially among the elite who could afford to purchase plows and draft oxen that allowed them to engage in more capital-intensive agriculture. Changes in the technology of agricultural production, missionary activity, and the calculus of indigenous political power under colonial overrule thus converged to diminish the economic and political value of polygyny and the economic and political alliances it once underwrote.

Problems related to polygyny are a concern not only of the past or of families living in rural areas, however. At the diamond mine at Jwaneng in the Kweneng district, for instance, the number of polygamous households is apparently high enough that the mine administration was compelled to impose limits on the availability of AIDS drugs to workers' spouses, stating that "they will stand firm on the one-spouse rule. Husbands will have to choose which wife will have access to the medicines."[14] It is not clear whether these measures were in response to demands by actual polygamous households in their employ or simply a strategy on the part of mine workers to acquire health care for more relatives by taking advantage of the "flexibility" to have more than one wife. Given the sometimes erratic nature of record keeping in the *kgotla,* proving the existence of any customary marriage— monogamous or polygynous—can be tedious. Even government employees who have married in a traditional way but have not registered at a magistrate's office or church have to return to their villages to obtain signed verification of their marriage by their parents and their chief, or *kgosi.* Compounding the problems of traditional marriage and polygamy, beginning in the 1920s and 1930s the scarcity of available men due to transnational migrant labor contracts resulted in a reevaluation of the institution of marriage on the part of both men and women who now "tended to engage in a series of relationships [outside marriage], investigating the potential of various marriage partners and testing the benefits of such associations before committing themselves to one partner."[15]

CONTEMPORARY MARRIAGE

Marriage and having children are two of the most central events affecting an individual's status and rights within the community. The family household of husband, wife, and children forms the basic building block of Tswana society. Among the Tswana, groups of households, affiliated agnatically around a *kgotla* and animal corral (kraal), are the grassroots, political and economic institutions that are organized into larger wards and sections that make up a *morafe*. On marriage, women are expected to leave their home *kgotla* and move to their husband's, to which their children become affiliated socially, economically, and spiritually. In this way, marriage establishes new relationships between the families of the bride and groom. In Tswana society, these relationships are often especially close because of an affinity for marrying close relatives, including first cousins.

With marriage, men and women are initiated into fuller participation as adults in the affairs of the community. Single men, on the other hand, are sometimes referred to as *makgope*, a synonym for "large yellow locusts" because, like locusts, they are "free agents" with few responsibilities; they can move around and stay where they like without familial obligations.[16] Full participation in *kgotla* deliberations, however, is denied them, regardless of age, while given to married men who may be chronologically junior. The effective social and kin networks established by marriage are thus valuable social resources, and individuals often "pursue different marriage strategies based on their position within households and in the political hierarchy."[17] Children also bring an increase in status—as well as responsibility. Young men and women often feel pressure to "grow up" by getting married and having children, although not necessarily in that order. Some couples may cohabit for a long time without any formal rites or traditional ceremonies, but the community at large looks down on such arrangements.

Unlike in the West, where a young couple may simply announce to their families that they intend to marry, negotiations between families in Botswana (*patlo*, from the term "to seek") are the foundation of a traditional marriage, and it can take many months, if not years, before a formal marriage ceremony (*lenyalo*) takes place. So important are these interfamilial relationships that in the past children—even those not yet born—were sometimes betrothed to one another. The bride and groom had little to say in the matter, as they were bound to comply with their parent's wishes as "dutiful children." In most cases, the choice of a marriage partner involved close kin, especially cousins: a mother's brother's daughter or a father's sister's daughter were often chosen. If there was no suitable prospect, "another girl will be sought, from among the more remote relatives or even from non-relatives. Normally men marry women of their own tribe; but marriages between people of different Tswana tribes are becoming fairly common."[18] The practice of cousin marriage is still prevalent, although not as much as in earlier times.[19]

Today younger people have a much greater say in the selection of their spouse, and marriage between people of different *merafe,* not just Tswana groups, is now fairly common among the more educated and among those living in urban areas. Intermarriage between patrilineal and matrilineal peoples poses different challenges, however, and such marriages are still uncommon, especially because of differences in marriage customs related to bride wealth and dowry. Among the Mbukushu, it was once customary for the bride's family to provide a dowry at the time of marriage. Changes are occurring as the country becomes increasing more "Tswana-ized" in some of its customs and practices. A dowry is no longer expected, and even among the Herero, the giving of bride wealth or *bogadi* has become customary. While the details of marriage customs in the country are different, there are overall similarities in many respects. The following discussion presents a somewhat idealized version of the betrothal and marriage rites among the Tswana peoples, who make up approximately 80% of the population.

The descriptions of Tswana betrothal and marriage ceremonies presented here represent the ideal or iconic situation. While many of the traditional elements such as *patlo* and *go laa* continue, there have also been many changes. In some cases, money is substituted for *bogadi* cattle, and today there is no required period of residence and cohabitation at the bride's home. While polygyny is still allowed under customary law, it is rare. Some men, especially Mbukushu, Yeyi, and Herero, still practice it, but for most it is now too costly or brings too little benefit for most men to consider it. Child betrothal is also no longer practiced, and young people generally choose whon they would like to marry, although "polite children" also respect that negotiations between the families must still take place following traditional and customary formats. Some Herero, however, continue to practice child bethrothal. Marriages of couples coming from different or unrelated *merafe,* particularly between Tswana and Kalanga, are also more common than in the past.

Betrothal

In the past, parents often made decisions about marriage with little consultation with the young couple to be married. In some cases, the couple may never have seen one another until after their betrothal was announced. Marriage was seen as a relationship between families rather than individuals, and betrothals of young or even unborn daughters (known as *"go opa mpa,"* "to strike the womb") were not uncommon, especially between close relatives.

Indeed, the relationship created between the families by a betrothal could be so strong that if the girl died before marriage, her family was expected to replace her with a younger sister under a custom known as *seyantlo*.

Today, betrothal and marriage continue to create strong bonds between families, and many of the same customs of respect and gift giving apply, even though the couples now choose whom they would like to marry. If a young man wishes to marry, the first step is for him to speak to his maternal uncle about his intentions. The maternal uncle will then bring the matter up with the boy's parents, and, if the family agrees, the prospective groom, his father, and a delegation of his uncles will formally visit the woman's family to begin negotiations for her hand in marriage.[20] During this visit, the man's family is expected to display good manners and be extremely humble, attributes that are often put to the test in a number of ways.

To begin with, only married men and women can participate in marriage talks. The men should dress in suit jackets and ties (and the women in dresses) to show their respect to the bride's family during the talks. On the day of the negotiations *(patlo)*, the groom's family must wake up before dawn and go to wait near the bride's place. The most propitious time for a *patlo* is in winter after the harvest. According to custom, the groom's delegation, composed of both men and women, must wait by the nearest stream to the bride's home; they should not cross the stream before getting permission from the bride's family. If the delegation arrives after sunrise or crosses the stream before getting permission, they will be regarded as disrespectful and may be required to give an extra cow when *bogadi* is given. In large villages or towns where there may be no rivers or streams convenient to the bride's homestead, the groom's delegation must wait at the last main road for consent to cross. To ensure that the rules are followed, a man from the bride's family known as the *mmaditsela* ("the one who controls the roads or paths") will be assigned to escort them across the barrier.

After waiting beside the stream or road, in some instances for most of the day to ensure that proper respect is given, the *mmaditsela* will grant the groom's family permission to enter the bride's homestead. At this stage, the women from both families gather in the front courtyard, while the men go to the bride's *kgotla*. It is important that the groom's maternal uncle, who according to custom should lead the delegation, be informed in advance of the particulars of the bride and her family: her name, her parents' names, and the location of their *kgotla*. If he is confused about these details, it shows a lack of seriousness and respect, and it will be assumed that the groom's delegation must have "made a mistake" and have come to the wrong place.

At the beginning of the negotiations, the groom's family is sometimes additionally humbled by being addressed as "hyenas" *(diphiri)* or scavengers who want to take girl away from her family.[21] The men will not be offered chairs (a sign of respect) until they explicitly state the purpose of their visit. The women gathered in the *lolwapa* sit on the ground on traditional leather mats known as *diphate* throughout the talks. The use of these mats and the seating of women on the ground rather than on chairs is done to respect customary practices with regard to the hierarchy of men and women in the family. Polite women sit on the ground; heads of families and other important men sit on chairs or stools. Only after the negotiations have been successfully completed will the bride's family become more lenient, providing food and perhaps beer—signals that the young man's request has been heard and that negotiations can go forward.

A week or two after the initial delegations have met, the groom's senior female relatives will meet with the bride's in a ceremony known as "washing the words of the men" *(go tlhatswa puo ya banna)*. After these discussions, the women are usually told to come back at a later date to hear the decision of the bride's family, which will generally be yes if the negotiations have been allowed to go this far. When the negotiations are completed, both families come together to officially confirm the betrothal. The groom's family will arrange for the slaughter of a cow if they can afford it or for gifts of clothing, blankets, and other apparel known as *perepetsha* or *maisiwa,* depending on the particular ethnic group involved. Once the *patlo* gifts have been accepted, the young man is free to visit his future wife's home as often as he likes; he will be treated there with great respect. In some groups, he will also be free to spend the night in a custom known as *go ralala.* The young woman, on the other hand, is not allowed to go to her fiancé's place until after they are married.

The Wedding Ceremony

Civil Law Marriages

Many marriage ceremonies today, particularly among the wage-earning and salaried class, combine both a Western component, which may include a church ceremony or an exchange of vows at the District Commissioner's (DC) or magistrate's office, with a traditional, community ceremony at the homes of both parents. The elaborateness of the ceremony generally depends on the social status and wealth of the families concerned. Three weeks before the marriage, the bride and groom are expected to fill out a public notice of their intent to marry at the DC's office. This is distributed to public notice boards in the places where the future bride and groom have lived. In some Spiritual Healing churches, the intention to marry is announced for several Sundays in advance to give the people the opportunity to raise objections.

In either case, if no one objects to the marriage, the couple may get married at the end of the three-week waiting period.[22]

The couple may choose to have the DC perform a civil marriage at his or her office, or they may choose to be married by a pastor at church. In either case, they will register the marriage at the DC's office before exchanging vows.[23] Couples married in church go through Christian counseling; the DC also counsels couples before marriage. In both cases, the wedding vows are Western style but translated into Tswana. Couples are expected to come with witnesses (normally the best man and woman or a cousin). In the past, only married women wore rings, but married men are now expected to wear them as well. Although Botswana is one of the largest producers of diamonds in the world, most people cannot afford diamond engagement or wedding rings, and most use gold bands. Another widely adopted Western custom is for the bride and groom to kiss at the conclusion of the marriage ceremony. In the past, such a public display of affection, especially in front of parents and elders, would have been unthinkable.

Regardless of whether vows have been exchanged in a church or at the DC's office, these rites are usually followed by traditional ceremonies at the homes of both the bride's and the groom's parents. If the families do not have money to pay for a complete traditional ceremony, which would generally include slaughtering of cattle and the provision of a feast, the couples may just sign their vows and postpone the traditional wedding ceremonies for later.

Customary or Traditional Marriages

When marriage celebrations are held in two tiers at the bride's and groom's homes, people generally start the first wedding celebration on a Saturday after signing the vows at the bride's place. The next week, a second celebration will be held at the groom's place. The whole marriage process, including negotiations, signing, and celebrations, is accompanied by singing and uluations by married women wearing traditional clothes *(mateitshe)*. Couples can be excused from a complete traditional ceremony only if one of them has to leave immediately for work or studies overseas. But they will not be considered fully married until they have had a traditional ceremony and the groom has paid *bogadi*. Procrastination cannot last too long, as a couple's children cannot receive *bogadi* until their father has paid his own.

The traditional wedding ceremony follows many of the same formal steps as betrothal, with the groom's family sending messengers to the bride's family to request permission to discuss the ceremony. A formal meeting follows in which the groom's spokesmen "request a gourd of water [to drink]" *(go kopa sego sa metsi)*. These discussions are later followed later by those of the women, who must "wash the words of the men." After agreement is reached, plans begin for the wedding celebrations. Among the Ngwaketse, the groom would at this time drive the *bogadi* cattle to his wife's village, where her family would slaughter one or more animals, depending on the size of the *bogadi*. In some cases, the bride's maternal uncle is also expected to slaughter an ox "to feed the *bogadi*" so that the herd will prosper and grow along with the marriage. The parents of the bride and groom are expected to inform the *Kgosi* of the marriage of their son and daughter. Thereafter, the couple will be considered married by the community, and today, the marriage will be recorded in ledgers kept in the *kgotla* offices.

The bride's family, following the marriage customs of the group involved, usually determines the number of *bogadi* cattle to be given. It should be emphasized that *bogadi* is seen not as a form of commodity payment to the bride's family but rather as a token of appreciation to them for giving the groom's family a wife. The number of cattle thought to be "respectable" varies from group to group and by social status, but eight cows is the standardized number of cattle expected among the Ngwaketse. The number is likely to be higher, however, if the bride has a college degree or is from a royal family. If the man's family is poor, *bogadi* may be lowered at the discretion of the bride's family. As a rule of the thumb, *bogadi* should not be given in odd numbers,

An elite wedding celebration and banquet held at the home of the bride. Drinks and food abound. Afterward, the guests will dance to CDs containing a mix of music especially created for use at wedding gatherings. Courtesy of Jennifer Denbow.

or it will be said that the "cattle are limping" *(dikgomo tsa bogadi di a tlhotsa),* an omen that could cause the marriage to be "unstable" or unhappy, just as an odd number of feet would cause an animal to stumble. However, if the mother of children passes away before marriage is completed by the passage of *bogadi,* the father may "marry the children" *(go nyala bana)* by paying an "odd-numbered" *bogadi* so that the children will be officially associated with his lineage. In this way, he gains legal right to the children. Otherwise, legal rights to the children will remain with the mother's family.

While cash may be used, it is still considered more prestigious to give cattle as *bogadi.* When there is great a distance separating the bride's and groom's villages, cattle may sometimes be bought near the bride's place rather than having them transported from the groom's homestead. Even so, it is not uncommon to see *bogadi* cattle being trucked along the national road from one end of the country to the other. The gift of cattle is so important that even urban families not familiar with herding still accept them as *bogadi,* only to sell them immediately after the ceremony. Even in these cases, a cash equivalent to the number of cattle agreed on as *bogadi* is used only when the groom's family has no cattle at all. Some ethnic groups, particularly those with matrilineal systems of descent such as the Mbukushu, Yeye, and Sarwa, who live in the north of Botswana, usually do not require payment of *bogadi,* although in the past Mbukushu women married with a dowry.

After paying *bogadi,* the Western custom of having a bride's shower is held to collect funds to support the new family. In a more African innovation, however, "stake parties" held for men are now becoming common among the salaried class in living in towns and cities. These fund-raising events are usually conducted a week before the exchange of marriage vows. Women are given household items, while men receive garden and farming equipment. Despite their intention to provide needed household goods, stake parties have a reputation of devolving into drinking fests. Baby showers are another celebration adopted from Western culture.

WEDDING CELEBRATIONS

A wedding feast and celebration at the bride's home is usually followed a few days later with similar festivities in the groom's village.[24] The celebrations carry on for the whole day as the two families, more distant relatives, and friends and neighbors gather together and get to know one another. At wedding ceremonies, traditional beer and treats such as *seswaa* are commonly served. Music and dance CDs are played. These CDs are made specifically for weddings and widely sold by street vendors and in local markets; they contain selections of traditional weddings songs along with modern African pop music. The ceremony begins with a procession of the bride, groom, best man, bridesmaids, and a flower girl to the family compound of the bride. The bride usually wears a white dress, while the groom wears a black suit.[25] After the ceremony, the bride changes into the traditional *mateitshe* "uniform" of German cloth *(Geremani; shiba)*, a small shawl-like blanket called a *mogagolwane*, and head scarf *(tukwi)*. While many families still insist on separate wedding ceremonies at their respective homes, it is becoming increasingly common for wealthier families to have a single joint celebration at a "neutral" location such as a lodge, with both families sharing the wedding costs. This has the convenience of not having to slaughter a beast in the backyard, but some people criticize it as too "Western," particularly because wedding invitations are restricted to a small group of invited people rather than being open to the entire village.

A bridesmaid standing in front of an elite private residence in Gaborone. The bridesmaid's dress is locally designed. The modern, brick home with a tile roof in the background is typical of newer middle class urban housing. The burglar bars covering the windows are also typical. Courtesy of Jennifer Denbow.

At the end of the traditional marriage celebrations (usually on the Sunday after the marriage), a smaller ceremony is held at the groom's residence to welcome the bride into her new family. The occasion is usually accompanied by mixed feelings. On the one hand, the groom's family is happy to receive the bride. On the other, the bride's family is sad to leave their child. To move to her new home, the bride must bring her new blankets, old clothes, and other personal items that were given to her. (The *bogadi* cattle, however, remain with her father and other relatives.) In the past, clay pots for cooking the family meals were also brought from the bride's to the groom's home. As was the case during the betrothal negotiations, the bride's family is expected to stop at the nearest stream or main road to the groom's place and await permission to begin their procession. The bride and her female relatives carry her belongings on their heads, while her maternal uncle and his wife head the delegation.[26] As they walk, they sing songs instructing the bride about her demeanor and duties in her new home:

O itshoke, o itshoke ngwana wa batho.
Re tsere dikgomo, re tsere di tsa batho.
Be patient, be patient everyone's [the new family's] child
We have taken the cows [bogadi], we have taken their cattle

The song requests the bride to be obedient and patient in her new home, as she is now a married woman living with a new family. In return, her family has received cattle as a token of appreciation. To westerners, this may sound as though the *bogadi* is a payment and women therefore have to submit to their marriage because the have been "bought," but in reality the situation is complex. In Tswana culture, a person is priceless and so cannot be bought.

In addition to welcoming the bride to her new home, one of the traditional customs that occurs at this time is for the bride and groom to be given "advice" (*go laa,* from *go laalana,* "to instruct") about their obligations and responsibilities to one another by the married members of their family. The new bride is instructed in the courtyard of her husband's residence, while the groom meets with the men at the *kgotla.* At the end of the wedding, depending on finances, the bride and groom may go on a Western-style "honeymoon." Otherwise, they go to the husband's family *kgotla,* where their new home will be located.

In the past, traditional marriages were recorded only in the minds and memories of the community. As a result, questions about whether a marriage had actually taken place and whether they had the consent of both sets of parents were sometimes open to endless discussion and reinterpretation, particularly if

The bride and her female relatives, dressed in traditional fashion, move in a procession from her home to that of her husband. After their arrival, the women will instruct her about her duties and behavior as a wife in a tradition known as *go laa*. Courtesy of Jennifer Denbow.

disputes over property or children were at issue. Because of the inherent male bias of traditional custom, women often experienced a difficult time obtaining an equable resolution if they had complaints.[27]

Traditional marriages sanctioned by the community and their families are still the most common everywhere. In addition, families that live in towns and district capitals usually include a church or civil wedding. As will be discussed later, lack of registration can lead to difficulties if the couple decides to separate or there are disputes over property. Witnesses are required for all traditional marriages performed at the *kgotla* regardless of ethnicity. In most cases, a signing ceremony will also be held in the bride's village.

Protecting Marriages

To protect the newly married couple from potential problems thought to be caused by jealousy or evil spirits within their community, rituals are usually conducted during the traditional wedding celebration. The form of these rituals varies depending on the family's religious orientation. Orthodox Christian families, for instance, may pray for the new family to be blessed with good health and prosperity. African independent churches such as the Zionist

The male relatives gather separately from the women at the front of the groom's residence to chat, get to know one another better, and to give advice to the new husband. Courtesy of Jennifer Denbow.

Christian Church may prefer to sprinkle holy water on the bride and groom to protect them against evil forces. Followers of African traditional religions may invite a traditional doctor *(ngaka ya setso)* to purify *(phekolo)*, the new family with his herbs and prayers to the ancestors.

Marriage and Totems

The use of totems is widespread in Botswana, and it is usually assumed that "groups who share a totem can be thought to have all come from the same source, regardless of the *merafhe* they now claim allegiance to."[28] Most totems are wild animals that were chosen in the distant past as symbols of a family group, or *merafhe*. People show respect to their distant ancestors through their totems by not killing, eating, or using their meat, skin, and other products.[29] Greeting someone by their totem is a sign of honor and respect in Botswana. Among the Tswana and other patrilineal groups, children take on the totem of their father. Children born outside wedlock, however, take their mother's totem unless *bogadi* is later paid during marriage. Matrilineal groups such as the Herero and Yeyi adopt their mother's totem rather than their father's. With changes in the inheritance of cattle and giving of bride wealth, however, many Herero and Mbukushu now pass their totems from father to children rather than from mother to children.

The Married Household

Especially in the past, the household was composed of a man and his wife or wives, their own or adopted children, and other relatives, perhaps including a husband's younger brothers or sisters and even unrelated dependents who lived with the family and acted as servants or retainers. Generally, members of the household live in a set of conjoined houses or dwellings known as a *lolwapa* (see chapter 4) that were arranged, along with the homes of patrilateral relatives, around a lineage animal corral (kraal; *lesaka*) and *kgotla*. In smaller villages, each married couple usually has its own house, which they share with their infant children. Older children sleep in a separate house or live with an older relative. Today it is common for younger children to be sent from rural areas to towns and villages where they live with their parent's brothers, sisters, or other relatives in order to gain access to schooling, hospitals, and other resources. Many of the large secondary schools also have facilities for boarding students who come from distant villages or more rural areas.

PARADIGMS OF GENDER AND MARRIAGE

Men and women enter into a new stage of their life when they marry and have children. After their first child is born, parents are commonly addressed by the name of their firstborn child rather than their given name with a prefix of *mmago* (mother of . . .) or *rrago* (father of . . .) and then the child's name. Along with their new status comes new codes of behavior, new obligations to parents and children, and for women even new modes of "traditional" dress they are expected to wear a blanket *(mogagolwane)* over their shoulders and "Geremani" cloth dresses for respectful occasions, such as weddings and funerals.

But women, especially the more educated or those belonging to the salaried class, also experience conflicts with traditional expectations and the relative status of men and women in traditional society. Many women no longer work in agricultural pursuits but have jobs in villages and towns in more skilled capacities as secretaries, clerks, and so forth as they take advantage of new job and wage opportunities in the modern economy. In her short story "Snapshots of a Wedding," Serowe-based author Bessie Head poignantly illustrated the contradictions of an educated woman as she awaits instruction from her relatives in the *go laa* ceremony. Her maternal aunts have gathered around her at sunset to instruct her in her behavior in her new home and to remind her not to neglect her duties as a "good wife" as she sits obediently, head down, on a skin mat:

> Daughter, you must carry water for your husband. Beware, that at all times, he
> is the owner of the house and must be obeyed. Do not mind if he stops now

and then and talks to other ladies. Let him feel free to come and go as he likes. . . . Be a good wife! Be a good wife![30,31]

Even today, Batswana men consider themselves the head of the household in very patriarchal ways, and it is generally still the case that they remain uncomfortable if their wives have more education, earn more money, or hold more prominent positions in the workforce than they do. Women who become exceptional in some way, on the other hand, are generally suspected to have done so through the manipulation of supernatural powers by witchcraft. As indicated by Bessie Head, within the home the negotiation of rights and the settlement of disputes continues to pay homage to an idealized paradigm of what it takes to be a "good" spouse, namely,

A woman always attends to her man regardless of when he returns home and where he has been. She is always prepared to cook for him, to wash his clothes, and to work hard to develop their household. She only complains about his affairs with other women if he neglects her or the children. She does not have affairs herself, or gossip about her husband, or bring his name into disrepute. Nor does she criticize him to his children or set them against him. Where real problems arise in their relationship, she acts by reporting them to both families and enlisting their assistance as mediators. Where this is unsuccessful, the help of the local headman is enlisted. For his part, a 'good' husband may have affairs but he does not ill treat, neglect, or fail to support his family. He does not leave his wife, or live apart from her without cause, and he does not use her household property to support another woman. It is also his duty to report any marital difficulties [to their respective families] where they arise.[32]

It is often difficult for modern women to completely live up to traditional expectations that they "carry water" for their husbands, and as one young, unmarried professor remarked after completing her Ph.D. at Cambridge, "Well, I guess I have just educated myself right out of the marriage market!"[33] Her point was that there were now very few Batswana men in a position to marry her because they would think that they had to have even more education, status, salary, or power before they would feel comfortable in the relationship. Yet despite all the cultural meanings embedded in the phrase "to carry water" *(go sego sa metsi),* women do hold important jobs in Botswana—many are professors, department heads, business owners, and even government ministers. But if they are married, it is usually to a man with even greater seniority or position, thus keeping the relative relations of power within the family intact. While younger couples are often at odds with such paradigmatic expectations of the "good" spouse, they must still conduct their lives "in the shadow of marriage," measuring their behavior in terms of either its conformity to customary models of gender and status or its deviation from them.[34]

The dominance of patriarchal relations was also seen in the fact that children born to non-Batswana husbands were not given automatic Botswana citizenship through their mother. This was challenged in the courts, and the constitution was changed to allow children to take their mother's identity.[35] In addition, married women could not take out bank loans without their husband's signature. This was also challenged in court with the result that women now have the same legal status as men in this regard.

DEATH AND FAMILY CONTINUITY

After marriage, if *bogadi* was given, the death of a husband will not necessarily end the marriage, and under the levirate, a custom known as *"go tsena mo tlung"* ["to come into the house"], a widow could, if she wished, choose from among her husband's close relatives a man to care for her in her husband's stead.[36] In other groups, the elders choose the man for her. Children born from this relationship, known as *"bana ba dikgomo,"* or "children of the [bride-wealth] cattle," were considered the legal children of the deceased husband and equal under the law in all respects to his biological children.[37] Similarly, as noted, if a man's wife died, the *bogadi* cattle entitled him to claim from her parents another woman *(seyantlo)* to take her place, usually a younger sister, after a period of ritual mourning and purification that could last up to a year. His wife's family could refuse his request if they thought that he had not treated his first wife properly. Arranged marriages and the customs of *seyantlo* and *go tsena mo tlung* are now rarely encountered, but they illustrate the close relationship that was established between families by traditional marriage customs. The point of these practices was to fulfill the most sacred purposes of marriage: continuity of the family, lineage, and community. Children bring honor and continuity to the family and lineage. It is they who will support their parents in old age, and it is they who will venerate the totems and ancestors of their family and *kgotla* with the passing of their parents.

CONCUBINAGE

Adulterous actions on the part of men are still often dismissed with phrases such as "a man is like an axe, he has to be borrowed from time to time" *(Monna, selepe o a adimanwa).* Such notions are even ingrained in the marriage ceremony, as new brides, during the *go laa* ceremony, are told never to ask a man "where he is coming from [where he slept]" *(monna ga a nke a bodiwa gore o tswa kae).* These and many other proverbs reinforced the idea that a man, as head of the family, should never be questioned as long as he does not use family resources to support his affairs.[38,39] Indeed, affairs between married men and unmarried concubines, termed "*nyatsi*," are almost institutionalized.[40] Any children born of such unions belong to the mother's lineage and would take her totem. In such a relationship,

> a man who is already married takes some other woman as a concubine *(nyatsi)*. The concubine may be a divorcee, or a widow who would formerly have been taken over by one of her husband's male relatives; but most often she is a *lefetwa,* i.e. a woman who has never been married and is held to have passed the suitable age for marriage. The man visits her openly and regularly at her own home, and her people acquiesce in the relationship, so long as he feeds and clothes her and the children he has by her, ploughs for her, and helps her in various other ways ... so long as they are not formally betrothed and especially as long as *bogadi* has not been paid, neither party is under any legally enforceable obligation towards the other.[41]

While these relationships were sometimes openly known, in many cases they were kept secret—a situation that was complicated by the fact that a wife could not question her husband directly about his affairs but had to go through the elders to complain about his cheating on her. If a man flaunted his relationship with a *nyatsi* openly, it could bring disgrace to his family name. One of the unfortunate outcomes of the secrecy is that many children born of such relationships grow up not knowing who their father's are, and many do not have the courage to ask when they are grown. While discrete extramarital affairs may not raise many eyebrows for a married man, the same is not true for the "yellow locusts," or unmarried men, who, in the past at least, would be "punished if discovered with the girls."[42] Such relationships are usually transitory and short term. But if a child is born, action will almost always be taken by the woman's family. Her power to win compensation, however, is greatly diminished if she has additional children outside wedlock. Because of the dangers of AIDS, *nyatsi* relationships are now more freely criticized than they were in the past.

DIVORCE

While there is a tendency to try to sustain marriage in Botswana, some marriages will eventually end in divorce. Divorces are routed through the same set of steps as marriage. First, the couple should consult their families, who will listen to their difficulties and try to advise them. The complainant's family first contacts the accused family about the possibility of divorce, following the same procedures they used during marriage talks/negotiations.

They take the same physical path that they used during the betrothal negotiations and wedding, and it is expected that the same spirit of cooperation
that was exercised during marriage talks will characterize the discussions
about divorce. Maternal uncles must still lead the delegation, but according
to some traditions, as they travel to the bride's home, they must drag a bush
behind their donkey cart or car as a sign that they have come to discuss a
marriage in trouble. The branch, usually from an acacia tree, is the sort that
would normally be used to close the entrance to a cattle corral. When they
reach the woman's compound, it is left at the gate, communicating their
intention to discuss a divorce. Just as the dead bush signifies a tree that has
failed to bear fruit and so should be destroyed, it also symbolizes a marriage
that has failed to be fruitful. In addition, it evokes an image of a cattle corral
that has been neglected and left open so that the cattle go astray. Dragging
the bush through the dust signals a desire to make "the woman's footprints
disappear from the man's homestead," erasing the memory of the failed
marriage.

Both men and women can initiate divorce, but in practical terms, given the
inherent bias toward men, the wife will generally find it difficult to prevail
except under circumstances such as obvious abuse or neglect by the husband.
If attempts at reconciliation fail, couples that were married in church will
have to pass their divorce through the church before the courts will finalize
the case. Similarly, those married in the DC's office will have to consult with
him or her before official permission to divorce will be granted. In the case of
a traditional marriage, if agreements cannot be made on the family level, the
couple will be expected to meet at the *kgotla* and present their case to the
elders assembled there. Women experience difficulties in such situations
because court and *kgotla* findings are tilted in favor of the husband not because
his behavior is necessarily in the right but "on the grounds of preserving the
children's inheritance under the control of their father as head of the household and representative of the male line with which they are affiliated."[43]
Although women may now present their cases directly to the *kgotla,* they
continue to experience gender discrimination because it is "based on a system
of male authority; while women today... may present their own disputes in
the *kgotla,* they are still operating within a predominantly male ethos and
domain. For this reason, the support of male relatives is often crucial to their
standing."[44] Women are commonly blamed for infertility and laziness—all
acceptable reasons for men to divorce. They could also be blamed for adul-
tery, an action that continues to be viewed more leniently for men. In almost
all cases, *kgotla* decisions almost always try to effect reconciliation rather than
place blame by requesting that the couple go back home and "try hard to
work things out." This search for compromise rather than a desire to affix

blame is a significant aspect of Tswana character that informs most negotiations, not just those associated with marriage, in Tswana society.

If a wife becomes pregnant in an adulterous relationship, her husband is still expected to shoulder some responsibility. Proverbs such as "you are the only man in this yard so you must be responsible for the pregnancy; do not complain because people will laugh at you" uphold male dominance in family relations.[45] During the colonial period, up to 40% of the men from some of the districts in southeastern Botswana were engaged as migrant laborers in the mines of South Africa.[46] They were often held to this tradition when they returned home to find that extra children had appeared during their absence whom they were expected to support.

Relations between married and unmarried people are treated more harshly than those between married couples, and fines comparable to those given as *bogadi* were sometimes leveled as compensation if such relations could be proven without a doubt. Even today, it is not uncommon to hear of single people who are engaging in relationships with married couples being warned that they should stay away to avoid a large fine. Rightly or wrongly, such relationships are often used by the public to place blame for the high incidence and spread of HIV/AIDS in the country.

In conclusion, gender and marriage relations in Botswana are dynamic and have undergone many transformations as people adapt to a changing world. Women, for instance, are now entering in the nontraditional workforce in larger numbers in areas such as laborers on road construction crews. One need only look at the dress of these modern women to see how engendered symbols are reworked to meet new circumstances: head scarves *(tukwi)* peek out from beneath hard hats, and knee-length dresses billow over the "male attire" of blue coveralls and high rubber boots. The fact that women work on construction crews at all marks a significant departure from the Western gender roles that missionaries and colonial administrators tried to impose. In addition, recent changes to the legal status of women now recognize their right to equal financial opportunities with men and to the constitutional right for their children to be recognized as Botswana citizens.

NOTES

1. Written in 1806. Hinrich Lichtenstein and O. H. Spohr, *Foundation of the Cape [and] About the Bechuanas* (Cape Town: A. A. Balkema, 1973), p. 76.

2. Anne Griffiths, *In the Shadow of Marriage: Gender and Justice in an African Community* (Chicago: University of Chicago Press, 1997), p. 25. Copyright 1997 by the University of Chicago Press. Reprinted by permission of the University of Chicago Press.

3. Isaac Schapera, *A Handbook of Tswana Law and Custom* (London, F. Cass, 1970), p. 231. Among the Ngwato, the custom of excluding the daughter's and widow's inheritance of cattle was changed at the beginning of the twentieth century by Khama III.

4. G. Gibson, "Double Descent and Its Correlates among the Herero of Ngamiland," *American Anthropologist* 58 (1956): 109–39.

5. Frank Vivelo, *The Herero of Western Botswana: Aspects of Change in a Group of Bantu-Speaking Cattle Herders* (St. Paul, Minn.: West, 1977), p. 183.

6. Lichtenstein and Spohr, *Foundation of the Cape [and] About the Bechuanas,* p. 77.

7. Schapera, *A Handbook of Tswana Law and Custom.* For a more up-to-date account of the same pattern of close kin marriage among the Kwena, see Griffiths, *In the Shadow of Marriage.* Copyright 1997 by the University of Chicago Press. Reprinted by permission of the University of Chicago Press. Even poor families may choose to marry close kin, however, since the cattle would still circulate within the family.

8. Schapera, *A Handbook of Tswana Law and Custom,* p. 128.

9. Among the Ngwaketse, a sheep (called *nku ya mokwele*) is slaughtered.

10. Griffiths, *In the Shadow of Marriage,* p. 115. Copyright 1997 by the University of Chicago Press. Reprinted by permission of the University of Chicago Press.

11. Schapera, *A Handbook of Tswana Law and Custom.*

12. J. Comaroff and J. L. Comaroff, *Of Revelation and Revolution,* vol. 1 (Chicago: University of Chicago Press, 1991), pp. 131–32. Reprinted with permission from the University of Chicago Press and the authors, John and Jean Comaroff.

13. Schapera, *A Handbook of Tswana Law and Custom,* p. xv.

14. Rachel Swarns, "Free AIDS Care Brings Hope to Botswana," *New York Times,* May 8, 1997.

15. Griffiths, *In the Shadow of Marriage,* p. 220. Copyright 1997 by the University of Chicago Press. Reprinted by permission of the University of Chicago Press.

16. Another term used is *lekgwatlhe,* which has the same (but less poetic) meaning.

17. Griffiths, *In the Shadow of Marriage,* p. 45. Copyright 1997 by the University of Chicago Press. Reprinted by permission of the University of Chicago Press.

18. Ibid. Copyright 1997 by the University of Chicago Press. Reprinted by permission of the University of Chicago Press.

19. Ibid. Copyright 1997 by the University of Chicago Press. Reprinted by permission of the University of Chicago Press.

20. A friendly and cooperative "joking relationship" of great freedom between matrilateral cousins known as *"go tlhagana"* is common. In contrast, a competitive relationship usually pertains between patrilateral relatives.

21. The term *diphiri,* or hyenas, is also used for gravediggers.

22. The British, throughout their African colonies, introduced the custom of posting the marriage banns. The appointment to meet with the DC to fill out the forms was sometimes used to lecture the prospective couple on the rights, responsibilities, and duties of marriage.

23. Most educated people living in larger villages and urban areas now realize the importance of a formal marriage certificate from the DC's office.

24. In the past, the ceremony at the groom's home took place the next day. But today, with marriages between families that often live very far apart, more time is needed to move from one location to another.

25. In an adaptation of Western custom, if the bride has been married before or if she has had a number of children with someone other than her husband, she will not wear a white dress, as she is not considered "pure."

26. If the marriage takes place at the DC's office, the father of the bride will lead the procession.

27. Griffiths, *In the Shadow of Marriage.* Copyright 1997 by the University of Chicago Press. Reprinted by permission of the University of Chicago Press.

28. Schapera, *A Handbook of Tswana Law and Custom,* p. 3. The present spelling of *merafe* is *"merafhe,"* meaning "tribes" or "ethnic groups."

29. Often a new totem was chosen when a segment of a tribe broke away to form a new group. Today a variety of totems are found in even the smallest village and even among people belonging to the same ethnic group, or *merafhe.* Some common totems associated with ruling Tswana households include *phuti*/duiker (Ngwato), *nare*/buffalo (Birwa), *kgabo*/monkey (Kgatla), *kwena*/crocodile (Kwena), *tlou*/elephant (Ngwaketse), and *tholo*/kudu and *tshipi*/iron for the Rolong (one of the exceptions to the animal theme). There are more than 20 other less common animal totems used by smaller groups, including *mutwa*/hare (Tswapong) and *sehudi*/duck (some Tsua-khoe or eastern Sarwa).

30. The same metaphor—to carry water *(go sega sa metsi)*—is used during the betrothal *(patlo)* and *go laa* ceremonies to evoke obedience and humbleness.

31. Advice offered to the bride, Neo, by her maternal aunts in "Snapshots of a Wedding," by Bessie Head, *The Collector of Treasures, and Other Botswana Village Tales* (London: Heinemann Educational, 1977), pp. 79–80.

32. Griffiths, *In the Shadow of Marriage,* p. 135. Copyright 1997 by the University of Chicago Press. Reprinted by permission of the University of Chicago Press.

33. Private conversation between J. Denbow and an educated *Motswana* woman, Gaborone, December 1995.

34. The sense of this phrase is taken from Griffith, *In the Shadow of Marriage.* Copyright 1997 by the University of Chicago Press. Reprinted by permission of the University of Chicago Press.

35. The plaintiff in the case was Unity Dow, Botswana's first and only female High Court justice.

36. "Levirate" is an anthropological term adopted from the biblical story of Levi.

37. They were also known as *"bana ba ditlhomeso,"* or the "children of the rafters." Schapera, *A Handbook of Tswana Law and Custom,* p. 165.

38. A similar but more oblique saying with the same meaning is "a dog urinates by lifting both his right and left legs."

39. In one case in Molepolole, the *kgotla* concluded that "in terms of Tswana custom it is wrong when a man has a *nyatsi* to move-out from his family and stay at the *nyatsi's* place and forget his wife and children altogether." Griffiths, *In the Shadow of Marriage,* pp. 171–72. Copyright 1997 by the University of Chicago Press. Reprinted by permission of the University of Chicago Press.

40. Some have translated the term "*nyatsi*" as being derived from the meaning "little houses," but the derivation comes from "*motho yo o nyatsegang*," meaning a secret lover who has no legal status. The opposite of *nyatsi* is *mogatsaka pelo yame*, literally, "the one who burns my heart."

41. Schapera, *A Handbook of Tswana Law and Custom*, p. 126.

42. Ibid.

43. Griffiths, *In the Shadow of Marriage*, p. 174. Copyright 1997 by the University of Chicago Press. Reprinted by permission of the University of Chicago Press.

44. Ibid., p. 160. Copyright 1997 by the University of Chicago Press. Reprinted by permission of the University of Chicago Press.

45. This Tswana saying, "You are the person of the house . . ." *(ke wena monna wa motse o, otla a re tshegisa batho)* is one that can be used by both sexes when referring to who has responsibility for bringing disgrace on the household.

46. In part, they did this to support their parents, purchase livestock and other goods for use at home, and, not insignificantly, to pay poll or hut taxes to the colonial government. See Isaac Schapera, *Migrant Labour and Tribal Life: A Study of Conditions in the Bechuanaland Protectorate* (London: Oxford University Press, 1947), p. 195.

7

Social Customs and Lifestyle

From beyond its borders, Botswana appears unrelievedly dull. . . . A place of large plains and largely plainspoken people, a place not known for extravagant couture, for elaborate, tourist-magnetic rituals, or for hip cultural products. Botswana does not draw much attention to itself. . . . Although Botswana has managed to sustain one of the more durable democracies on the continent, it has always lived in the shadows of its more newsworthy, noisy neighbors. Happily so. And yet, beneath its surfaces, hiding in the light of everyday life, lies a world of enduring fascination, a world of quiet cultural depth . . . in which indomitable people fashion coherent, meaningful lives, shoring up their meager material resources by seeking to create social wealth.[1]

As an ethnic minority, Kalanga, like Tswana as an ethnic majority, are what some Africanists would call a "super-tribe." . . . I call it mirrored super-tribalism, because each super-tribe reflects the other in relation to whom it imagines itself to be. . . . What is important for mirrored super-tribalism is much tolerated diversity and incorporation of strangers, because that, rather than intolerant exclusiveness, is often foregrounded by the people themselves. "Scrambled eggs" is President Mogae's sound bite for that concept.[2]

When writing about the customs and lifestyle of a country as diverse as Botswana, it is appropriate to begin with the malleable nature of its cultural politics and the ability of its peoples to activate multiple and sometimes even contradictory identities, depending on context. A contrast is sometimes drawn between kin-based or tribal societies whose social boundaries are open and accepting of diversity and in-migration and those where societal boundaries are more rigid and defended, resulting in so-called hard ethnicities.[3] Textbook and news accounts of African "tribalism" often embrace, if not reify, a timeless view of static and "rigid" ethnic differences as the source of most conflict on the continent, but in Botswana ethnic identities and politics are usually more tempered and fluid as people daily negotiate the social spaces open to them. Even for its minorities, urban Botswana is often a "society of choices, in which ... being Herero [or any other ethnic identity] ... becomes something of an optative performance, a membership enacted much as other church, school, job, and associational memberships, a simple uniform over the universal citizen's body—and not a form of resistance to Setswana hegemony."[4]

When rights to scarce resources such as land, water, educational facilities, health care, or political representation are contested, however, social boundaries may be "hardened" through choice of language, dress, and other means of signaling distinctiveness through ethnicity. Political mobilization along ethnic lines can be an effective way to get the attention of the state. But in Botswana such strategies of difference are almost always tempered by an awareness of the benefits to be derived from allegiance to what is widely regarded as one of the most democratic and economically successful governments in Africa. The Kalanga, among the most vocal critics of Tswana dominance, have often mobilized themselves along ethnic lines as they negotiate for increased political power and economic participation in the country's affairs. Yet at the same time, as a group they are also at pains to make it clear that their first loyalty is to a unified Botswana state, not to a transnational identity that would amalgamate them with the inhabitants of Zimbabwe— a country that, in Botswana eyes, "is poor, conflict-ridden, criminal, violent, non-Tswana, [and] in short subject to negative stereotypes."[5] In similar fashion, Herero women, when they wear their colorful and distinctive dresses, can appear as a quintessential symbol of ethnic difference. Yet at the same time, "in spite of the clearly Tswana hegemonic discourses within the nation, Mahalapye Herero often embrace the official line of ethnic nondiscrimination (perhaps in contrast to Herero in northwestern Botswana)."[6]

Like the Herero, the Yeyi and Sarwa have also used ethnicity as a principle around which to organize themselves as they attempt to compel the government to be more sensitive to and representative of their interests and rights with regard to political representation, access to traditional land, and hunting rights. These actions attest to less homogenized networks of relationships between Botswana's varied ethnic groups than a "scrambled eggs" analogy. Depending on circumstances, cultural differences can be either accentuated or downplayed, depending on need. Perhaps a more apt comparison—and one commonly used to describe the politics of multiethnic diversity in the United States—is a "salad bowl" in which the ingredients retain their distinctiveness even as they are incorporated into the same salad.

But even this is an oversimplification because tomatoes cannot marry radishes to produce a salad with new ingredients. Such "mixing" has in fact taken place many times over the course of the nation's past as people have interacted, married, or otherwise assimilated themselves into cultures whose regional dominance has varied over time. The result is that almost everyone in Botswana is multilingual, and no village can truly be said to be homogeneous with respect to ethnicity. At the same time, over the past century and a half, changes in language and customs such as bride wealth, inheritance, and even religious belief have resulted in increasing "Tswanaization" as well as incorporation of Western influences. The Tswana language, for instance, is now spoken almost everywhere in the country, although sometimes, if people wish to voice their dissatisfaction with the Tswana-dominated government, they may insist on speaking in English or their native language as a form of resistance to this dominance.

Stereotyping of cultures along a scale of ethnic or racial superiority also continues to plague relations between ethnic groups despite a national credo of "unity in diversity" and the often-used phrase "we are all Batswana here." Besides characterizing their lifestyle as "primitive hunters and gatherers," people of Sarwa or Khoisan heritage are stereotyped by their skin color, and there is often an undercurrent of prejudice against anyone with a skin color that is "too light" because it is assumed that they have a "mixed" ancestry with Khoisan peoples. Conversely, the Kalanga, Mbukushu, and Yeyi are often characterized as "too dark," also with implications of racial inferiority, although this time doubtlessly influenced in part by Western or apartheid-derived prejudices. Such fault lines in the terrain of national unity are amplified by the government's resistance to the use of non-Tswana languages, such as Kalanga, Yeyi, or Herero, in early education or on radio and television. Although such attitudes are gradually moderating among more urban and educated people, they are still common enough to remark on despite the tolerance otherwise shown by Tswana for peoples of other ethnicities. Even in the West, racial and ethnic prejudices are hard to eradicate, and in Botswana they pose similar challenges to the creation of conditions for greater social equality.

CATTLE AS A METAPHOR FOR PROSPERITY AND WELL-BEING

Despite the differences in culture found in the country, most of Botswana's ethnic groups would subscribe to the view that a man's wealth was traditionally measured by the number of cattle he possessed. Even today, with many more investment opportunities available, it is still true that one's wealth is often thought to be "incomplete" or less prestigious if it does not include cattle.

They are a cultural good, not simply a commodity. Without them, a man could not plow his fields, pay *bogadi* at marriage, or feed his guests to honor his ancestors during funerals. In addition to their meat, cattle provided milk for drinking, skins for sleeping mats, dung for building houses, fertilizer for fields, and even fuel for cooking fires when wood was scarce. Long strips cut from their hides were dried and stretched from tree branches to make ropes for guiding the draft oxen and donkey carts and leather thongs that were laced over the frames of *kgotla* chairs to make softer seating for old men. In the past, their hides were also fashioned into the shields used by warriors in battle, giving another meaning to the common praise-poem name for cattle—"stout-one of weapons." Finally, in the contemporary world, cattle can be sold to buy land or pay fines, school fees, and hut taxes.

But the ideological dominance of cattle in Tswana thought sometimes makes it difficult for Tswana to understand or appreciate other values and ways of living. Some of the Sarwa living in the Central Kalahari Game Reserve, for instance, have resisted resettlement outside the reserve—even in exchange for a "herd" of five cows, which the government believes would set them on a "proper" track to "progress and prosperity."[7] As much as anything, it is resistance to a cultural ideology that equates cattle ownership with well-being, which most Tswana see as "self-evident" progress from a "stone age existence," that confounds negotiations between the government and those Sarwa who wish to continue living as hunters, gatherers, and herders in the Central Kalahari Game Reserve.

Although Tswana culture and customs have come to dominate the ethnic ingredients of the national "salad," adaptations to differing cultural values and practices have not been entirely one-sided. The Tawana living on the margins of the Okavango Delta, for instance, have adopted Yeyi methods of fishing using traps, nets, and reed barrages. Many Tswana also consult Sarwa healers and use their herbs and medicines. In the Central District, cattle owners whose animals have strayed during the rainy season often prefer to visit Sarwa diviners who throw leather divining disks to help them locate their animals; the cattle owners believe that the Sarwa are better at this than other diviners. Nevertheless, the general trend that has developed is for non-Tswana ethnic groups to adopt cattle ownership as the most acceptable symbol of wealth, and almost all now give them as *bogadi* or bride wealth in marriage transactions. Few would thus dispute the Tswana idiom that a cow is a "god with a wet nose" *(modimo o o nko e metsi)* or the popular saying that "I have no cattle, I have no sleep; I have cattle, I still have no sleep" *(Ka e tlhoka ka tlhoka boroko, ka e bona le gone ka bo tlhoka).*[8]

SOCIAL CUSTOMS AND LIFESTYLE

The Old and the New: Villages and Cities

In the past, most Tswana lived a lifestyle of seasonal transhumance as they moved from the villages to the lands and cattle posts during the rainy season and then back to town again until the harvest season. Even people living in the cities of Gaborone and Francistown participated in this annual movement, especially during long holiday seasons, such as Christmas, when visits to the lands and cattle posts usually meant a plethora of milk, *madila* (sour milk), and evenings around the fire filled with choral singing and stories. Children, who by necessity had to stay in town to be close to schools, were especially attuned to the contrasting lifestyles of town and lands. As one child remembers it,

> Life at the lands, which I was part of on weekends and on school holidays, was so far removed from life at the village that it often seemed to me that the people changed as well. They walked and talked differently, I thought. The neatly thatched rondavals [round houses] with the gaily decorated walls of the village compounds were nowhere to be seen at the lands. Instead, the compounds [were] comprised of huts thatched with less regard to aesthetics. Further, the compound perimeter fence was thorn bushes while at the village there were sturdy decorated walls. The lands compounds seemed to melt into the bushy surroundings while the village ones seemed to be designed to stand out. . . . In April, the husbands would come back to the lands, bringing a few of the cows and other calves, and dispatch the boys to the cattlepost . . . the sweet reeds, watermelons, beans, and many other . . . foods would be ready and the days would be one long string of feasting. A goat might be killed if the rains were particularly good . . . [then] April became a month of much whistling by men and humming by women. We children played and helped and played and helped. At night we listened to stories by my mother and grandmother and then we collapsed with exhaustion.[9]

While the cyclical movement of families between the different lives of village and town is still familiar to most Batswana, as the population has become more urban, fewer and fewer children and young adults now participate in this annual migration. As a result, clear divisions are beginning to develop between Batswana who live in rural areas and those who live in cities regardless of ethnic origins. Conservative rural families, most of whom continue to subscribe to a more traditional way of life, for instance, are sometimes referred to by those living in cities as "people of the bush or wilderness" (*managa*). The *managa* are the butt of countless jokes about their naïveté and the cultural shocks they experience when they come to town and are confronted by its differences and affectations of modernity. Andrew Sesinyi's 1981 novel *Love on the Rocks* captures these difficulties well.[10]

Those who live in towns and follow a more Western lifestyle sometimes try to differentiate themselves from the *managa,* whom they see as unsophisticated country bumpkins, by calling themselves "cats." To them, the cat is an appropriate symbol because it "is a clean and smart animal. It walks nicely and carefully. It is tender, gentle, modern—as opposed to wild."[11] Young city "cats" generally try to speak English rather than Tswana as a mark of their sophistication and worldliness, often affecting as heavy a British or American accent as they can muster. While they take this is a sign of their being cosmopolitan, to others it seems an arrogant affectation, and instead of "cats," they call them "capitalists" or "people who like things" *(ba ba ratang dilo).*

Even within the towns and cities, there are conflicts between tradition and modernity. Children who attend English medium primary schools, for instance, are encouraged by their teachers to speak English at home as a way of improving their language skill. But this is sometimes unpopular with their parents, who expect them to use English at school and Tswana or other indigenous languages at home. It is thus fairly common to hear parents sardonically announce, "Welcome to Botswana," when their children arrive home after school. There is thus an inherent contradiction between the feeling of

Beginning in 1995, the Botswana government began to resettle people, such as those shown here, from the Central Kalahari Game Reserve. While life in the reserve may be seen by many as harsh, some Sarwa have protested the removal from their traditional homes and the changes in their way of life that result.

pride that parents feel in their children's accomplishments at school and the general sense they have that the status and respect for cultural traditions they expect at home are being threatened by "Western" education. As a result, conflicts between what children have learned at school, particularly high school and the university, and the sometimes more traditional expectations and beliefs of their parents at home are fairly common. Discussions about the causes and consequences of AIDS, for instance, often spiral into this type of confrontation.

Except in the most remote areas, most people today have a lifestyle that combines traditional and Western elements. It is fairly common, for instance, for middle-class villagers to live in houses made of cement blocks, with grass thatching or tin roofs, running water, and electricity; a satellite dish may even be attached to the house to pick up local or international television programs. In the front yard, goats graze around modern German or Japanese vehicles, while donkey carts, fashioned from wood or the beds of old pickup trucks, rest under shade trees in the backyard waiting for the next movement to the lands. Almost everywhere, manufactured goods have replaced homemade leather clothing, carved wooden bowls and spoons, handcrafted pottery. Even rituals such as rainmaking ceremonies have been affected. Yet many traditional values and practices remain, and some, including traditional music and dance, are enjoying a renaissance as performances are played on Botswana radio and television. Traditional diviners, healers, and herbalists are also being consulted in growing numbers by people seeking jobs, by young people trying to attract girlfriends or boyfriends, or to obtain relief from illness and other problems.

Greetings

Generally, Batswana are friendly and welcoming. A visitor can feel free to visit most places, although in towns and cities one must keep an eye out for pickpockets, thieves, and troublemakers, sometimes known as *ditsotsi*. Except for when one is on a crowded street, it is customary for people to greet one another when passing—to not do so is insulting because it implies that the other party is insignificant and beneath notice. Even strangers riding in public transport are expected to acknowledge one another and to strike up a conversation. Reading in public, instead of talking to people, is considered rude. Batswana appreciate being greeted in their language, and as almost everyone understands Tswana, it is polite to use it in greetings even if one knows nothing else of the language. The customary greetings begin with, "*dumela, rra/mma*" (due-MAY-la, *rra* [rolled "r"] or *mma* [long "m"]; hello, sir/madam). It is polite to add "*rra*" or "*mma*" (literally, "father" or "mother") after the greeting, although some visitors have difficulty rolling the "r" in Tswana (or Spanish) fashion.[12] Depending on the time of day, in the southern part of the country this is usually followed by "*Le kae?*" (LAY-kai), which translates as "How are you (all)?" The answer, of course, is "*Re teng*" (RAY-teng), "We are here." Greetings in the northern dialects involve variations on the theme "How did you awaken?"

Age, seniority, and status are important in social matters, so when addressing an older person, people from northern Botswana usually use the polite "third-person plural" form "*Le*" instead of the "second- or third-person singular" form "O" (Oh), which are differentiated from one another only by tone. Despite the importance of gender in most daily activities, the Tswana language does not have words for "he" or "she." As a result, it is not uncommon for Tswana speakers to confuse these words in English, resulting in sometimes surprising sentences, such as "He is wearing such a pretty dress today."

Different from common Western practice where greetings carry little content and have become almost pro forma, in Botswana questions of "How are you?" are expected to be answered factually. If one has a headache, one says so; if one has stubbed one's toe, one will mention it. But even for Batswana, the etiquette of greetings can quickly become complicated. For instance, although it is accepted for a person in the southern part of the country to ask an older person the state of his or her health when greeting, the Ngwato and Tawana consider this impertinent. For them, it is a matter of status and respect: an elderly person may greet and ask a younger person how he or she is, but it is impolite for the younger person to ask first or to answer back. These differences in custom can result in delicate situations when greeting strangers. One must first try to guess from the accent which part of the country they are from and then estimate their age relative to one's own before deciding whether it is polite to ask about their health. Children and subordinates may show additional respect by slightly bowing when greeting their superiors or elderly people.

Visitors are usually not censured for violating the rules of greeting, but there are some subtle traps nonetheless. Many Tswana now work in nontraditional settings in hotels, stores, and banks, where the status roles may be reversed or contradictory for the foreign tourist and the Tswana clerk. For both the clerk and the visitor, the customer has the higher status. But because of the complicating factors of age and status in Tswana greetings, the response from each side may appear inappropriate to the other. When Western visitors enter a bank for the first time, for instance, they may feel disconcerted if they are met with (polite) silence. So they respond in kind by making curt demands for service rather than taking the time to exchange greetings. The teller has quite different expectations. According the customers (particularly if older) higher status, the teller waits for the customers to extend the first greeting. When this does not happen, the teller assumes that the customers do not consider him or her important enough to be greeted and so responds brusquely in kind. The result is surly service and an interaction in which both parties feel slighted. The bad feelings left by such encounters can result in the cutting Tswana criticism, "*Makgowa oa rata dilo, fela*" (literally, "White people only like [material] things [as opposed to people]," indicating that one is acting in a pompous and arrogant manner).

The Kalanga show respect to an older or senior person by using a custom called *go buchila,* in which they go down on their knees, put their hands together, clap them three times, and then extend them to the visitor to greet. The senior person, in turn, kisses both hands. Another sign of respect is to take off one's hat when greeting seniors. Members of some churches, including the Zionist Christian Church, greet one another with terms such as *kgotsong,* or "peace be with you." They recognize one another by the silver star or dove they wear on their clothing. Teenage boys often greet more informally with *ita da* or *go jwang,* meaning "what's up?" "Homeboy," "homegirl," or "homie" are additional terms used to greet those from the same home village, town, or district.

Shaking hands is another aspect of customary greetings. As a sign of respect, this should always be done "with both hands" by holding the right forearm at the elbow with the left hand while shaking. This same mannerism is used in "polite" company when passing something from one person to another.[13] This mannerism is used even in urban settings as, for instance, when coins are passed to the bus conductor to pay the fare.

Age, Seniority, and Respect

With age comes privilege, and in Botswana it is further assumed that wisdom comes with age. Young people are taught to respect senior citizens and to accord them respect because they are considered to have contributed significantly to the development of society. Seniority not only guides relations between parents and children and between bosses and workers but also is a factor in every social gathering—even if it is just two people. Age differences are so important that within a week of beginning a new school year, all the students in a class will have determined the respective ages and ranks of all their classmates—"sorting out the line of command" is how it has been put.[14] Even if the difference in age is minimal, this can have important consequences because the "older" person is permitted to command those more junior to carry out tasks and errands that can include anything from fetching books and bringing drinks to washing dishes and other daily tasks. The younger person should never complain publicly, even though he or she may grumble in private. Sometimes elderly people use their seniority to bully their subordinates in the workplace, but this is gradually changing as more educated people come to hold senior positions. But regardless of their position at work, even the most senior civil servants may become subordinates when they return to their home villages where traditional rules of age and seniority trump status in the workplace. Status and age are delicately balanced, however. Even a chief, for instance, will always be junior among his mother's brothers while senior among his father's brothers regardless of their respective ages. And elderly people will always accord respect and seniority to a child of royal birth.

According status and respect to the elderly is not confined only to the Tswana; it is observed by all of Botswana's peoples. As the following vignette illustrates, age and status are not simply a function of chronological age; they also encompass more complex characteristics that are claimed and tested through daily behavior, as in this example from the Herero community in Mahalapye:

> One of the most telling forums for the management of age is the men's circle at weddings and funerals. Here older men sit around a fire on chairs provided by the host, on their own wooden folding chairs, and on overturned buckets and the like, and they talk, are served tea or food, and occasionally direct their juniors in some task. Younger men, those with tenuous claims to status, and those who want to signal respect to seniority will approach and greet the men in the circle deferentially, partly bent at the waist ... the junior men then sit on logs and overturned buckets outside the main circle. At around the age of 30 ... young men begin to sit in the inner circle in a manner that is not quite as deferential and subservient. A man may assert his claim to that space by not moving from a seat when another man comes into the circle. Or he may carry a walking stick and wear a felt hat, or even an overcoat [all symbols of age and status]. To do so is risky and takes confidence—any of these acts may ... invite good-natured ridicule or chiding, or be overturned when a senior commands the young man to fetch something or to respect his "parents." ... As men get into their forties, their claims to be seated in the inner circle around the fire become more secure, but never entirely so. Even much older men may take a junior role, showing deference or giving up an inner circle seat for one in the outer circle on the arrival of an elder man or the chief. Some men in their fifties and even older, herdboys or others who have failed to gain dependents and household independence, sustain very fragile claims to the men's circle.[15]

In the past, all the men and women in a Tswana community were organized into age sets (*mephato*) at initiation. This provided a clear demarcation of age, and those belonging to different regiments were often assigned communal tasks under the oversight of the *kgosi*. When there were important national projects or operations to be undertaken, the *kgosi* would call a specific *mophato* (singular) by name to undertake it. These projects included protecting villagers and their livestock from predators such as lions and leopards as well as the construction of roads, dams, and national granaries. Regiments completed many important projects in Botswana, including the construction of Moeng College near Palapye and the construction of a dam and a community hall in Kanye and Serowe. The last regiment was named in Mochudi in the late 1980s, when *bogwera* and *bojale* initiations were briefly resumed. With the abandonment of initiation, except in very attenuated form, regiments are now a thing of the past, and many of the duties once carried out by them are now done by informal associations sometimes based around high school classmates or other affiliations.

Recently, the government has recognized the importance of its senior citizens by giving everyone over the age of 65 a small pension—about $40 a month. This small pension is emblematic of the ways in which the Botswana government, whatever its other failings, consistently tries to direct its finances toward the improvement of ordinary citizens' lives rather than to the financing of high-profile public works and statues of more symbolic than practical value. While it is a small amount even by rural standards, it does meet many old people's tastes for Five Roses tea and sugar, luxuries in which most indulge themselves. The gesture is even more significant because the funds come directly from government revenues rather than private retirement accounts. Rural herders who never received a cash wage in their lives collect pensions— even though some have to travel a considerable distance from their homes to the nearest village to do so.

Character

While conversations are often very relaxed in the context of family and friends, from the British the Batswana have inherited a liking for formality and titles in the workplace. Many insist on wearing suits, ties, or formal dresses at work, and in villages and towns some clerks and receptionists are known to change their outfits at lunchtime so as to appear "fresh" for the afternoon.[16] At work, most prefer to be addressed by their titles as Mr., Mrs., Miss, Dr., and Professor. On business cards and letterhead stationery, the initials of associations or other organizations with which they are associated may also be listed after their names.[17]

Outward signs of status are also popular, and many urban people purchase expensive cars with government-subsidized loans as a sign of their success;

their homes, on the other hand, may remain very modest. An important aspect of the vehicle as status symbol, like the decorated *lolwapa* in front of a house, is that it should always be spotlessly clean. In both cases, however, the tin cans, plastic bags, and other rubbish that build up are simply tossed outside the yard or from the car into the "no-man's-land" between houses or into the roadside ditch. In rural areas, the household midden is often just outside the front entrance gate to the homestead, so this leaves an impression of immense untidiness until one enters the fenced *lolwapa* and house, which are generally impeccable. The roadsides for a mile or two before and after a village are also usually littered with soft-drink cans, plastic bottles, and other detritus of modernity without refuse collection.

Like people everywhere, Batswana can be vain, and if someone in a family has an important position or is of high status in society, this will generally "come up" in conversation. Yet at the same time, outward signs of self-aggrandizement are tempered by a crosscutting current in Batswana culture that places a high value on humbleness and dignity. People may boast and talk loudly, yet a person who speaks quietly in a subdued manner is typically afforded a subtle respect as exemplifying characteristics enshrined in the indigenous meanings of the term *"botho"* ("character").[18] One should never lose one's temper in public, and if someone appears likely to lose control, he or she will be reminded that "the heart is like a young goat, it needs to be tied up with a rope" *(Pelo potsane, e boswa ka kgole).*[19]

Another dimension of self-control is that jealousy, anger, and angry words and gestures are believed to disrupt the spiritual harmony of the community, leaving both the offender and the community at large open to danger through the withdrawal of ancestral support. If someone is unhappy about what another has done to them, for instance, it is believed that the social disruption that ensues will cause the ancestors to "withdraw their protection," exposing the arguing parties—and perhaps even the community itself—to danger. Even the land can become "ill" and unproductive if reconciliation is not effected by healing the social breach followed, in some cases, by ritual purification of the land.[20] Consequently, arguments and verbal assaults are taken quite seriously in Botswana, and if disputes are not quickly cleared up, the parties may turn to the *kgotla* or to *dingaka* not for the apportionment of blame but for compromise, resolution, and "healing."

For the Tswana, the concept of *botho* also combines elements of fatalism with self-determination. Each individual is considered to be unique yet at the same time subject to forces of "human nature" that are not entirely under his or her control. As one Kgalagadi elder summarized it,

A person's conduct can be shaped by good upbringing. But a person does not necessarily act the way he's been taught, because he is born with certain qualities that training does not change. "I weeded for the tiny thorn, and after it grew, it pricked me." Children can grow up to disappoint and hurt their parents who have tried to mold them properly. A person's conduct can be shaped by events which a person is powerless to change. "The well dries up even as I am looking at it."[21]

Some people have blamed bad behavior and a perceived loss of *botho* in modern society as resulting from the cancellation of traditional initiation ceremonies during the colonial era (*bogwera* and *bojale* for men and women, respectively) that taught young people to respect their elders and to understand the nature of their responsibilities to their families and community. While in some ways the call for a return to "past traditions" represents a romanticized correction for the problems of the present, in the 1980s Kgosi Linchwe II briefly reintroduced initiation schools in Mochudi, the capital of Kgatleng district, to teach young people about their history, moral behavior, and family values.[22] Many more traditional Batswana thought that issues of *botho* were not being addressed in the formal, westernized educational system. The initiation schools were conducted during the holidays and attracted a large number of teenagers from within and beyond the Kgatleng district. The program was popular among some, but it could not be entirely "traditional" because circumcision, an important part of the old ceremony, could not be done in the traditional fashion by the *rathipana* ("men with the little knives") because of problems such as the possible transmission of AIDS during circumcision.[23]

Other people will point out that children learned much about good behavior and *botho* from their families as they grew up. But today, many children from rural areas are sent to live with relatives in town so that they can attend school. With the expansion of educational facilities to include community junior secondary schools in most towns, there are often not enough boarding facilities to meet the demand. If students have no relatives in town, even students as young as 14 or 15 may have to resort to living in rented rooms while at school, with little or no adult supervision or guidance. Even in earlier times, the cost of boarding fees made junior high school attendance prohibitive for many rural families. When Maun Secondary School first opened its doors in 1970, for instance, several nonboarding students were discovered to have been sleeping out in the open in the bush, throwing their blankets into the thorn trees for safekeeping during the day while they were at school.[24]

Home and Family

Batswana enjoy visiting and conversation. Face-to-face encounters are preferred, but the vast distances, low population densities, and propensity for Batswana to travel back and forth to the lands and around the country have provided a ready market for cell phones. There are now twice as many cell phones (more than 270,000) as landline phones in the country, and it is fairly common to see 15 or 20 phones going off all at once when a bus arrives within range of a cell tower on the long journey across the Kalahari. The costs are high, as it is a pay-as-one-goes system. When the minutes are exhausted, people can still receive messages, but they must wait to answer them until they have saved enough money to buy another card to recharge it. Cell phone cards are for sale practically everywhere in shops and markets and even from street vendors.

The ubiquitousness of the cell phone has had an impact on the way that people interact. Whereas formerly people did not make appointments to meet one another at their homes for visiting or for meals, today it is becoming customary to "phone ahead" to avoid being a surprise guest. Before cell phones were common, many Batswana families cooked an extra dish at dinnertime just in case someone turned up unexpectedly. In Tswana custom, no one should ever be turned away at dinnertime. But a person who consistently appears just then may be teased as someone who "cooks with his feet" *(o apaya ka lonao).*

SOCIAL GATHERINGS AND CELEBRATIONS

Holidays and Festivals

Botswana holds several annual celebrations to mark important secular and religious events. These instill a sense of identity and national pride as well as provide amusement and entertainment. They are also a time when praise is given to the ancestors and when prayers for rain and other blessings are typically offered. Secular holidays include New Year's Day (January 1), Labor Day (May 1), Sir Seretse Khama Day (July 1), President's Day (July 18), and Botswana Independence Day (September 30). Christian holidays include Good Friday, Easter Monday, and Christmas Day. Most Batswana leave their homes in the city to celebrate Christmas in their district capitals or rural homes where traditional choirs and other festivities are customary. Boxing Day is another holiday that is used mainly for parties and picnics. This holiday, which comes the day after Christmas, started as a tradition in colonial households as the day when servants and other workers were given their Christmas gifts (in boxes). Batswana Muslims celebrate Ramadan from new moon to new moon in March or April, but it is not a national holiday.

Planting and harvest ceremonies in the spring and fall provide additional opportunities for celebration. In the past, the agricultural cycle was centrally regulated by the *kgosi,* and families were not permitted to go to their lands to plow until given permission to do so by the chief. People were also not permitted to eat from their harvest until the *kgosi* gave the order to do so in the "first fruits" ceremony (*go loma thotse;* "to bite the seed"). During the following harvest ceremony *(dikgafela),* people presented a portion of their grain to the *kgosi,* who, as a representative of God and the ancestors, received it in thanksgiving for the harvest. Traditionally, age regiments *(mephato)* were assigned to plow the chief's fields (*masotla;* "tribal" fields) before the rest of the community could begin to plow theirs. In the past, violation of this custom was punishable by traditional law, and in egregious cases chiefs were known to have the offender's homestead burned to the ground. Prayers for rain also brought the community together to ask God, through the *kgosi's* ancestors, for rain. Produce from the *masotla* was stored in tribal granaries *(sefalana)* where it could be drawn on during drought or other national emergencies. The needy and those who had fallen on hard times were also fed from the *sefalana.* Much like the current government pension system, these communal institutions were meant to ensure that no one had to live with an empty stomach.[25]

Today, versions of these ceremonies are incorporated into most Christian calendars as well as into the observances of those following more traditional religious practices. Celebrations usually include traditional songs, dancing, poetry, and drama. Batswana are not shy when they express themselves in public through song and dance. In the past, for instance, it was fairly common to see someone stop their job for few minutes to dance a "bump jive" before continuing work.[26]

Amusements and Sports

Indigenous games and leisure provide a window into Botswana's customs because they contribute to the general health, well-being, and physical development of the individual and society. Two Tswana men, for instance, were the first Africans to ever participate in the Olympic Games, where Len Tau finished in ninth place in a marathon marred by many irregularities at the 1904 Olympics held in St. Louis in conjunction with the World's Fair.[27] Indeed, he would likely have made a much better standing had he not had to run more than a half a mile off track to escape a dog that began chasing him.

There are many traditional indoor and outdoor games for boys and girls, although most are segregated by gender. Girls and boys both play hide-and-seek. They also make a variety of toys and musical instruments, such as banjos and guitars, from clay, wood, fencing wire, and even discarded tin cans. Ingeniously detailed trucks, cars, and even motorcycles and airplanes fashioned from coiled wire were once seen in almost every village, where they were driven along dusty paths by boys imagining the joys of such travel and work. These homemade toys are becoming rare as mass-produced plastic toys, television programming, and other activities have taken their place. Girls still play jump rope and a jacks-like game known as *diketo* that involves filling a small hole with tiny, smooth pebbles. As one of the stones is thrown up into the air, as many pebbles as possible are removed before catching the thrown stone on its way down. When all the stones have been removed, they are put back in the same manner, sometimes in patterns of multiple numbers.

Morabaraba, one of Africa's oldest board games with a history going back to ancient Egypt, is played in a variety of ways throughout eastern and southern Africa.[28] In its most common form, it involves making four parallel rows of 12 holes in the ground, with each player taking one side of 24 holes. To begin, two pebbles are put into each hole, and the game begins as one player takes the pebbles from one of the holes and begins to move them by placing them one by one into the holes until he is out of pebbles. In so doing, he may try to capture his opponent's pebbles that lie in the hole opposite where his last pebble has landed. But he can "eat" his opponent's pebbles only if he has two or more stones already in that hole. If he ends with only a single stone in a hole, it becomes the opponent's turn. One can choose to begin from any one of the 24 holes, and as the game progresses the number of pebbles in each hole rises and falls as the game takes on a chess-like quality in its strategy. Good players are known for the lightning speed with which they can assess the numbers of stones in each hole across the board and make their moves quickly; slow players and those who must count out the stones before moving are ridiculed.[29]

Another popular board game with an ancient African pedigree, *mohele,* is played on a board (often simply scratched into the ground or on a rock outcrop or sidewalk) with three squares nested inside each other. A cross drawn through the middle of the squares, along with diagonal lines connecting their corners, creates 24 points of intersection that are sometimes marked with circles. Each player is allotted 12 "cows" (represented by stones, bottle caps, beans, and so on), and the aim is to take as many of one's opponent's herd as possible by ringing them in with two of one's animals. (A cow that is surrounded on two sides by those of an opponent can be captured; a herd with three in a row is "safe.") The game is won when the opponent has so few that it is impossible to have three in a row. The Botswana National Sports Council is considering adding such traditional "war" games to local and international sports contests as a supplement to such Western sports as soccer, netball, volleyball, martial arts, boxing, and athletics.[30] These traditional African games are now being played in many parts of the world, and in 1996, South Africa even sent a *mohele* team to Thailand for the Traditional War Games Championships.

Hunting with dogs is a favorite pastime at the grazing lands and cattle posts, and most herders carry slingshots and throwing sticks for hunting birds and rabbits. Dog fights and races are common pastimes, and those who own the fastest and bravest dogs are respected. Racing both horses and donkeys is also popular. Boys often engage in a variety of "war games" with their herding sticks while at the pastures tending their livestock. Each household had its own grazing areas, and any attempt to disrespect the territory of one family by another could result in fights. Seniority is reinforced at the pastures, and older boys often bully younger ones by taking their lunch packs of sorghum, corn, milk, and meat. Older boys sometimes take the kills of younger ones if they cannot defend themselves. But attempts to report such bullying to adults is usually met with further punishment for being a "coward."

Soccer is the most popular sport in the country, but because Botswana has a small population, the national team, the Zebras, has consistently ranked as one of the poorest in Africa. Until very recently, they had never won a game in international competition. Nonetheless, Batswana are patriotic and fully support the Zebras as their national team regardless of differences in ethnicity and politics. The Zebra's poor performance was in part due to the absence of a professional league because most of their players had to work at other jobs during the day to afford to play for their teams after hours and on weekends. In recent years, however, the team has improved, and there are now talented Batswana playing in European and American professional soccer leagues. They have participated in the Africa Cup games and are taking part in the World Cup qualifying matches for 2006.

When the Zebras play, everyone comes together to celebrate "unity in diversity" and to cheer them on with their own "praise song." The fans beat drums and blow horns, and almost everyone dresses in the national colors of blue, black, and white. Tickets are usually sold out a week before Zebras games, so some must stay home to watch the game on television because the national stadium cannot accommodate everyone. When the Zebras win, there are celebrations across the country, and traffic jams the streets of Gaborone.

Parties

Batswana enjoy social gatherings, birthday celebrations, and parties, and it is common to hear a person saying, "*ke a throwa,*" a corruption of the English, "I am throwing [a party]." If someone decides to "throwa" a party, he or she is expected to provide all the food and beverages for their visitors. Bringing one's own bottle is a foreign concept but is becoming increasingly common. Most people are also uncomfortable with the idea of a "potluck" because it may be taken as a sign that the hosts do not have the wherewithal to provide for their guests. Another "code switch" that occurs in relation to celebrations includes "*ke a turna*," for "I am turning [a certain age; it is my birthday]."

Other Public Gatherings

Public gatherings around election time offer people opportunities to freely express their opinions about the government, including accusations of corruption, unequal distribution of wealth, unfair land and representation rights, and other concerns. At election time, pickup trucks with bullhorns are commonly heard driving in the early morning through neighborhoods loudly extolling the virtues of their candidates while freely maligning their opponents—or those who are alleged to be corrupt or to have conducted themselves badly in public office. The fact that such criticisms can be made fairly freely is a tribute to the principles of freedom and democracy that have formed the philosophical foundation of the Botswana government since independence. The recognized right to freedom of expression is one of the fundamental factors that has enabled Botswana to become Africa's oldest, most stable, and perhaps freest multiparty democracy.

Another type of public gathering less appreciated by outsiders includes public floggings at the *kgotla* carried out to humiliate those found guilty of crimes. During some of these gatherings, poets and singers may also be on hand to make ribald jokes. The flogging, which uses a cane, is often announced with livestock metaphors, such as when a *kgosi* and his council announce a sentence as "goat teats" *(mabele a pudi)*[31] for two strokes of the cane or "cow teats" *(mabele a kgomo)* for four. After the punishment, the guilty party is given the opportunity to insult everyone present without further punishment—the comments being excused as being due to the "pains of the cane" *(manokonoko a thupa)*. After the caning, the guilty party is often mainstreamed back into society. With overcrowding in prisons, such corporal punishment has come to be more accepted as an alternative to imprisonment for minor crimes. In the view of many Batswana, the cane is preferred because it cheap, involves no lawyers, and affects the guilty party directly. In addition, by avoiding prison, it is seen as a way to prevent petty thieves from becoming more hardened criminals through association with tougher gangsters in prison. Whether true or not, most serious crime in Botswana is blamed on more "sophisticated" or desperate immigrant criminals from the streets of Johannesburg, Cape Town, and Zimbabwe.

In the past, caning was a common punishment for misbehavior at school, especially at boarding schools, where principals and headmasters are expected to act as the parental surrogates. Given the almost universal belief in the adage of "spare the rod and spoil the child," headmasters could be criticized if they neglected what parents saw as their disciplinary responsibilities. The process was highly ritualized, and the child to be punished was usually sent to the bush to cut his own cane, "which he or she knows to be the appropriate thickness" for their punishment. Three swipes are the norm, with the expectation that the cane will break on the last one.[32] Each instance was supposed to be recorded in a school ledger. According to custom, the heir to a chief could be corporally punished only if one of the teachers was also of royal blood and thus of high social status—but even then, the punishment was hard to administer. Today, more progressive views have led to the outlawing if not the complete disappearance of school canings.

COMMUNITY ORGANIZATIONS AND SELF-HELP COMMITTEES

Village Health Committees

Village health committees (VHCs) have been in existence since the 1970s to promote public health measures to reduce illnesses in the community. They encourage villagers to build latrines, to keep their homesteads clean, and to remind patients with tuberculosis and pregnant mothers to attend meetings at the clinic. The VHCs also encourage mothers to make small garden plots where they can grow vegetables to ensure that their children are properly nourished. They distribute donated clothing to those in need and participate in AIDS support issues, such as home-based care. Under the guidance of a family welfare educator, the VHC works closely with the staff of government clinics. In some villages, prominent traditional doctors *(dingaka)* are also committee members. They often complain that it is difficult to work with the trained medical personnel in village clinic, who may discourage or condemn traditional medicine. On a positive note, incorporating them into the VHC keeps *dingaka* from working completely outside the health care system while letting them know that their work is appreciated. At the same time, the other committee members can point out that there are some diseases, such as tuberculosis and AIDS, that are better left to medical practitioners trained in scientific techniques.

Red Cross

One of the oldest community organizations in Botswana, the Red Cross, with membership throughout the country, is still relatively active, although its membership appears to be gradually declining. In the decade after independence, many village Red Cross committees were established under the patronage of the late Ruth Khama, wife of the first president of Botswana, Sir Seretse Khama. Presently, in rural areas, often in simple thatched houses, members give lectures on first aid, and in many places they provide the only focal point for community health issues. A high percentage of Red Cross volunteers are women who, in addition to attending to community health concerns, participate in projects such as building houses for the poor and, through the Food for Work Program, help cater to the needs of undernourished children in some communities. Other areas of activity include peer education about HIV/AIDS, village beautification and tree-planting campaigns, and teaching basic first aid.

Tirelo Sechaba (National Service)

Tirelo Sechaba, similar to the Peace Corps or Teach for America, encourages Botswana's young people to contribute to their country by providing their labor to community development projects in villages in rural or disadvantaged parts of the country. At the same time, it was expected that the young participants would gain skills and knowledge that would be of use later when they entered the job market. While one of the objectives was to get young people to learn more about their culture, another aspect was to enable them to get to know and appreciate cultures different from their own by posting them to villages far from their homes in other parts of Botswana. Beginning in 1980, students who completed high school (Form 5) participated by working as teaching assistants or at other volunteer tasks before going on to college or entering the job market. In 1992–93 more than 6,000 young people participated in the volunteer program.

Despite the good intentions of Tirelo Sechaba to increase social awareness among young people by using their skills and energies to benefit the nation, the scheme soon came under fire. It was never able to fully absorb the number of young people available and was also criticized for delaying young men and women from obtaining higher job qualifications. In addition, poor oversight in some areas meant that student skills were often underused or not adequately engaged in appropriate projects. The Botswana government consequently abolished the scheme, but there is currently a motion in Parliament to revive it. For instance, the *Tautona Times,* the weekly electronic press circular of the Office of the President distributed over the Internet, recently concluded that the program could be made "more effective and productive if more young people obtain higher qualifications before entering into their national service. The educational aspect of Tirelo Sechaba should become less necessary as the system of education in Botswana improves."[33]

Pregnancy, Naming Ceremonies, and Other Rituals

The Tswana, like most southern African peoples, mark important stages in life, such as the naming and presenting of a newborn baby to the community, puberty, marriage, and death, with ceremonies. Naming, marriage, and death are also among the most costly rites of passage in Botswana. To cope with these expenses, bridal showers, stake parties, burial societies, and other opportunities for gift giving occur at most of these life cycle events as the community comes together to both recognize and financially support families as they assume new roles and responsibilities.

Pregnancy

When a woman becomes pregnant, according to custom she is expected to follow a regimen that will ensure that the baby develops properly. Interestingly, most taboos are centered on meat products. She should not eat intestines, for instance, because it is believed that this will cause her to have a painful delivery and perhaps diarrhea. Eating liver is also considered dangerous because it might cause bleeding. During pregnancy, she is not supposed to eat reptiles, such as monitor lizards, because some believe that this will cause the baby to crawl forever like a snake. Finally, she is not supposed to eat eggs or drink alcohol for fear that they could deform the child's brain or cause other complications. For the birth of her first child, a mother is usually assisted by her mother; for subsequent children, her mother-in-law may also be present to share in the birthing procedure, as both will be involved in the child's upbringing.[34]

According to Botswana custom, members of the public should not see an infant until it is three months old. At the end of this confinement period, the newborn baby is introduced to the community for the first time and it is given a name *(mantsho/ go ntsha botsetsi)*. An old Tswana proverb says, "Children are a gift from the ancestors" *(Bana ke mpho ya badimo),* and during the period of confinement it is believed that the child is "hovering between this life and the realm of the 'badimo,' [and so] the 'gift' must be acknowledged."[35] Those who see or touch the child during confinement should refrain from sexual activity because that could cause a dangerous condition of impurity known as "hot feet" *(maoto a a molelo),* which it is believed can be passed on to the baby.

Naming

The end of the confinement period, with its special rules and customs, is marked by a naming celebration. In some ethnic groups, an elder gives the child its "official" name *(mantsho)* when it is presented to the community after confinement. Naming a child "Keneilwe," for instance, meaning, "I have been given," could be done to show appreciation to ancestors for the "gift" of the child.[36] *Mantsho* names often reference specific circumstances or events that marked the child's birth. A boy born on a rainy day, for instance, may be called "*Rrapula,*" or "Mr. Rain," or a girl born to parents who have had a difficult time conceiving may be named "Surprise" *(Kgakgamatso)*. All names in Tswana have such meanings. Phenyo, for instance, means "victory," and "Thebe" is the word for a warrior's shield. When combined with an English middle name of "Churchill," the combination is formidable. Later in life, additional names may be added at other important stages in the life cycle, such as puberty and the birth of a first child. In the past, a father's surname would become the child's given name. At the *Mantsho* celebration, gifts of livestock, bags of grain or clothing, and money are presented to the parents to help them with the expense of raising the child. After the birth of a couple's first child, the parent's will afterward generally be called by their firstborn's name, with the prefix "Rra" (father of) or "Mma" (mother of) added, according to the sex of the parent.

At the end of the naming ceremony, the baby's head is shaved for the first time and "doctored" in a cleansing ceremony *(phekolo)* conducted by a traditional doctor *(ngwaka ya setso)* or a spiritual healer *(moporofiti,* from the English "prophet"), depending on the religious beliefs of the parents.[37] In either case, at the naming ceremony a tied-up piece of cloth or small leather pouch stuffed with traditional medicine will usually be tied around the baby's waist or neck to provide protection against jealous people or witches *(baloi)* who may have evil intentions toward the child. The doctored items are supposed to be worn until they fall off, after which they should be left on the ground where they fall, as they represent gifts to the ancestors.

In some traditional households, it is believed that the blood of a sheep or a goat (never a cow) should be spilled *(madi a tshologa;* "overflow") and beer prepared in honor of the ancestors who have "provided" the child. Some Christians and educated citizens disregard these social customs, but in some churches such customary rites are still implicit in the shadows of the Christian ceremonies of baptism and christening.

Puberty Rites

When a girl reaches puberty and has her first menstruation, it is said that "she sees the moon" *(go bona kgwedi)* or "needs to wash" *(go tlhatswa)*.[38] While in the past young girls were then expected to undergo a period of confinement when she would learn from her elders how to take care of herself, in most places this transition to womanhood is now handled more casually in the home or at school. In the more traditional setting, cow dung was in some cases applied to her body to "help with the flow of blood." Later, her body was ritually covered with a mixture of fat and red ocher as elderly women taught her how to handle her periods and warned her of the consequences of having sex. While in confinement, she was not supposed eat with her hands because they were considered impure. Dishes, pots, and other household goods were also placed inside the confinement hut with her to "make her a good wife." At the end of the confinement period, the young woman was taken to the river to wash. After that, she had to run home while an elder brother or cousin chased her with a cane. As she entered her home compound, the female relatives welcomed her into womanhood with ululating and clapping. Many traditional prohibitions regulated the behavior of menstruating women. They were not allowed to use the same chairs as other people, for instance, and in some cases they were not supposed to cook food for others.

FUNERALS AND MOURNING

Burial Societies

Almost everyone in Botswana belongs to a burial society because they are one of the most important village institutions that provide economic and emotional support at one of the most difficult points in a family's life. All societies pay toward the cost of the coffin, the food served to guests at the funeral, and other funeral expenses.[39] The amount varies from society to society and for different categories of coverage. Members are also expected to act as mourners at one another's funerals so that one does not pass into the next world in silence. Interestingly, women seem to dominate burial societies. In two society meetings observed in Kanye, for instance, of the 40 members present, only three were men.[40] In both cases, however, the men chaired the meetings. Burial society meetings are so important in some small villages that local policemen may be called on to summon members to the meetings by blowing their whistles.

While the members of a burial society are generally homogeneous with respect to ethnicity, they are heterogeneous in terms of family status, age, profession, social position, and economic status. The name of the Segotsamolelo Burial Society in Kanye, for instance, translates as the "one who lights the fire," meaning there should always be life (fire) in the village.[41] According to Tswana custom, fire is the essence of life, and there should always be a fire at the *kgotla*. Because more than half the population now lives in urban areas, however, there are few people to light the fire in a village *kgotla,* and in general the only time one is now lit is when there is a funeral or a marriage.

Each month, burial society members meet to pay their subscription fees, attend to the cases of those who have violated regulations, and discuss general matters affecting the management of the society. When a society is formed, members are expected to pay a joining fee, which typically ranges from $5.00 to $6.00, followed by annual dues of $6.00 to $8.00. Subscription fees are generally low enough that most people can afford them.

Everyone who joins must pay back dues equivalent to the accumulated payments of a founding member. This is done to ensure the financial security of the society because most do not have a large number of members. If a society is 10 years old when it accepts a new member, for instance, it will suffer a loss if that member dies shortly after joining without paying back dues. Joining a long established society can thus become quite expensive, and young people joining for the first time usually register with a newly formed society to get out of paying back dues. This creates a problem of a different sort for older societies whose membership tends to become fixed relatively quickly. To compensate for dwindling membership over time, existing member's children are often allowed to join the society without any obligation to pay back dues. Although an extremely high percentage of people in Botswana belong to burial societies, the destitute and the poor who may be cut off from the support of friends or family for a variety of reasons are buried with little ceremony at government expense.

Burial societies are also a source of loans for members who may not qualify at a commercial bank, although interest rates can run as high as 20 to 30 percent a month. No members can borrow money unless another member acts as a guarantor who will be held responsible if the person fails to pay back the loan. Most people borrow money at the beginning of the plowing season with the expectation that they will be able to repay it when the crops are harvested. Members can usually borrow up to the amount of their contribution to the society, but if they fail to repay the loan, their membership can be terminated without a refund.

Funerals

Ceremonies for the dead mark the last stage in the life cycle. In general, a person's status in life correlates closely with the degree of ceremony and expense he or she is accorded at death. Important and rich people are buried in dignity with lavish and elaborate funerals. To receive such a burial, one must grow to an old age, have children, and be considered to have lived a successful life. Ceremonies for the death of a child, especially an infant, are usually not public and are attended only by the immediate family. Funerals serve as a forum where a family's genealogy is made public; they are a time to mourn as well as an occasion used to wish the deceased a peaceful journey to the ancestral world. While the death of an elderly person is a generally accepted as a natural occurrence, the passing away of a young person is always thought to be associated in some way with witchcraft, evil spirits, spurned ancestors, or harmful rivalry and jealousy within the community. In addition to respecting and honoring the dead, in the days of colonialism and apartheid, funeral attendance was also used as a subtle form of resistance or work stoppage as "kin from far and wide gave up their daily occupations from which their livelihood is earned, much to the annoyance of their European masters and overlords, to attend the funeral services of relations."[42]

Burial practices vary in different parts of the country according to differences in ethnicity and religion. In rural areas, where there are no mortuaries, people are buried immediately. For Muslims, according to Islamic prescription the deceased should be buried as soon as possible, typically within a few hours of death. Approached within an overriding Muslim framework, the funeral is usually brief and understated. On the other hand, the Kalanga, when possible, usually wait a week before the body is buried in order to allow time for family and friends to gather. Personal items of the deceased are sometimes buried with them, along with traditional herbs associated with cleansing and purifying. Funerals are usually held very early in the morning. A black or blue cloth is pinned around the shoulders of people who have lost someone in the immediate family; other mourners may wear a black or blue necklace or armband. In the mid-nineteenth century, parasols made "from the black feathers of the ostrich" served the same purpose as a sign of mourning.[43]

Among the Tswana, funerals are typically carried out on weekends so that more people can attend. Nightly radio programs such as *Ditatolo* or *Dikitsiso tsa Dinstho* come on around 8:00 P.M. and announce the names of people who have recently died so that people who are living in rural areas or traveling or working far from their homes can listen and learn if any of their friends or loved ones have passed away. With the impact of AIDS on the overall mortality rate and especially that of young people, even those in their twenties and thirties now listen to such programs every evening in hushed silence. They may then decide to attend a funeral if it is not too distant and there is enough time to get there.

In traditional funeral rites, the corpse is brought to the deceased family's home the evening before the burial, where people come to pay their last respects, say prayers, and partake of tea and snacks. Funerals are expensive because the deceased's family is expected to provide food for everyone who attends; it is standard practice for those who can afford it to kill a number of cows.[44] Migrant miners in South Africa started the *Tebelelo,* or "night vigil," ceremonies. The miners came from many different countries, and when one passed away, his coworkers were expected to attend the funeral in lieu of family. There was generally no place for mourners to stay, and even when there was it was expensive. So they developed night vigils or wakes where they could stay all night and talk, sing, and cite proverbs to pass the time until the burial in the morning. Christian congregations have elaborated on these early, all-night *tebelelo* ceremonies by using them to preach and to console mourners as well as to sing, eat, and make speeches extolling the virtues of the deceased.

The songs sung at the graveside the next day are generally choral adaptations of Christian hymns sung to "tunes composed in foreign lands, but now appropriate and made their own ... the various parts blending in glorious harmony, the strains wafting in the highveld breeze, seeming to make the Savanna grass tilt and bow in reverence to the weight of their deep-felt meaning."[45] As the family and mourners file by, each casting clods of earth on the coffin, the singing continues until the grave has been filled in and boulders are placed over it. Prayers and invocations for ritual "coolness" *(a go nne tsididi)* follow. In the past and still sometimes today, chiefs and family eldermen were buried in the family cattle kraal situated next to the *kgotla.* Women and children were buried under the *lapa,* or courtyard, of the house. This pattern has been found in archaeological sites dating to more than 1,000 years in Botswana, indicating at least some continuity in ritual over this period. In the distant past and among those who continue these traditions today, the body was placed in flexed, fetal or sitting position facing the west—the direction of the setting sun and the ancestral world. In some parts of Botswana, burials still take place in the *lolwapa,* although most villages now have official cemeteries on the outskirts of town.[46] People suspected of witchcraft or those who are believed to have died from it, such as those struck by lightning, are treated differently. Their graves are doctored with ritual medicines to keep them from coming back to disturb the living, and they are often buried away from town in ritually "cool" places, such as the wet earth along the banks of streams, where their spirits may be calmed and of less danger to the living.[47]

After the funeral, all the members of the deceased's immediate family shave their heads and apply traditional herbs or holy water, depending on their religious orientation. Some members of the Zionist Christian Church require a widow to wear a blue cloth, similar in color to her church uniform, over her shoulders for the entire mourning period, which lasts for a year. In other traditions, women are expected to wear black dresses that symbolize darkness or sadness, while men wear black hats and pin a piece of black or blue cloth on their sleeves. Men and women should not shake hands during the mourning period, and widows are not supposed to take long trips or leave the place where their deceased clothes are stored until the yearlong mourning period has ended. At the end of the mourning period, family members and very close relatives hold another ceremony, *kapolo,* in which the widow's black or blue mourning attire is removed; a traditional doctor or spiritual healer then conducts a death announcement ceremony. If the *kapolo* is for a man, the blood of a bull should be spilled; if for a woman, a cow is sacrificed. At this time, the clothes and goods of the deceased are distributed among the immediate family, who may disperse them as they see fit.

Some authorities, such as Kgosi Seepepitso IV, have argued that black mourning clothes are a foreign concept and should be abolished because they are too costly. Indeed, since the early 1990s the amount of money spent on funerals has increased in tandem with the numbers of deaths related to AIDS. Perhaps it is because the country is now more prosperous, with more people with expendable income to spend on funerals, that expensive coffins, elaborate headstones, and small tents are now erected to honor and shade ancestors in addition to the simple fieldstones that are placed over their graves. No doubt the bereaved gain a certain amount of status and respect in their communities by burying their dead in a "respectable" fashion. But with the average cost of a funeral now topping $1,500, a figure that strains most family budgets, the topic of "impoverishment by funeral" now resonates with many families. Belief that the ancestors may become jealous and visit sickness or harm on their descendants if they are not praised or remembered sets an additional undertone to these newly elaborated rituals, especially in the context of increasing mortality rates among the young caused directly and indirectly by HIV/AIDS.

NOTES

1. Foreword by John Comaroff, in P. Motzafi-Haller, *Fragmented Worlds, Coherent Lives: The Politics of Difference in Botswana* (Westport, Conn.: Bergin & Garvey, 2002), p. ix.

2. R. P. Werbner, *Reasonable Radicals and Citizenship in Botswana: The Public Anthropology of Kalanga Elites* (Bloomington: Indiana University Press, 2004), pp. 67–68.

3. J. Lonsdale, "Moral Ethnicity and Political Tribalism," in *Inventions and Boundaries: Historical and Anthropological Approaches to the Study of Ethnicity and Nationalism,* ed. P. Kaarsholm and J. Hultin, Occasional Paper no. 11 (Roskilde: Roskilde University, International Development Studies, 1994), p. 141.

4. D. Durham, "The Predicament of Dress: Polyvalency and the Ironies of Cultural Identity," *American Ethnologist* 26 (2, 1999): 402.

5. W. vin Binsbergen, "Minority Language, Ethnicity and the State in Two African Situations," in *African Languages, Development and the State,* ed. R. Farden and G. Furniss (London: Routledge, 1994), p. 167.

6. Durham, "The Predicament of Dress," p. 398.

7. Those Khoisan resettled to Kx'oensakene found a community with an elementary school, a clinic, and a police station. To compensate them for their move, the residents were given farmland and a choice of either 15 goats or five cattle. Government also employed the resettled as construction workers and other income-generating projects. J. Maruyama, *Resettlement, Livelihood and Social Relationships among the /Gwi and //Gana in Central Kalahari* (Kyoto: Graduate School of Asian and African Area Studies, 2002).

8. Sometimes proverbs and sayings are woven into praise poems and vice versa. This saying can be found incorporated in many longer poems, such as that translated in H. Alverson, *Mind in the Heart of Darkness: Value and Self-Identity among the Tswana of Southern Africa* (New Haven, Conn.: Yale University Press, 1978), p. 125.

9. U. Dow, *Juggling Truths* (North Melbourne: Spinifex Press, 2003), pp. 4, 34. Reproduced with permission from *Juggling Truths* by Unity Dow (2003) published by Spinifex Press.

10. A. Sesinyi, *Love on the Rocks* (London: Macmillan Education, 1983).

11. Personal communication by e-mail to J. Denbow, May 26, 2005.

12. It is even more polite to use the forms "rre" and "mme," which literally translate as "my father" or "my mother." Another step up in politeness and respect would be to address someone as a fictional "uncle" *(ntati)* or, even better, by his totem: *"Dumela tlou"* ("Hello elephant").

13. In some cases, this can become complicated. When working on an archaeological excavation in central Botswana, for instance, workers passing heavy buckets of earth from their units up to their supervisor always held them up over their heads with one hand while using their other to grasp their right forearm in respect.

14. It is common for people to ask someone his or her age, but some women have now adopted the Western fashion of not responding.

15. D. Durham, "Disappearing Youth: Youth as a Social Shifter in Botswana," *American Ethnologist* 31 (4, 2004): 593–94.

16. Durham, "The Predicament of Dress," p. 397. Durham notes that in Mahalapye, Herero are also "meticulous about cleanliness, usually bathing twice a day and washing clothes often."

17. This is much like the way in which F.R.S. after a British surname indicates "Friend of the Royal Society" or OBE means one has been named to the Order of the British Empire.

18. The term *botho* is also central to the country's development plan for itself, known as "Vision 2016," which expresses how the country wishes to find itself in the year 2016. Botswana Government Presidential Task Group for a Long Term Vision for Botswana, *A Framework for a Long Term Vision for Botswana* (Gaborone: Government Printer, 1996).

19. Cattle and village metaphors are again appropriate. If a child acts in good ways, just like parents, one may say, *"e e mashi e a itsale,"* or "a cow with good milk produces a

calf that does the same." On the other hand, when a child turns out badly despite having good parents, it may be remarked that *"molelo o tswa molora,"* or "a fire produces ash."

20. G. Ntloedibe-Kuswani, *Bongaka, Women and Witchcraft,* Women's Worlds 99: the 7th International Interdisciplinary Congress on Women. Session VII: Gendering the Past, Tromso, Norway, 1999.

21. Quoted in Alverson, *Mind in the Heart of Darkness,* p. 113.

22. M. N. Mosothwane, "An Ethnographic Study of Initiation Schools among the Bakgatla bo ga Kgafela in Mochudi (1874–1988)," *Pula: Botswana Journal of African Studies* 15 (1, 2001): 144–65.

23. A team of student doctors from the then Medical University of South Africa (MEDUNSA) were called in to do the circumcisions instead.

24. While working at Maun Secondary School between 1970 and 1973, J. Denbow observed several students camping in the bush. They had come from poor families and could not afford to pay for boarding.

25. On the other hand, the needs of the community need to be balanced by the resources at hand to meet them. If the *kgosi* demanded too much, he could be met with complaints that "the [number of] tasks of a chief can kill an ordinary worker" *("tiro ya kgosi e bolaya lesilo").*

26. The bump jive is a sexual dance that involves two people, usually a man and a woman, bumping their buttocks against one other. But if there is no one to dance with, they may even bump against the nearest object—a pole or a house wall, for instance.

27. Len Tau and Jan Mashiani were not actually trained Olympic runners but happened to be at the World's Fair as part of a Boer War exhibit. The initial winner of the race was later disqualified after photographs were produced showing him catching a lift to the finish line in an automobile.

28. This is the Tswana term; there are a variety of others, including *mankala* and *bau.* In West Africa, it is known as *Wari* or *Waro* and many other terms.

29. One can play a variation of *morabaraba* online at http://www.max99kbgames.com/mancala.html.

30. "BNSC Brings Traditional Games into Sports Code," *Botswana Daily News,* August 4, 2003.

31. *Mabele a Pudi* is also a common name for villages in Botswana that have two rocky peaks resembling "goat teats" near them.

32. As deputy headmaster of Maun Secondary School in 1972–73, J. Denbow was once berated by a local member of Parliament (MP) for neglecting his duties as "parent in absentia" for not whipping the MP's child. The MP instructed him on the formalities of the process. Unity Day described a harsher system in Mochudi during the 1960s when "'Ninety Degrees' was what Mrs Monyatsi called bending over at a ninety-degree angle, without touching your ankles, and receiving nine strokes from a cane." Dow, *Juggling Truths,* p. 26. Reproduced with permission from *Juggling Truths* by Unity Dow (2003) published by Spinifex Press.

33. *Tautona Times,* no. 18 (May 21, 2005), http://www.utexas.edu/conferences/africa/ads/716.html. (The term *"Tautona,"* or "president," is derived from the word meaning "male lion.")

34. One proverb related to the sharing of responsibilities in the rearing of a child is "*kgetsi ya tsie o a tshwaraganelwa,*" or "a child is like a bag full of locusts, it has to be shared."

35. G. Setiloane, *The Image of God among the Sotho-Tswana* (Rotterdam: A. A. Balkema, 1976), p. 187.

36. As Dow writes in *Juggling Truths,* the name Keneilwe, meaning "I have been given," signifies "gratitude to God and the ancestors" (p. 5). Reproduced with permission from *Juggling Truths* by Unity Dow (2003) published by Spinifex Press.

37. In some families, the first shave happens within a week or two of giving birth and was done by the grandmother or close aunt.

38. *Kwedi* is also the Tswana term used for month, again because of its cyclical nature.

39. Some funeral parlors are now entering this business by selling insurance policies, paid monthly, to cover the costs of the coffin and funeral.

40. The meeting in Bokaa was observed by Phenyo Thebe in May 2005.

41. The term *segotsamolelo* is also a more general name given to societies that provide labor, food, and resources on the first or second day after death or that provide money after the funeral.

42. Setiloane, *The Image of God among the Sotho-Tswana,* p. 192.

43. C. J. Andersson, *Lake Ngami, or, Explorations and Discoveries during Four Years' Wanderings in the Wilds of Southwestern Africa* (New York: Harper and Brothers, 1856), p. 257. Ostrich parasols were also used "for the preservation of the complexion."

44. Funerals for the poor or infamous are likely to be poorly attended and less costly.

45. Setiloane, *The Image of God among the Sotho-Tswana,* p. 193.

46. The Tlokwa who live on the southern outskirts of Gaborone are one of the groups that still do this. After burial in the courtyard, a small structure or house is usually built over the grave.

47. I. Schapera, *Rainmaking Rites of Tswana Tribes* (Leiden: Afrika-Studiecentrum, 1971), pp. 111–12.

8

Music, Dance, and Theater

The "boguera" is a civil rather than a religious rite. All the boys of an age between ten and fourteen or fifteen are selected to be the companions for life of one of the sons of the chief. They are taken out to some retired spot in the forest, and huts are erected for their accommodation; the old men go out and teach them to dance, initiating them, at the same time, into all the mysteries of African politics and government.[1]

The Bamangwato are a cheerful people, especially the women. They dance and sing nearly every night, keeping up the revels till next day. . . . The only musical instruments the bechuanas have are reeds, monotonous and discordant at their moonlight dances, and a musical bow, with a hollow calabash at the back on one end, on which is stretched a twisted string of sinews; it is struck with a thin stick and the tones modified by running the fingers along the string. The instrument is a favourite with the Bushmen as well, and they while away many an hour with it.[2]

More than 100 years after these descriptions, the drums, flutes, songs, and traditional chants of religious prayer and thanksgiving that once echoed "nearly every night" through Botswana villages are now largely silent because of the combined impact of missionary activity, colonial censure, and the impact of radio, television, and other forms of entertainment on community life and religious practice. While mainline Christian denominations did their best to eliminate the fusion of religion, divination, and healing that was an integral part of the life of all of Botswana's cultures, most indigenous Christian churches such as the Zionist Christian Church (ZCC) have co-opted spiritual healing with its songs and dances of purification and renewal as part of their ritual liturgy. In addition, new generations of ancestor-inspired priests, prophets, and healers continue to practice and sometimes even flourish by erecting faith-healing centers on isolated hilltops outside major centers such as Serowe and Francistown where they call on the ancestors *(badimo)* and God to aid in the well-being of their followers. Thus, the ceremonies and rites of old have not disappeared but have been transformed and relocated from the center of village life to more isolated and hidden settings where dance, song, and prayers continue to raise offerings to the ancestors.

The performing arts are thus an integral part of the culture and customs of Botswana. As part of every community's entertainment, song and dance instills a spirit of togetherness and belonging while at the same time providing Batswana an embodied means through which to express their feelings of joy and grief. In the past, songs and dances were also an integral part of the *bogwera* and *bojale* initiation ceremonies for young men and women. Songs and "steps" also accompanied communal work groups when women pounded grain together in heavy wooden mortars or joined together in work parties to help one another ready their fields for planting. Today, all Batswana continue to take pride in the variety of dance forms and music that have been inherited from the pasts of the different cultures that make up the country. While there have been rapid changes in many other aspects of social and cultural life, the nation's political unity is founded on respect for these different traditions and the freedom that people have to express their diversity through cultural performance.

The call to dance is thus close to the core of all the cultures of Botswana, and the phrase that is still used in Tswana to ask someone the name of their totem is, "*O binang?*," or "What do you dance?" Yet, curiously, there are no traditions or remembrances of dances dedicated to totemic animals. Nor did the earliest European visitors describe dances held in veneration of crocodiles, monkeys, duikers, elephants, hares, buffaloes, or any of the other animals that make up the pantheon of Botswana totems. Indeed, most of the Europeans who first encountered the varied cultures of Botswana in the nineteenth century had difficulty in perceiving the cosmological and cultural connections between dance, song, religion, and healing that were intrinsic to most "traditional" musical performances. Used to dividing the cultural and natural world into discrete and separate categories of "medicine," "religion," and "dance," Europeans had difficulty in seeing how these divisions and categories could be blurred or even nonexistent in the cultural worlds of the Batswana. The only indigenous practices that early missionaries and adventurers recognized as "medicinal," for instance, were those that mimicked their own use of roots, herbs, and unguents; African use of prayer, song, dance, amulets, and spiritual embodiments they termed "fetishes" to ward against evil were dismissed as primitive "magic" that was qualitatively "different" from their own entreaties to the Almighty. It is, therefore, not surprising that when they did encounter Africans singing and dancing, they interpreted it by analogy with their own cultures as simply partying, secular entertainment—or, as noted in 1822, "recreation purely corporeal, and perfectly independent of mental qualification or refinement…a recreative mode of exercising the body and keeping it in health, the means of shaking off spleen, and of expanding one of the best characters of the heart—the social feeling."[3] Sometimes European observers were right, but often the significance of the dances and songs they observed eluded them.

Blinded by the refractions from their own cultural lenses, European descriptions of nineteenth-century music and dance were seriously flawed. A description of Herero and Yeyi dancing in the 1850s as a "stupid and uninteresting" mimicking of "the awkward gallop of the giraffe, the quick trot of the zebra, and the lively caperings of the beautiful springbok" foregrounds the aloof disdain that most European travelers had for the cultural complexities of the local cultures that entertained and accommodated them.[4] With few exceptions, Europeans found what their cultures had already prepared them to see: an Africa rich in game and an exemplar of life at the dawn of humanity, a primitive and atavistic continent. To the misguided views of local rituals and dances held by European hunters and adventurers, one can add those of missionaries who often saw such performances as unabashedly wonton and greatly in need of Christian intervention. As one missionary commented in 1839, "I feel happy also in saying that the bechuana customs and ceremonies are considerably on the wane. The native dance is in some instances kept up; but I frequently go at the time of the dance, openly oppose it and preach to those who are waiting to hear."[5]

Even sympathetic observers often failed to see the deeper spiritual import of much of what they saw. For instance, in an otherwise accurate description of a Sarwa trance dance, J. Burchell accurately described the distinctive bent-over posture, complete with use of two sticks to support the upper body, of healers going into trance. But to him, the dance was simply an entertainment, and his description of the inexplicable posture as "constrained, and as unsuited for dancing, as imagination could devise" completely misses its intention—which was to allow the supernatural potency some call *n/um* to enter into the dancer's bodies where the dance would cause it to heat up or boil, activating its potency and imparting the ability to cure.[6] As one !Kung healer described it a century and a half later,

You dance, dance, dance, dance. Then num lifts you up in your belly and lifts you in your back, and you begin to shiver. Num makes you tremble; it's

hot...you're looking around because you see everything, you see what's trou-
bling everybody. Rapid shallow breathing draws num up. What I do in my
upper body with the breathing, I also do in my legs with the dancing....Then
num enters every part of your body, right to the tip of your feet and even your
hair.[7]

While references to dancing and totems in the Tswana language could
index a past now long forgotten, dances that call on the supernatural potency
of animals to assist with curing or as an aspect of menarcheal dances continue
to be a part of Sarwa cultures. In eastern Botswana, however, only fragmented
memories of such dances remain, as the elders who once performed such rituals have become dispersed throughout cattle posts and villages, making it
difficult to resurrect the sense of community such rituals require. In northwestern Botswana, however, trance dancers continue to call on the eland,
giraffe, gemsbok, and other spiritually charged objects to aid in the protection of their community from sickness and evil. But even here, especially in
more westernized locales such as the leasehold farms around Ghanzi, curing
dances that once involved the whole community have been transformed into
more individualized performances where specialist shamen collect money
from their "clients" for their services.[8] More recently, staged trance dances
that are more evocative than real have become a regular part of the "tourist
experience" at many safari camps. Yet despite such instances of commodifica-
tion, the deeper association between dance, song, and spiritual power remains
strong throughout Botswana.

TRADITIONAL MUSIC AND DANCE

It is unrealistic to try to separate music from body movement in African
musical compositions because many of the instruments—especially drums
and dance rattles—incorporate complex combinations of hand, arm, torso,
and leg movement. In addition, while each musician may contribute only a
single musical note, when these are combined, complex polyrhythmic and
polymetric compositions are produced. Voices are often used in a similar fashion to produce both harmonic and antiphonal call-and-response performances,
with the different elements of the "choir" sometimes performing differing
parts and entering at staggered or even overlapping intervals in the composition. Another common feature of Botswana choral music is that the melodic
phrasing and instrumental accompaniment is sometimes slightly "offset" or
"off-beat," adding a momentum to the music as it builds up complex, interlocking structures from simple elements. And contrary to popular belief,
multipart harmonic singing, which is often associated in people's minds with

hymns introduced by missionaries, was a characteristic of earlier musical performance such as the reed dance—it is not a product solely of acculturation.[9]

TRADITIONAL MUSICAL INSTRUMENTS

The oldest musical instrument recovered from excavations in Botswana is a bull roarer *(seburuburu)* made of a roughly carved bone fragment. It was unearthed at an Early Iron Age site at Matlapaneng on the outskirts of Maun.[10] This artifact, which had been broken and repaired, had holes drilled through both ends (some as repairs), where it would have been attached to a string and whirled around the head to make a roaring sound; it is a little more than 1,000 years old.

A slightly younger instrument, a one-holed stopped flute or whistle, was recovered from the Bosutswe site about 80 kilometers west of Serowe. It was exposed about a meter below the surface of the ground in a prehistoric cattle kraal where it must have been dropped and lost by its owner, perhaps a herd boy, about 900 years ago.[11] Approximately six inches long, this instrument would have been blown something like a panpipe using a finger to alternately open or close the lower end and the single side opening to produce a variety of notes. Made from the hollowed-out leg bone of a large bird, it was decorated along its length with closely spaced circular grooves that had became highly polished and worn through use. No other musical instruments have been recognized from archaeological contexts in Botswana, but that is not unusual, as most would not have been preserved because they were constructed of wood, reeds, gourds, and other perishable materials.

Both the prehistoric flute and the bull roarer show evidence of long and careful use, a characteristic that was continued through the nineteenth and twentieth centuries, when it was fairly common to find that favorite musical instruments were conserved and cherished by their owners for many decades. Some were considered community "treasures" that could not be sold without the permission of the chief; others had such sentimental value to their owners that in one case, "before parting with the instrument, [the old man] actually sang a farewell to it; had he not had another (a very unusual thing), I could not have taken it from him."[12]

Language also plays a part in the way traditional instruments are played and music is performed in Botswana. All southern African Bantu languages, including Tswana, Kalanga, Herero, and Yeyi, are "tone languages," which means that many words are distinguished from one another only by the differing pitches or tones given to their syllables. The difference between "sorghum" *(mabele)* and "breasts" *(mabele),* for instance, is only a matter of tone. Native English speakers often find it impossible to hear these distinctions, and even those with some familiarity with the language need to be careful; David Livingstone, for instance, found this difficult and wrote a list of sometimes embarrassing words that could be easily confused by using the wrong tone or aspiration after a consonant.[13] Traditional flutes and whistles sometimes made use of the tonal structure of the language to send understandable "messages" by varying the pitch of the notes to mimic words or short sentences.[14]

Other examples of using tonality to create what sound like meaningful phrases include birdsongs such as that of the honey guide, which is believed by those living in the Okavango to direct people to the location of "honey trees." As it flies, in the Tswana language the tonal call of the bird is heard as, "*kwa pele; kwa pele*," or "come ahead; come ahead."[15] Once the tree is cut down and the hive removed, local lore says that some of the honeycomb must always be left as a reward for the bird—or else the next time it will guide one not to the sweetness of honey but to the more bitter reward of a hungry lion. Sounds such as the running hoofbeats of animals are also sometimes mimicked on the musical bows played by young Sarwa boys who while away many hours with the instrument when relaxing.

Finally, in the past, musical instruments were not simply devices used to make musical notes or rhythmic beats; many were also believed to be endowed with supernatural potency embedded in the materials from which they were made. In many cases, drums, flutes, and whistles were also "doctored" by prayers and blessings. As a result, their sounds could be used to draw down the attention of the ancestors, thereby helping to create the kind of ritual environment necessary for rain to be made, for crops to prosper, for warriors to be victorious, and for human ailments to be cured. Other whistles were for more personal use, and in the nineteenth century, Tswana men were often seen to wear beads and other items around their necks and on their arms as charms to protect them from evil; one of these was a small whistle that was blown when in danger.

Percussion Instruments

Drums

In the more forested regions of northern and northeastern Botswana, drums were fashioned in many sizes from segments of large tree trunks that were cut and then hollowed out with an adze. Skins of wild game, such as springbok or monitor lizards, were often the preferred coverings because they were thin and provided good resonance. The hides were applied "wet" so that they would shrink and tighten over the top of the drum as they dried; "doctored" pegs of wood or thorns held the head in place. Particularly fine drums were sometimes given names that were incised or burned into their surfaces along with geometric designs. The drums, some more than four feet in length, had different "voices," depending on their size and shape. Before being used, they were usually "tuned" by tightening their heads by heating them near a fire. In some cases, a thick circle of beeswax was also applied to the center of the head to help with the tuning process. Very large drums were played with the hands, with the body of the drum held at an angle between the legs of the drummer, and the bottom opening of the instrument pointing behind.

A more unusual type of wooden drum—a friction drum—continues to be used by some Batswana, especially the Mbukushu, who live on the western margins of the Okavango delta. Usually less than two feet in length, this drum has a reed that hangs down inside and that is tied with sinew to the center of the drumhead. Holding the drum under one arm, the player rubs a wet hand up and down the internal reed, causing the drumhead to vibrate and produce a very loud and distinctive roaring sound.

Most drums these days are not single-headed wooden drums but rather "double-headed" instruments made by stretching a wet cowhide over both ends of a paraffin tin or a large segment cut from a 44-gallon galvanized steel barrel. The Herero also use a more traditional double-headed drum called *ongoma,* which is played with sticks rather than hands and is used mainly for religious and wedding ceremonies.[16] In the past, drums were sometimes also fashioned from clay pots, perhaps because large trees are scarce in many parts of the country. Apart from the friction drum, most are played by striking with the hands or with a wooden baton. A drum that has been used by Kgatla women since 1871 in their *bojale* initiation ceremonies is housed in the Phutadi Kobo museum in Mochudi. During the ceremony it symbolized the womb, with its open end representing the birth canal.[17]

Dance Rattles

While ensembles of variously sized drums playing in complexly interwoven tempos are one of the most common elements of traditional music in most of Africa, in the dry savanna grasslands of the Kalahari, trees large enough in diameter to make drums are often hard to come by. Perhaps as a result, the percussive beat found in the traditional music of most of Botswana's peoples— especially the Tswana and Sarwa—usually comes from clapping hands (always done by women) and dance or leg rattles (depending on the culture, both men and women may dance with them).

Dance rattles, essential equipment for all traditional dances, are often found for sale in the traditional markets of larger towns. They are manufactured from the cocoons of two species of wild silkworm. The cocoons, which are found

Dance rattles made from dried cocoons of wild silkworms provide much of the percussive sound, along with hand clapping, in the traditional dances of the Sarwa and Tswana.

only on mopane and some species of acacia trees, need to be harvested and processed carefully, as they are covered with thin, spiny hairs that can penetrate and irritate the fingers.[18] The stiff, fibrous, oblong pods about two inches long are soaked in water to soften them. They are then slit along one end and filled with small stones. The slit end is then pressed closed and allowed to dry and seal shut before the cocoon is tied at each end onto a double string of rolled fiber or leather cord. More than 100 cocoons are generally used to make a single leg rattle, which is six feet or more in length. Known by a variety of names in different languages, the rattles are wrapped around both lower legs between the ankle and the knee and played by the rapid stomping or shuffling of the dancer's feet. Because the dancing is vigorous, most rattles last only a year or two before needing to be replaced. In areas where *Gonometa* cocoons were unavailable, leg rattles were in the past sometimes also made from dried springbok ears that were filled with small pebbles.[19]

Clapping

Hand clapping combines with dance rattles to form a complex, percussive, often syncopated counterpoint to the drum, which, especially among the Tswana, generally lays down a basic 4/4 or 2/4 beat. By cupping the hands in different ways, the clapping, which is done only by women, can produce a variety of percussive sounds used to accompany both spiritual and secular dances. Rock paintings of women clapping hands are common in the rock art of southern Africa, where they are often associated with other motifs that suggest trance dancing.[20] Some authorities even suggest that some of the paintings were purposely hammered, cut, and flaked to produce sounds that were associated with their use as numinous objects.[21]

Wind Instruments

Whistles and Flutes

While simple drumbeats are an important aspect of traditional music and dance compositions in Botswana, the most emblematic instruments among the Tswana and Sarwa were flutes, whistles , and one-stringed bows. Tuned reed flute ensembles, sometimes incorporating up to 100 players, were often remarked on by early missionaries. David Livingstone included an etching of a "Reed dance by moonlight" in his *Missionary Travels,* but the description accompanying the picture is of a different dance done by the Kololo in which men, without flutes, "simultaneously lift one leg, stamp heavily twice with it, and then lift the other and give one stamp with that" while the women "standby, clapping their hands."[22]

According to one source, the Tswana reed dance could last up to 10 hours with the men playing a variety of different-sized flutes while dancing counterclockwise in a circle surrounded by an outer ring of women and young girls who clapped hands and occasionally ululated. A description from 1812 reads,

> When the dancers, who were all men, had tuned their reeds, they formed themselves into a ring, which sometimes consisted of about thirty persons, and at others, of not more than ten or twelve, according to the inclination of those who joined or left the party; but without attention to any observable order, or to any pre-arranged figure. The ring was drawn as closely together as their number would conveniently allow; but each person danced separate without any attempt at a particular step or acquired movement of the feet; nor at any time did they join hands. In this form they moved round in a body, keeping time together, by the assistance of a small party of women and girls, who, without joining in the dance, followed them round, and regulated their steps by

clapping hands in exact measure; but without singing or any other noise . . . the music was pleasing and harmonious. It was not of a sprightly cast, nor noisy, neither was it sluggish or heavy; but possessed something agreeably soothing, which prevented it . . . from wearying the ear.[23]

The flutes, made from river reeds that had been hollowed out by poking a stick through them, ranged from one foot to almost six feet in length. The pitch of each flute could be adjusted or "tuned" by using a stick to alter the position of a fiber or goat-skin plug or stop placed in the lower end of the reed. The short, higher-pitched reeds were called *mpenyane,* while the longer, deeper-toned ones were known as *meporo.*[24] To produce the deep or low notes, several reed sections were lashed together to form a single long pipe, but it was often difficult to seal the joints properly. By the 1930s, the long pipes made of conjoined reeds had been replaced by long sections of metal tubing. Tuning of the instruments was under the direction of a leader who took care to tune each instrument so that the chords or harmonies produced by the simultaneous sounding of the single note flutes were not discordant. The techniques used by the reed ensembles of the Kalahari past thus resembled the bell choirs found in some churches in the southern United States where each bell sounds a single note but forms chords when several are sounded simultaneously.

One musicologist fortunate enough to witness a re-creation of a reed flute ensemble in the 1930s reported that "the system of tuning is the same as that of the four highest principal flutes of the Nama Hottentots. . . . I was told that the idea underlying this song, with which words used to be associated, was the lamentation of the women for the old customs which had been abandoned by the chief Makaba [of the Ngwaketse] on the advice of the missionary Moffat."[25] The songs composed for and played by reed-flute ensembles were thus not only praises or songs extolling the successes of the community but also songs that could be admonishing and critical of current practices. After the performance, the flutes and tuning sticks were stored in goat-skin bags that were looked after by a curator who kept them safe near the rafters under the grass thatch of his house.

Other flutes and whistles were constructed of duiker horn and hollowed-out bone. In the past, these were used for a variety of purposes: herders used them to communicate with one another and to call their cattle in the pastures, young cadets played them during dances carried out at initiation, and traditional doctors sometimes sounded them to summon spirits for the purposes of divining and curing. The whistles worn around the necks of traditional doctors or *dinaka* often had plugs or stops inside them that contained medicines. In fact, the term *dinaka* means "horns" because traditional doctors often wore necklaces of small animal horns containing medicines around their necks. In one example, the fibers taken from a tree called *phefo* ("wind") were mixed with fat taken from around the kidneys of an ox and inserted into "doctored" whistles that were believed to be able to "blow away" the plague. The owner of one such whistle, a Lete doctor in Ramotswa, also kept a "feather from the legendary 'lightning bird,'" in the tube, since the whistle is also used against lightning [strikes]."[26] Nonmedicinal flutes and whistles also used feathers and other materials inside them to keep them lubricated and prevent splitting or cracking, which would render them useless.

Bow Harps and Lutes

One-Stringed Bow Harps

Almost all the peoples of Botswana—but especially the Tswana and the Sarwa—play a variety of one-stringed bows known by names such as *nkokwane* in Tswana or *//gwashi* in some Sarwa dialects. In its simplest form, this was simply a hunting bow that was played by striking the bowstring with a stick or arrow. The player formed notes by touching or "stopping" the string with his fingers; the arrow also produces an accompanying percussive sound when it strikes the string. To serve a resonator, the player can put the end of the bow in his mouth, a calabash, or even a discarded tin can. "Harps" made with resonators of gourd or leather permanently attached to the instrument are known as *segwana*.

A related, combination string and wind instrument that superficially resembles the bow harp but is played quite differently is known as a *lesiba* or *kwadi* in Tswana or *gora* in some Sarwa dialects. With this instrument, one end of the bowstring is attached directly to the wooden bow, while the other end is first fixed to a piece of quill that is then run through a hole or slit in the other end of the bow. The quill can be made to vibrate by placing it between lips, without actually touching them, while the player inhales and exhales. By varying the opening of the mouth, different tones are produced that are "very pleasant, partaking of the qualities of both string and wind, reminding one of an Aeolian harp; and it can be varied in power from a faint whisper to a strong, vibrant sound, the air column of the mouth and throat acting as a resonator."[27]

Another one-stringed instrument something like a violin is the *segankuru* or *segaba,* which is played by stroking a friction bow strung with hair from a cow's tail across a single string. Pushing the string down onto the wooden neck or shaft of the instrument, varying its length, creates the different notes, while a tin can, fixed to the other end of the neck, serves as a resonator.

A traditional *segwana,* or bow harp, with
a gourd attached as a resonator.

In some cases, a wooden tuning peg inserted through the neck of the instrument is used to tighten or loosen the single string.

Multistringed Lutes

A final stringed instrument is still sometimes encountered in the northwestern parts of Botswana, where it is played by Sarwa and, in the past, Mbukushu musicians. Called a *daukashe, ≠gou kha:s, dzoma,* or *lohi* in different Sarwa dialects, it is a stringed lute-like instrument that has four to seven small, bow-like necks attached to one end of a resonator made of wood or on some occasions a large tortoise shell. The lengths of sinew that run from the resonator box to ends of the bows are tuned to different notes that the player, who sits on the ground with the resonator toward the body, produces by plucking the strings with his fingers to produce notes and chords. This manner of playing is nearly identical to another type of instrument, the finger piano or *setinkane,* which is of considerable antiquity among the Kalanga in northeastern Botswana.

A four-stringed lute, or *daukashe,* played by a Sarwa woman in Ngamiland. The resonator is made from a hollowed-out log with sinew used for strings.

Thumb Piano

The earliest record of the thumb piano *(setinkane)* comes from a detailed description of the *"ambira"* in 1586 by the Portuguese friar Joao dos Santos, who described the Shona using them to produce "altogether a sweet and gentle harmony of accordant sounds."[28] James Chapman, a later traveler in Botswana, was also favorably impressed by the quality of the music that could be produced by experienced players. He provides this description of the instrument from the 1840s:

> The Mashuna and Banabea have [an] . . . inventive genius for musical instruments, some of which produce excellent music in the hands of a competent performer. I have seen two of these worthy of notice. In one, 16 iron keys, 8 long and 8 short, are fixed inside a large calabash; the keys are attached by one end to a piece of wood, and raised halfway with a thin crosspiece of wood to give the keys free play. The performer vibrates them with his thumb.[29]

Today, a tin can often acts as a resonator, sometimes with metal beads attached that "buzz" when the instrument is played. It is fairly common for two or three thumb pianos to be played together as an ensemble. A second instrument that dos Santos describes is an indigenous marimba or xylophone, also called an *"ambira,"* which features more commonly in the traditional music of the Venda and Shona than the Batswana, although marimba ensembles are occasionally heard in Serowe and Francistown. While the xylophone is limited in its distribution, the *setinkane* is played almost everywhere in Botswana, although it was taken up only in the late 1950s by *zhu/oasi* or Sarwa musicians in the northwest. And even in this area, the instrument is now gradually replacing the multistringed lutes *(daukashe),* also played by plucking with the thumbs, among younger musicians. As one anthropologist noted, "Older people rarely even pick up the instrument [thumb piano], preferring to stick to the older musical hunting bow or to the . . . five- and four-stringed lute-like instruments."[30] Because the instrument is so new, few songs had been composed to accompany it until recently. Called by such names as *sitengena, dongu,* and *!goma,* by the early 1970s several young Sarwa artists, including a performer known as !Kaha or "Jack," began to compose songs for the instrument, which, in Jack's case, also served "as a vehicle for trance and a medium for speaking to God."[31] In an excerpt from one of his songs, Jack attributes his talent (and his destiny) on the thumb piano to the will of God *(//gauwa)*:

A young soul lives in the western sky
And is still learning.
These are my tears.
I mourn at death, for years and years—

The thumb piano, or *setinkane,* is played by snapping the fingers off the metal keys. This instrument has only recently been adopted by the Sarwa living in northwestern Botswana, but it has been popular for centuries among the Kalanga in the northeast.

This is what I have to tell.
God spoke, telling me to take up
These metal bits and this scrap of wood
And with them to sing.[32]

Horns and Trumpets

A variety of animal horns—kudu, gemsbok, goat, and cow—were used in the past but are seldom heard today, perhaps because the ceremonies and activities such as war that they were mostly associated with are now rarely encountered. The Herero, for instance, used a side-blown gemsbok horn known as *ohiva* on ceremonial occasions as well as to warn people of immanent danger in time of war, although it was never used directly as a battle horn. A Tswana instrument known as a *lepapata* was fashioned from the horn of a kudu or sable antelope and was also used for a variety of ceremonial occasions, including being blown "for war, during a circumcision ceremony, or when a lion or leopard was killed."[33] The instrument was made by soaking the horn in hot water to loosen the outer keratin layer from the bony core. The hole or embouchure was then cut in the outer layer at a point near the tip where the keratin covering ceases to be solid and becomes hollow. In elaborate examples, the embouchure was raised by carving down or thinning the exterior of the horn, leaving a raised surface surrounding the mouthpiece. Although very large and elaborately carved, side-blown ivory horns are well known from central Africa, they do not appear to have been made by any of Botswana's peoples.

TRADITIONAL RITES INCORPORATING MUSIC AND DANCE

Music and musical instruments accompanied all important rites and ceremonies, including menstruation and initiation rites, rainmaking prayers, exhortations for war, marriage, naming ceremonies, and funerals. In some cases, songs and dances were also used in protest, such as on those occasions when chiefs, through neglect of their ancestors, were believed to have failed in their obligation to make rain or prevent drought and famine. While early travelers and missionaries often recorded secular dances such as the reed dance and dances associated with rain, war, and fertility, they often did not recognize the many dances the Batswana people addressed to ancestral and other spirits for the purposes of curing or healing.

Prayers and Songs for Rain

In the nineteenth century, one of the major responsibilities of the chief was to work with his ancestors to produce the rain needed for the crops to grow, the pastures to become verdant, and the rivers, streams, and springs to fill with water to ensure the sustenance of his people and their animals. In many cases—and especially in times of drought—ritual specialists or "doctors" known as *moroka ya pula* were called on to help produce rain. Part of the rites involved "pegging the land" by driving stakes at crossroads and other locations to prevent the intrusion of malevolent forces that could stop or even "steal" the rain. In addition, special medicines consisting of wild bulbs, the fat of lions, and even portions of sacrificed human victims were burned in a "rain enclosure" constructed near the chief's residence. The rain medicines were placed inside horns, and the oily, black smoke that was emitted when their ingredients were set on fire was meant to empathetically cause the clouds to release their rain *(pula)* with the blessing of the ancestors. According to one description,

> As soon as it was learned that the first rains had fallen in any part of the country, the rain doctor went there with selected young girls and boys who were still innocent of sexual experience. The girls carried completely new pots, not yet used for cooking or any other purpose, into which medicines (melemo) had been put. As they went along, "they sang songs for rain in a heart-rending manner." When they got to the spot, the boys smeared themselves "all over" with mud, while the girls filled their pots with the rain water. Then, "still singing songs for rain," they headed for home. When they were within earshot of the village, the girls smashed their pots by throwing them to the ground, and the boys wiped off the mud with which they had anointed themselves. Then they all went home, still singing the rain songs.[34]

The last rainmaking rites held by the Ngwato occurred in the 1860s because Khama III forbade them after his conversion to Christianity. The Reverend W. Willoughby, who lived for more than 25 years with the Ngwato, recorded a mysterious fragment of an early rain song from this final ceremony as it was related to him by an unnamed informant in 1893. The ceremony, which took place after the more usual prayers and rites for rain had failed to ease a severe drought, began with the sacrifice of a totally black bull, after which the people

> stood and worshipped, under the presidency of their chief, intoning the "praise songs" of their dead chiefs, and saying, "we have come to beg rain by means of this ox, O chief, our Father!" The rain-songs also were chanted; and the people dispersed with a great shout, "Rain! Rain! Rain! Chief, we are dead—we who are your people! Let the rain fall!" As they wended their homeward way, they continued to make the welkin ring with their rain-songs; "and," added my old friend, "on the evening of that same day there was a drenching rain." Of the rain-songs sung upon this occasion my informant could remember but one

Kololo a éé kaka ea komakoma;
Kgomo co moroka di letse di sa nwa,
Megobyane e kgadile.

The first line is somewhat obscure, but I venture the following translation:

Let the klipspringer go, grappling with the gentle rain;
The cattle of the rain-doctor's folk lay down thirsty last night,
The rain-pools having dried up.[35]

As it turns out, the renowned hunter R. Gordon Cumming was in the vicinity of the Ngwato capital around 1846, 15 years earlier than Willougby's informant's account. He confirms the use of the cries of live klipspringers in rainmaking ceremonies with this remarkable description:

It often, however, happens that the relentless clouds decline attending to the solicitations of the rain-maker, and the fields of young corn become parched and withered. Other schemes are then resorted to. A number of the young men sally forth, and, forming an extensive circle, enclose the surface of some mountain-side in which the rock-loving klipspringer is likely to be met with, when, by gradually contracting their circle, like our Highlanders of old, they generally manage to catch alive sundry klipspringers, whose voices are supposed to attract rain. The unfortunate little antelopes thus captured are paraded round the kraal, while the rain-maker, by pinching them, induces them to scream.[36]

Why the klipspringer (and also the eland and rock dassie or hyrax) were chosen as consistent components of rainmaking rites is unclear. For the dassie and the klipspringer, it is possible that their habit of living on rocky hills and the distress "song" of the klipspringer, which is described as a roaring sound made with the mouth wide open, are what led to their association with rain. Live klipspringers and human sacrifice were generally resorted to only in unusual cases of drought, and if that occurred, regiments might also be called to search for "unnatural" or other "astonishing objects" in the bush that might have been placed there by sorcerers to block the rain from falling.

Dance and Healing

Contemporary cleansing and curing rites (*phekolo*) now incorporate more heterogeneous groups of people drawn from many more ethnic groups than was the case in the past.[37] In addition, healing dances and prayers that were once carried out communally in the village *kgotla* now take place in more guarded locations—especially isolated, rocky outcrops in the bush or even at ancient archaeological sites such as Khubu la Dintsha (Hill of the Dogs) near Mmashoro and Khubu Island on the Makgadikgadi pans, where ancestral associations are particularly strong. Songs and dances addressed to the ancestral spirits, along with spirit possession, are integral features of these ceremonies, and, as one priest remarked,

> no medicine is given to people. They are healed, their problems are solved, and they get luck by dancing. If people say they want promotion [in their jobs], we tell them to go with the dust [from the dance midden] on their feet and ask for it, and then wash them the following day. That is how they are healed, blessed, and their problems are solved. We believe that the *badimo* [ancestors] and their spirits live in people's veins *(ditshika)*. They are what make western medicine work or not. If people resist treatment in the hospital, they would be healed after dancing and praying to the *badimo*.[38]

The songs performed during the dances at *phekolo* ceremonies, such as that held every July at Khubu la Dintsha, are not usually ones that have been handed down from antiquity; rather, they are contemporary call-and-response compositions that sing of the glory of the past while welcoming the arrival and aid of "generalized" ancestral spirits to the curing ceremonies.[39] As Mothofela Molato, the founder of the *Tumelo mo Badimong* ("Faith in the Ancestors") Church, put it, "When I get here I use any *badimo* who will respond first, and I communicate with them."[40] The songs sometimes also include biblical metaphors with references to Jesus interspersed with songs to the *badimo*. During the evening curing ceremony, which takes place in complete darkness on the hilltop, a female "choir" leads the singing, stamping out rapid, synchronized beats with their legs wrapped in leg rattles while the drums pound out simple rhythms that vary somewhat depending on whether Kalanga or Tswana songs are being sung. Those wishing to be cured or cleansed dance as well, circling the dancers with rattles, each in their own individual fashion while singing. As the dancing progresses, clouds of dust from the ancient midden where the dancing floor has been cleared rise above the dancers' heads, creating a halo effect in the starlight as it settles onto them. Occasionally, a few of the dancers become possessed by spirits, moaning, growling, or speaking in tongues as other members of the congregation attend to them. Although the details differ, some ZCC congregations hold similar curing rites.

Purifying or healing *(phekolo)* basins used to address the ancestors by members of the *Tumelo mo Badimong* traditional
church. At an annual ceremony, the basins are filled with traditional beer that is then blessed by the priest before congregation members are permitted to enter the enclosure to beseech
their ancestors for help with healing or other troubles. Each
basin is for the ancestors of a different tribe, or *morafe*.

TRADITIONAL MUSIC AND DANCE

Movement and vocals that use repetitive forms of call-and-response in
which a soloist sings the stanzas to which the other singers respond in a chorus
are characteristic of Botswana's traditional dances. Most dancing is accompanied by rhythmic hand clapping and usually ends with an exuberant and
high-pitched ululation by the female participants. Men and women of varying
ages dance using creative leg and body motions with women, in particular,
emphasizing the movement of hips and changing facial expressions; the ele-
gance of the body and facial gestures are intended to go hand in hand with
the beauty of the music.

Clothing is another important aspect of traditional dance. Most Batswana
today, for instance, wear Western clothing except when they put on traditional costumes for tourist or ceremonial purposes. But even when dances
such as the trance dance are done "at home" for their traditional purposes,
Sarwa men in eastern Botswana—where skin loincloths have long been
abandoned—will still remove their shirts and roll up their trouser legs or put

on shorts for these dances. During Tswana performances, the young women who dance don leather skirts and headdresses made of beads, porcupine quills, animal tails, and even tortoise shell. Both Sarwa and Tswana wear the traditional ankle rattles.

Different traditional dance forms are associated in the popular mind with different parts of Botswana. The *setapa,* for instance, is a coordinated processional dance done by both men and women—and especially among the Ngwaketse by men—in celebration of weddings or the harvest season. During the dance, the men's leg and arm movements mirror one another in choreographed fashion as they change styles during the dance. *Tsutsube* was originally a dance associated with the Kgalagadi and Ghanzi districts. In it, the dancers sometimes act out events, such as a traditional doctor trying to cure a patient or men going on a hunt. The dance is popular because it usually includes handsprings, backflips, and other exciting acrobatic movements. *Phatisi* is a dance that originates in the Kweneng district and includes both men and women dancing together. The vigorous foot-stomping movements of the dance are reminiscent of the "gumboot" style associated with the mines in South Africa. The dance often begins with lively impromptu solo performances, common among the Kwena. *Borankana,* a dance named after the term *"go rankana,"* or "to jump about or behave in a boisterous manner," because it combines the styles of many dances, is performed throughout the country. Some people call it the Botswana dance, a combination of all the mentioned dances. It is usually

Young children learn and practice traditional dances at school that are then performed at holiday festivals and other special occasions. In recent years, many more dance troupes have formed in response to the popularity of traditional performances on the newly established Botswana Television.

performed with the arms raised as a form of praise to cattle. Another dance, *Hosanna,* originally prominent among the Kalanga in the North-East district, uses female performers who dance to appease God *(Mwali),* the giver of rain.[41] *Diware,* another traditional dance not as widely performed, is derived from an Mbukushu healing dance in which the performers dance while shaking their shoulders, which are draped with animal skins. It is danced when healing the sick. Mbukushu also dance *Thiwinji* to give thanks for the harvest and *Diboki* to celebrate a girl's reaching puberty.

In 1991, in an attempt to rejuvenate interest in traditional dance in Botswana, a group named Mogwana was formed in Gaborone. Comprising both youth and adults, the group practices and performs the music and dance of many of the country's ethnic groups. This pioneer group visited many parts of the country to study different traditional dance forms that they have now incorporated into a routine that has made them popular both nationally and abroad. The group has performed for many national and international charities in addition to traditional dance competitions. More recently, the group has turned its attention other issues, including the environment, teenage delinquency, and HIV/AIDS.

Traditional Setswana Songs

Traditional songs composed to praise, to anger, or simply to entertain are another important aspect of the culture and customs of Botswana. In a song meant as a life narrative, for instance, Seleng describes how he was affected after returning to his home after working as a migrant laborer to find that people were only to ready to mock and cheat him. Other songs, such as the one sung by the women of Mmashoro, criticize chiefs such as Tshekedi Khama for not being strong leaders and dividing the tribe. Sometimes the lyrics are combined with poetry or are written simply to educate about Tswana life in general. Finally, there are a large number of songs composed and recorded for use at ceremonies such as marriage, initiation, planting and harvesting, and death. Traditional instruments such as the *serankure* and *segaba* accompany many solos by contemporary artists such as Seleng, Boruru Oageng, Speech Madimabe, and Sticker Sola. Group songs usually feature drums, reeds, and horn instruments.

CONTEMPORARY MUSIC

Because Botswana's traditional music and dance was rarely appreciated by Europeans during the colonial era, little was written about it. Nonetheless, music and dance continue to be an integral part of the intangible heritage of the country—a heritage embedded in people's minds and memories that continues to find expression in religious and folk music as well as in more contemporary compositions. Indeed, in the Tswana language, a single word, *maitisong,* captures the idea of a place where people come together in the evening to converse, play games, and enjoy one another's company. In recent years, particularly with the impact of Botswana television, there has been a surge of interest in traditional dancing, with dancers dressed in replica costumes that include skin aprons and loincloths. The beat of the dance continues to be kept by hand clapping and ankle rattles as the dancers move their bodies in an exuberant and energetic fashion. The dances, done by both men and women, are often performed as competitions between different villages as well as for official holidays and other cultural occasions. Many new favorites, such as the song *Malalaswi*—which relates a story about an uncle who attempts to seduce his younger cousin while on the way to the cattle post, justifying it by claiming that "in our culture it is done that way"—crosscut ethnic differences and are sung as "traditional" by both Tswana and Sarwa performers.

Traditional Music in Contemporary Settings

Choral Ensembles

Choral music is popular in Botswana. Many of the songs, some of which have been passed down from one generation to the next, incorporate melodic harmonies that are practiced throughout the year and performed in villages across Botswana during holidays and family gatherings. On Christmas Eve, for instance, choirs made up of family members often sing their rehearsed songs in competition with other family choirs from the village. Christmas, which falls in the middle of the rainy season, is the time of the year when extended families who have been dispersed at the lands, cattle posts, villages, and towns come together to celebrate the holidays. More than half of Gaborone's residents head out of town to the cattle posts and lands for the festive season. Few Batswana lived in urban settlements until about 40 years ago, so almost all have a rural home, and their ties to the countryside are especially strong. Although there is usually no electricity or running water, the rural cattle post is seen by most Batswana not as an arduous place but as a cultural icon that exemplifies well-being and family life. During the holiday season, a family elder may slaughter a cow or goat, the choral harmonies to traditional songs will be rehearsed, and dances, stories, and gossip will entertain those who gather every evening under the stars to enjoy one another's company around the campfire. Older men perform traditional songs of panegyric triumph or praise as well as laments known as *dikoma* while accompanied by one-stringed violins, homemade guitars, or other instruments.

To conserve the country's music and dance, children are now taught traditional songs and dances at school. Every morning school assembly begins with the national anthem, usually followed by a gospel chorus or traditional song. Even at the University of Botswana, there is a traditional dance group called *Ngwao Boswa,* which performs both nationally and overseas. On the commercial level, the choral music choir Kgalemang Tumediso Motsetse, popularly dubbed KTM, is one of the most talented and appreciated choral music groups in the country.

Traditional Ensembles

The group Machesa won a prestigious All-Africa Kora music award in 2003 for the best African traditional group for their album *Tshipidi,* which means "a child's first steps." Made up of three musicians, Batsile Lesetedi, Keduetse Lesetedi, and Lebitso Galemorone, their music incorporates traditional instruments such as whistles, one-stringed violins, and hand clapping with a modern beat. The song "*Seponono*" appeals to mothers-in-law to look after and take care of their daughters-in-law. The group's album *Kora,* named after the award, was released in 2004. According to Keduetse Letsedti, "We called this album Kora because the Awards have now become synonymous with African musical excellence. We feel this is an excellent album."[42] Onstage, the audience response to the group's traditional songs, which included "*Bojalwa jo re a bonwa jo*" ("Let's drink that traditional beer") was enthusiastic because they evoked memories of times past when traditional song and dance were the principal forms of home entertainment.

Modern Folk Music

Ndingo Johwa is one of the new stars of Botswana's folk or ethnic music genre. His music reflects the proud history of the Kalanga, who have a saying, "*Boshe Bagele Dombo balanda pasi, dziha ko buzwiza Njiba,*" which translates as "Kings live on the hilltop while everyone else lives below." Johwa's musical style pays homage to such traditions of social hierarchy while using well-known folkloric images to evoke the spirits of the land. While the music thus resonates with the past, it also addresses contemporary issues of identity and the changing social conditions that confront the Kalanga in Botswana's multiethnic society. One of his hits, "*Makungulupeswa,*" is an uncompromising critique of the impact of colonial administrators such as Colonel Rey on interethnic politics and the institution of chieftainship. In this idiomatically rich song, he argues that the roots of chieftainship go deep into the past so that no chief, no matter what ethnic group he represents, should be seen as more important than another. Kalanga leaders thus have as much right as any others to "*lebeleka*," or "speak up," in the contemporary political arena about the issues affecting their people. In another work, "*Tjililo Africa*," performed with Albert Malikongwa, the ravages of the HIV/AIDS on community life are compared with being attacked by a machine gun.

Kwaito

Odirile Sento, affectionately referred by his fans as "Vee," is a self-proclaimed king of *kwaito,* a style of music with an resounding beat that developed from a blend of earlier urban styles that include *marabi* of the 1920, *kwela* of the 1950s, and even hip-hop and jazz. The name, which derives from the Afrikaans term "*kwaai,*" meaning angry, is grounded in the tough life and culture of the urban townships of South Africa and presents a somewhat "gangsta" image with its booming bass notes and associations with smoky bars (shebeens), crowded taxis, and late-night parties. In harmony with its "tamed" *Tsotsi* roots, it is associated with particular ways of walking, dancing, and dressing. Vee's album, *Kasi Angel,* is a clear testimony of the young artist's roots and his emotional attachment to ghetto life. In it, he entertains viewers with adaptations of dances such as *Dziwanzenze* and *kwasa kwasa* in a style he calls *Taku-taku,* which incorporates flashes of Michael Jackson's moonwalk and break-dance steps. His ability to mix Zulu with Setswana and English lyrics contributes to his broad appeal.

Street Music and Dance

One of the most popular music and dance genres in the 1980s was the Street Dance *(Pantsula),* which was characterized by athletic movements and an "I'm cool and funky" style. Derived from the South African townships where gangs vied with one another for territory and respect, Pantsula music, with its "Queen," the late Brenda Fassie, dominated the local disco scene during this period.

Kwasa-Kwasa

Another popular music genre that began in the 1980s in the Republic of Congo (Zaire) is known as *kwasa-kwasa.* Similar to the shake-your-body hip-hop style popular in the United States, the *kwasa-kwasa* dance incorporates rhythmic hip and waist gyrations while the feet remain relatively motionless.

The music, which incorporates a fusion of soukous and rhumba rhythms, is characterized by intricate guitar solos with less of the heavy bass found in *kwaito*. While its origins are in Congo, one of the acknowledged greats of the *kwasa-kwasa* genre is the Tswana singer Franco, who in one of his hit albums titled *Ba Ntatola,* laments the unfortunate consequences of a death that is mistakenly announced while the person is still alive. Another group, the Loxion Kwasa Kwasa All Stars, have produced a recent hit with their song "Zebras Anthem," which capitalizes on the popularity of the country's national soccer team.

The female singer Olebile Maxy Sedumedi, or Maxy for short, has also been an inspiration to many Botswana artists through her performances of traditional music that include both popular and "Bushman music" sung with many clicks. Maxy is one of the most gifted and celebrated musicians in Botswana, where she is sometimes hailed as the "lady with the golden voice." Many have compared it with that of the international star from South Africa, the late Brenda Fassie. Her albums include *Maxy-Maxymam* in 2001, *Makorakoretsa* in 2003, and *Kothikothi* in 2004. Maxy is socially conscious artist who is actively involved in fund-raising for causes that include HIV/AIDS patients, orphans, and the elderly and disabled. Maxy's social activism has led Kgalalele Ntsepe, the winner of the first "Miss HIV stigma free" beauty contest held in Gaborone in 2004, to point to her as one of her inspirations.

Jazz

South Africa was once one of the major jazz venues in Africa—not only because the music was widely enjoyed but also because of its associations with blacks and "black power" in the United States, which made playing it a form of resistance to apartheid cultural repression. While the form lost popularity during the 1990s, it is seeing a resurgence of support among fans, and Gaborone and its suburbs have several nightclubs, including the Meropa Jazz Club and Eros, that are dedicated to it. Batswana audiences have also met recent jazz concerts and performances in Gaborone and Francistown with much appreciation. Louis Mhlanga, Nick Ndaba, and Magic Diau are among the most popular jazz performers, along with Moses Khumalo, who has played with such international greats as Hugh Masekela and Sebongile Khumalo. Puna Gabasiane, a female jazz singer on her way up, shows that talent is not restricted by gender. Another jazz great returning to the scene after a decade of silence is Socca Moruakgomo, one of the most talented jazz players in the country. In keeping with the social commitments of most of Botswana's contemporary performers, the lyrics to one of his most popular recordings, *Lefatshe* (our country), laments that "*Ke cholera e dira thoromo ya lefatshe la rona...HIV/AIDS ke sefofane sa yone...e merwalela, dikotsi tsa dikoloi,*

Oh re tla di tshabela kae?" ("Cholera is causing our country to quake... HIV/ AIDS... is its airplane... they fly [flood] everywhere, these dangerous witch-things... to where will we flee from them?").

Rock and Street Musicians

Noisy Road, a Lobatse-based group, is one of Botswana's leading rock bands. It is difficult to describe the rock music scene, however, because of the short life span of many groups, such as Tjoint, Unik Attractions, and Divine, that briefly come together only to split up over disputes about royalties and other matters. Other popular groups include BY2, Marulelo, Mokorwana, and Marabi.

Johnny Kobedi, a well-known musician who goes by the nickname "DJ Scientist," is referred to jokingly by some as the "Paramount Chief of Botswana." He can usually be heard at "his corner" next to the Gaborone Bus Rank, where he shouts and sings his "Radio Knockout Quiz Festival," attracting an appreciative crowd of onlookers ready for a good laugh. He argues that his Knockout Quiz was "the first commercial radio studio in Botswana—way ahead of RB II, Yarona FM, and Gabz FM." One should come prepared, however, because he sometimes appears wearing women's panty hose over his shorts, a bodice, and a "*stapora*," or rich man's hat, on his head. DJ Scientist is known to kick people out of his "festival" if they do not agree with his opinions, and his sharp tongue knows no bounds.

Sitting cross-legged on the sidewalk and smiling mischievously, his equipment includes a crude loudspeaker, a pair of battered two-band Tempest radios, a homemade guitar, and drums, although in recent years he has upgraded to a better microphone, a tape recorder, an amplifier, and less battered speakers. But he still keeps his homemade tin-can guitar. His latest self-produced album, *Moswi Mogatsake,* includes a lament for a dead spouse that is well worth listening to. DJ now markets and sells his own albums because he claims that the promoters and entrepreneurs who once sold his tapes cheated him—a complaint shared by many musicians who relate that there is little reward in being a full-time musician in Botswana.

Entrance to DJ's shows is obviously free, but his audience is expected to pay to hear him play. A battered tin cup, which has been around for many years, is passed around for people to throw in "something." But it is only when "enough" has been collected that Johnny will agree to play for a few minutes, sometimes warming up with a few amplified coughs and belches through his microphone. If he fails to get sufficient offerings in his cup, he often resorts to mocking and taunting his audience. Part street comedian and part musician, his "fan club" knows that the mocking is an integral part of his repertoire, shouting, "I usually charge P8 for a song and I have slashed the price by half, but you still refuse to pay. You idiot. Do you want me to perform for free?" DJ often targets civil servants who all get paid on the same day—the twentieth of the month. For several days afterward, the lines at the banks extend out the door as people wait in to deposit or cash their checks. DJ Scientists never one to miss an opportunity, implores them from the sidewalk, *"Batho ba di 20, a ko lo ntshe mogoshane o ke o gelele. Mose o tsoga o fedile, lo be lore tlhomola pelo"* ("You people who get paid on the twentieth of every month, give me your paltry wages. You know your money will be exhausted by tomorrow anyway, and then you'll just be sad").

Because of his cutting commentary and acerbic wit, Kobedi's songs are seldom given airtime on the nation's radio stations, even though he maintains that people "love his songs." And like many other musicians in Botswana, one of his ambitions is to help contribute to the national welfare by using his talent to fight HIV/AIDS, especially by encouraging people to get tested. Recognizing that there can be many paths that lead to a successful conclusion, his more comedic approach may produce results—at least among some segments of the population.

THEATER

Maitisong (named for the place where people traditionally gathered around the fire for an evening of conversation and games) is a cultural center in Gaborone that includes a 450-seat theater built on the grounds of Maru-a-Pula Secondary School.[43] It sponsors a variety of art, drama, and cultural events throughout the year, including the annual nine-day Maitisong festival held every March or April. Many international artists that have taken part in the festival since its inception in 1987 including the famous Cape Town jazz pianist Abdullah Ibrahim. Another highlight of the festival was the play *Super Patriots and Morons* presented by a troupe of performers from Zimbabwe. Their play was banned in Zimbabwe because its depiction of an African leader obsessed with power and opposed by an impoverished population was thought to be implicitly critical of the Mugabe regime. Other leading Botswana theater groups such as Reetsanang, Maruapula, Phakama, Letsatsi, and Bopaganang, have also participated in the festival. The center also organizes music lessons for a variety of instruments—both European and African—and sponsors a music camp that caters to more than 100 participants annually.

Through entertainment, most drama groups—like the contemporary musicians discussed in this chapter—have charged themselves with the additional responsibility of disseminating information about the HIV/AIDS pandemic that is devastating the country. A drama group at the University of Botswana under the guidance of Patrick Ebewo, for instance, uses theater and drama as

an interventionist and empowerment tool to aid in AIDS awareness education. The group has written and put on plays in both Botswana and Lesotho
that encourage the spectators, through audience participation, to learn about
the causes and prevention of the disease. The Francistown-based Ghetto Artists, in partnership with Youth Health Organization, have also traveled to a
number of venues in Botswana spreading information on AIDS prevention.

BEAUTY PAGEANTS

While not strictly in the category of music and dance, it would be remiss
not to mention the crowning of 19-year-old Mpule Kwelagobe of Botswana
as Miss Universe in 1999. This honor made her only the third black woman
to ever hold that title in the pageant's 48-year history. Her victory was even
more impressive because it was the first time that Botswana was represented
at the pageant. Kwelagobe, a student at Columbia University with an interest
in electrical engineering, is a global activist on behalf of victims of HIV/
AIDS; in 2000, she was appointed as a United Nation's Population Fund
Goodwill Ambassador.

In 2004, another Botswana beauty contestant, 17-year-old Sumaiyah
Marobe, a Muslim, was invited to participate in the Miss European Union
pageant. According to some accounts, she was favored to win the contest but
was denied the crown because she was from Africa rather than the European
Union. She was awarded the title of Miss Africa, instead—a somewhat hollow
title because she was the only African participant.[44]

Finally, in July 2005, Kaone Kario of Maun won the Nokia Face of Africa
contest, bringing home a contract worth $125,000. But while modeling and
beauty pageant success have encouraged many young Batswana girls to entertain visions of stardom, as with most fields founded mainly on popularity and
glamour, reality only occasionally meets dreams. Nonetheless, Botswana's
women are now taking their place on the international stage for their beauty,
poise, grace, and intelligence—an excellent complement to the resources of an
African country already well known for its ethnic and racial inclusiveness, freedom of speech, democratic principles, and sound economic management.

NOTES

1. D. Livingstone, *Missionary Travels and Researches in South Africa* (New York:
Harper and Brothers, 1858), p. 147.

2. J. Chapman and E. C. Tabler, *Travels in the Interior of South Africa, 1849–1863:
Hunting and Trading Journeys from Natal to Walvis Bay & Visits to Lake Ngami & Victoria
Falls,* vol. 1 (Cape Town: A. A. Balkema, 1971), p. 152. The diary entry was made
around October 20, 1854.

3. J. Burchell, *Travels in the Interior of Southern Africa* (London: Batchworth Press, 1822), p. 413.

4. C. J. Andersson, *Lake Ngami, or, Explorations and Discoveries during Four Years' Wanderings in the Wilds of Southwestern Africa* (New York: Harper and Brothers, 1856), pp. 193–94. Commenting about him and his companion, he wrote, "We did not join in the dance, but amused ourselves with admiring the ladies. What with their charms, which were by no means inconsiderable, and [perhaps most importantly] the wonderful regard they evinced for us, these damsels all but ruined our peace of mind."

5. Richard Giddy, a missionary to the Tswana at Thaba Nchu in South Africa in 1839. Quoted in G. Setiloane, *The Image of God among the Sotho-Tswana* (Rotterdam: A. A. Balkema, 1976), p. 92.

6. Burchell, *Travels in the Interior of Southern Africa*, p. 63.

7. R. Katz, *Boiling Energy: Community Healing among the Kalahari Kung* (Cambridge, Mass.: Harvard University Press, 1982), p. 42.

8. M. G. Guenther, "The Trance Dancer as an Agent of Social Change among the Farm Bushmen of the Ganzi District," *Botswana Notes and Records* 7 (1975): 161–66.

9. Performances that exemplify some of the traditional polyrhythmic, harmonic, and "offset" or "off-beat" characteristics of Tswana music can be heard (and purchased) on the Smithsonian Institution Web site at http://www.smithsonianglobal-sound.org/containerdetail.asp?itemid=2856.

10. J. Denbow's excavation notes for Matlapaneng, winter 1984.

11. J. Denbow's excavation notes for Bosutswe, July 2002.

12. P. R. Kirby, *The Musical Instruments of the Native Races of South Africa* (Johannesburg: Witwatersrand University Press, 1968), p. 199.

13. D. Livingstone and I. Schapera, *Family Letters, 1841–1856,* vol. 1 (Westport, Conn.: Greenwood Press, 1975), p. 206.

14. Kirby, *The Musical Instruments of the Native Races of South Africa*, p. 80.

15. For English speakers, the call of the gray lowry, "gawaaay," elicits a similar linguistic interpretation, resulting in its nickname as the "go away" bird.

16. Kirby, *The Musical Instruments of the Native Races of South Africa*, p. 46.

17. M. N. Mosothwane, "An Ethnographic Study of Initiation in Schools among the Bakgatla ba ga Kgafela at Mochudi (1874–1988)," in *Pula: Botswana Journal of African Studies* 15(1): 152.

18. The *Gonometa postica* silkworm is found widely in Botswana, as it feeds on a variety of acacias, especially *Acacia erioloba, A. melifera, and A. tortilis. Gonometa rufobrunnea* is more restricted in its distribution to northeastern Botswana, where it feeds exclusively on mopane trees *(Cholophospermum mopane).* There is a lively trade in dance rattles to those parts of Botswana where these trees and their silkworms do not live.

19. Kirby, *The Musical Instruments of the Native Races of South Africa*, p. 4.

20. J. D. Lewis-Williams, *Believing and Seeing: Symbolic Meanings in Southern San Rock Paintings* (London: Academic Press, 1981).

21. S. Ouzman, "Seeing Is Deceiving: Rock Art and the Non-Visual," *World Archaeology* 33 (2, 2001): 237–56.

22. D. Livingstone, *Missionary Travels and Researches in South Africa; Including a Sketch of Sixteen Years' Residence in the Interior of Africa, and a Journey from the Cape of Good Hope to Loanda on the West Coast; Thence across the Continent, Down the River Zambesi, to the Eastern Ocean* (Freeport, N.Y.: Books for Libraries Press, 1972), p. 225.

23. Burchell, *Travels in the Interior of Southern Africa,* pp. 411–12.

24. Kirby, *The Musical Instruments of the Native Races of South Africa,* pp. 149–50.

25. Ibid., p. 150.

26. Ibid., p. 97.

27. Ibid., p.189.

28. G. M. Theal, *Records of South-Eastern Africa* (London: William Clowes and Sons, 1899), pp. 202–3.

29. J. Chapman and E. C. Tabler, *Travels in the Interior of South Africa, 1849–1863,* p. 152. The diary entry was made around October 20, 1854.

30. M. Biesele, "Song Texts by the Master of Tricks: Kalahari San Thumb Piano Music," *Botswana Notes and Records* 7 (1975): 172.

31. Ibid., pp. 171–88.

32. Ibid., p. 171.

33. Kirby, *The Musical Instruments of the Native Races of South Africa,* p. 78.

34. I. Schapera, *Rainmaking Rites of Tswana Tribes* (Leiden: Afrika-Studiecentrum, 1971), pp. 126–27.

35. W. C. Willoughby, *The Soul of the Bantu: A Sympathetic Study of the Magico-Religious Practices and Beliefs of the Bantu Tribes of Africa* (Garden City, N.Y.: Doubleday, Doran & Company, 1928), p. 209; Schapera, *Rainmaking Rites of Tswana Tribes,* p. 120, translates this as "let the rain drip." He also records the klipspringer as being "the first animal sought in the rain hunt" and on page 130 mentions E. Lloyd remarking on the same practice in 1895. An account of the use of live klipspringers for rainmaking is also found in H. A. Bryden, *Gun and Camera in Southern Africa: A Year of Wanderings in Bechuanaland, the Kalahari Desert, and the Lake River Country, Ngamiland* (London: E. Stanford, 1893), pp. 440–41.

36. R. Gordon Cumming, *The Lion Hunter of South Africa: Five Years' Adventures in the Far Interior of South Africa, with Notices of the Native Tribes and Savage Animals* (London: John Murray, 1911), pp. 337–38.

37. The *Tumelo mo Badimong* church (Faith in the Ancestors) at Khubu la Dintsha, for instance, has separate clay *phekolo* basins dedicated to the ancestral spirits of the Pedi, Kalanga, Kgalagadi, Hurutshe, and Ngwato. The church also has many members with Sarwa ancestry, although there is no special basin for them (J. Denbow interview with Mothofela Molato, Khubu la Dintsha, July 2002).

38. J. Denbow interview with Mothofela Molato, Khubu la Dintsa, July 15, 2002.

39. These terms are taken from two of the refrains recorded in July 2002 at Khubu la Dintsa.

40. Interview with Mothofela Molato, J. Denbow, Khubu la Dintoha, July 2002.

41. *Hosanna* is also a term for a type of ancestral spirit that could take possession of a dancer's body in some religious sects. In Francistown, one of these sects staged dances wearing black, white, and red uniforms.

42. L. Mooketsi, "Machesa, Mr Magic Diau to Feature at St. Louis Concert," *Mmegi wa Dikgang,* February 23, 2005. This festival was held at the Blue Tree Club in Gaborone, not St. Louis, Missouri, and the favorite tunes were from Louis Armstrong, or "St. Louis."

43. Maru-a-Pula, meaning "rain clouds," was one of the first privately run secondary schools in the country.

44. Morongwa Phala, "Motswana Girl 'Wins' EU Beauty Contest," *Mmegi wa Dikgang,* May 6 2004.

Glossary

Terms are in Setswana unless otherwise indicated.

=Gaishi, N!adima, or =Gao N!a: (Khoisan) creator god distant from humanity.

//Gauwa, //Gauwa-si, G//awama, or G/ama dzi: (Khoisan) trickster spirit associated with spirits of the dead is also thought to cause sickness or misfortune.

amarula: liquor made from the fruit of the morula tree, exported throughout the world.

badimo: ancestors.

baloi: witches, ghosts; people with personal jealousies or grudges.

baporofiti (pl.): prophets who claim to communicate with ancestral spirits

baroka (pl.), moroka or moraka ya pula (sing.): rainmaking specialists.

Batswana: people of Botswana

biltong: (Afrikaans) type of jerky made from long, thin strips of meat coated with salt and sometimes additional spices. This is known as *segwapa* in Tswana.

bogadi: cows or money offered to the bride's parents as a token of appreciation for the loss of their daughter and her children to their lineage. Sometimes also known as *lobola*.

bogobe: porridge made of sorghum flour and water.

bogwera: traditional initiation school for boys; rite of passage.

bojale: traditional initiation school for girls; rite of passage.

bojalwa: traditional sorghum beer.

bokgosi: kingship and chieftainship.

boloi: witchcraft.

botho: character.

Chibuku: commercially produced, traditional beer brewed from sorghum.

difalana: centralized granaries under chief's supervision.

Difaquane/Mfecane: referring to the raids and population dislocations that occurred in southern Africa during the first two decades of the nineteenth century.

dikgafela: ceremonies traditionally used to thank the ancestors for the harvest.

dikgosi (pl.), kgosi (sing.): Tswana chiefs; kings.

dikobo: warm fur blankets (also known as karosses).

dingaka (pl.), ngaka (sing.): traditional doctor, after the small animal horns filled with medicine worn around the traditional doctor's neck.

dipitso (pl.), pitso (sing.): *kgotla* meetings.

ditlhare: traditional medicines (literally, "trees or bushes").

ditoropo (pl.), toropo (sing.): cities.

go alafa: to treat diseases.

kapolo: death announcement ceremony.

kgotla: institution through which Tswana communities govern themselves in family and community matters. Also the physical place where political discussions are held.

khadi: alcoholic drink traditionally made from honey, Grewia berries, and cream of tartar made from baobab seeds.

kraal: central animal corral (also known as *lesaka*).

lebelebele: millet.

Leina (sing.), maina (pl.): name; refers also to a person's oration in praise of himself or another person.

lenyalo: marriage.

lesaka: central animal corral (also known as kraal).

lolwapa: walled courtyard that connects the area in front of the principal houses of a family homestead; open courtyard synonymous with family, home, and household (also known as *lelapa* and *lelwapa*).

maboko: praise poetry.

madila: sour milk.

maere: (Herero) traditionally made butter.

mafisa: system of lending out animals to attract followers.

magwinya: deep-fried fat cakes.

maitisong: traditionally a place near the fire where people would come together in the evening to converse, play games, and enjoy each other's company.

Makgowa (pl.), Lekgowa (sing.): white people.

managa: people of the bush.

mantsho: naming ceremony.

mashi: milk.

mashimo: farmlands.

mateitshe: traditional women's clothes—a uniform of German cloth, a small shawl-like blanket *(mogagolwane),* a head scarf *(tukwi; doeke),* and soft sandals.

mephato (pl.), mophato (sing.): age sets at initiation.

merafe (pl.), morafe (sing.): nations, tribes, ethnic groups.

meraka: cattle posts.

Modimo: God.

mogwana: (Khoisan) Sarwa healing dance.

mopane worms: dried, spiny-backed caterpillars that consume mopane leaves; adult stage is emperor moth *(Imbrasia belina).*

mosese: skirt with various ornaments.

Mosi o a Thunya: "smoke that thunders," referring to Victoria Falls.

Mwari/Ngwale: (Kalanga) God.

n/um: (Khoisan) supernatural curing potency or power.

Ndjambi: (Herero) God.

nyatsi: unmarried girlfriend with whom a married man is having an affair.

okuruo: (Herero) sacred fire located on eastern side of the homestead.

paletshe: porridge or stiff paste the consistency of mashed potatoes made from maize flour (mealie meal) and water.

patlo: betrothal or negotiations between two families leading to a betrothal.

phekolo: ancestral cleansing or healing ceremony.

pitso: kgotla meeting.

pula: rain; Botswana's national cry meaning, "Let there be rain"; a national unit of currency.

samp: (Afrikaans) coarsely stamped maize.

Sangoma: spiritual diviner and healer.

Sarwa: generic term used in Botswana to refer to all the Khoisan-speaking peoples of the country.

sefalana: huge grain storage baskets more than two meters in diameter, made exclusively by men (also called *sesigo*).

seswaa: boiled meat that has been salted and pounded until it has a shredded texture.

setilo sa dikgole: kgotla chairs; folding hardwood chairs with rawhide thong seats.

shabeen: neighborhood bar where traditional beer is brewed and served.

tebelelo: night vigil ceremony; wake where mourners could spend the night.

thapo: mourning.

tukwi: cloth scarf tied around the head.

tokolosi: in folklore, a tiny trickster figure that can be used for good and evil intentions.

tsotsi (sing.), ditsotsi (pl.): colloquial term for a criminal, thief, or troublemaker.

tsotsitaal: slang language used by *ditsotsi;* a mixture of Afrikaans and other Bantu languages.

Selected Bibliography

INTRODUCTION

Botswana Presidential Task Group for a Long Term Vision for Botswana. (1996). *A Framework for a Long Term Vision for Botswana.* Gaborone: Government Printer.

Comaroff, J., and J. L. Comaroff. (1991, 1997). *Of Revelation and Revolution.* Vols. 1 and 2. Chicago: University of Chicago Press.

Denbow, J., and J. Denbow. (1985). *Uncovering Botswana's Past.* Gaborone: National Museum Monuments and Art Gallery.

Ehret, C. (1998). *An African Classical Age: Eastern and Southern Africa in World History, 1000 B.C. to A.D. 400.* Charlottesville: University Press of Virginia; Oxford: J. Currey.

Lee, R. (1979). *The !Kung San: Men, Women and Work in a Foraging Society.* New York: Cambridge University Press.

le Roux, W., and A. White, eds. (2004). *Voices of the San.* Cape Town: Kwela Books.

Main, M. (2002). *African Adventurer's Guide to Botswana.* Cape Town: Struik.

Maruyama, J. (2002). *Resettlement, Livelihood and Social Relationships among the / Gwi and //Gana in Central Kalahari.* Kyoto: Graduate School of Asian and African Area Studies.

Motzafi-Haller, P. (2002). *Fragmented worlds, coherent lives: the politics of difference in Botswana.* Westport, Conn.: Bergin & Garvey.

Nyati-Ramahobo, L. (2000). "The Language Situation in Botswana." *Current Issues in Language* 1 (2): 243–300.

Parson, J. (1981). "Cattle, Class, and State in Rural Botswana." *Journal of Southern African Studies* 7: 236–55.

Rey, C. F., and N. Parsons. (1988). *Monarch of All I Survey: Bechuanaland Diaries, 1929–37.* New York: L. Barber Press.

Schapera, I. (1930). *The Khoisan Peoples of South Africa: Bushmen and Hottentots.* London: Routledge.

Schapera, I. (1941). *Married Life in an African Tribe.* New York: Sheridan House.

Schapera, I. (1970). *A Handbook of Tswana Law and Custom.* London: F. Cass.

Schapera, I., and J. L. Comaroff. (1991). *The Tswana.* London: Kegan Paul International in association with the International African Institute.

Thomas, S., and P. Shaw. (1991). *The Kalahari Environment.* Cambridge: Cambridge University Press.

Tlou, T. (1985). *A History of Ngamiland, 1750 to 1906: The Formation of an African State.* Gaborone: Macmillan Botswana.

Tlou, T., and A. C. Campbell. (1997). *History of Botswana.* Gaborone: Macmillan Botswana.

Vansina, J. (2004). *How Societies Are Born: Governance in West Central Africa before 1600.* Charlottesville: University Press of Virginia.

vin Binsbergen, W. (1994). "Minority Language, Ethnicity and the State in Two African Situations." In *African Languages, Development and the State,* edited by R. Farden and G. Furniss, 142–88. London: Routledge.

Vivelo, F. R. (1977). *The Herero of Western Botswana: Aspects of Change in a Group of Bantu-Speaking Cattle Herders.* St. Paul, Minn.: West.

Vossen, R., and K. Keuthmann. (1986). *Contemporary Studies on Khoisan: In Honour of Oswin Köhler on the Occasion of His 75th Birthday.* Hamburg: H. Buske.

Werbner, R. P. (2004). *Reasonable Radicals and Citizenship in Botswana: The Public Anthropology of Kalanga Elites.* Bloomington: Indiana University Press.

Wilmsen, E. N. (1989). *Land Filled with Flies: A Political Economy of the Kalahari.* Chicago: University of Chicago Press.

Wilmsen, E. N. (1989). *We Are Here: Politics of Aboriginal Land Tenure.* Berkeley: University of California Press.

Zaffiro, J. J. (1993). "Mass Media, Politics and Society in Botswana: The 1990s and Beyond." *Africa Today* 40 (1): 7–25.

Religion and Worldview

Alverson, H. (1978). *Mind in the Heart of Darkness: Value and Self-Identity among the Tswana of Southern Africa.* New Haven, Conn.: Yale University Press.

Campbell, A., J. Denbow, and E. Wilmsen. (1994). Paintings Like Engravings: Rock Art at Tsodilo. In *Contested Images: Diversity in Southern African Rock Art Research,* edited by T. Dowson and D. Lewis-William, 131–58. Johannesburg: Witwatersrand University Press.

Comaroff, J. (1985). *Body of Power Spirit of Resistance: The Culture and History of a South African People.* Chicago: University of Chicago Press.

Comaroff, J., and J. L. Comaroff. (1991 and 1997). *Of Revelation and Revolution: The Dialectics of Modernity on a South African Frontier.* Vols. 1 and 2. Chicago: University of Chicago Press.

de Heusch, L. (1980). "Heat, Physiology, and Cosmogony: Rites de Passage among the Thonga." In *Explorations in African Systems of Thought,* edited by I. Karp and C. Bird, 27–43. Bloomington: Indiana University Press.

Denbow, J. (1999). "Heart and Soul: Glimpses of Ideology and Cosmology in the Iconography of Tombstones from the Loango Coast of Central Africa." *Journal of American Folklore* 112: 404–23.

Fu-Kiau, A. (1969). *Le Mukongo et le Monde qui l'Entourait: Cosmogonie-Kongo.* Kinshasa: Office National de la Recherche et de Developpement.

Guenther, M. G. (1975). "The Trance Dancer as an Agent of Social Change among the Farm Bushmen of the Ganzi District." *Botswana Notes and Records* 7: 161–66.

Guenther, M. G. (1999). *Tricksters and Trancers: Bushman Religion and Society.* Bloomington: Indiana University Press.

Hagenbucher-Sacripanti, F. (1973). *Les Fondements spirituels du pouvoir au royaume de Loango, République populaire du Congo.* Paris: O.R.S.T.O.M. [Office de la recherche scientifique et technique outre-mer].

Jacobson-Widding, A. (1979). *Red—White—Black as a Mode of Thought: A Study of Triadic Classification by Colours in the Ritual Symbolism and Cognitive Thought of the Peoples of the Lower Congo.* Uppsala: Stockholm University.

Janzen, J. (1982). *Lemba, 1650–1930: A Drum of Affliction in Africa and the New World.* New York: Garland Publishing.

Karp, I., and C. Bird, eds. (1980). *Explorations in Systems of African Thought.* Bloomington: Indiana University Press.

Katz, R. (1982). *Boiling Energy: Community Healing among the Kalahari Kung.* Cambridge, Mass.: Harvard University Press.

Larson, T. (1985). "Death Beliefs and Burial Customs of the Hambukushu of Ngamiland." *Botswana Notes and Records* 17: 33—37.

Lewis-Williams, J. D. (1981). *Believing and Seeing: Symbolic Meanings in Southern San Rock Paintings.* London: Academic Press.

MacGaffey, W. (1986). *Religion and Society in Central Africa: The Bakongo of Lower Zaire.* Chicago: University of Chicago Press.

MacGaffey, W. (1993). *Astonishment and Power.* Washington, D.C.: Smithsonian Institution Press.

Mosothwane, M. N. (2001). "An Ethnographic Study of Initiation Schools among the Bakgatla bo ga Kgafela in Mochudi (1874–1988)." *Pula: Botswana Journal of African Studies* 15 (1): 144–65.

Ngubane, H. (1977). *Body and Mind in Zulu Medicine: An Ethnography of Health and Disease in Nyuswa-Zulu Thought and Practice.* London: Academic Press.

Ouzman, S. (2001). "Seeing Is Deceiving: Rock Art and the Non-Visual." *World Archaeology* 33 (2): 237–56.

Schapera, I. (1978). *Bogwera, Kgatla Initiation.* Mochudi, Botswana: Phuthadikobo Museum; distributed by the Botswana Book Centre.

Setiloane, G. (1976). *The Image of God among the Sotho-Tswana.* Rotterdam: A. A. Balkema.

Thompson, R. and J. Cornet. (1981). *The Four Moments of the Sun: Kongo Art in Two Worlds.* Washington, D.C.: National Gallery of Art.

Willoughby, W. C. (1928). *The Soul of the Bantu: A Sympathetic Study of the Magico-Religious Practices and Beliefs of the Bantu Tribes of Africa.* Garden City, N.Y.: Doubleday, Doran & Company.

LITERATURE AND MEDIA

Biesele, M. (1975). "Song Texts by the Master of Tricks: Kalahari San Thumb Piano Music." *Botswana Notes and Records* 7: 171–88.

Biesele, M. (1993). *Women Like Meat: The Folklore and Foraging Ideology of the Kalahari Ju/hoan.* Johannesburg: Witwatersrand University Press; Bloomington: Indiana University Press.

Crowder, M. (1988). *The Flogging of Phineas McIntosh: A Tale of Colonial Folly and Injustice: Bechuanaland, 1933.* New Haven, Conn.: Yale University Press.

Dow, U. (2000). *Far and Beyon'.* San Francisco: Aunt Lute Books.

Dow, U. (2002). *Screaming of the Innocent.* North Melbourne: Spinifex Press.

Dow, U. (2003). *Juggling Truths.* North Melbourne: Spinifex Press.

Finnegan, R. H. (1970). *Oral Literature in Africa.* London: Clarendon Press.

Head, B. (1969). *When Rain Clouds Gather: A Novel.* London: Gollancz.

Head, B. (1971). *Maru: A Novel.* London, Gollancz.

Head, B. (1973). *A Question of Power: A Novel.* London: Davis-Poynter.

Head, B. (1977). *The Collector of Treasures, and Other Botswana Village Tales.* London: Heinemann Educational.

Head, B. (1981). *Serowe, Village of the Rain Wind.* London: Heinemann.

Head, B. (1986). *A Bewitched Crossroad: An African Saga.* New York: Paragon House..

Hewitt, R. (1986). *Structure, Meaning and Ritual in the Narratives of the Southern San.* Hamburg: H. Buske.

Kunczik, M. (1999). *Ethics in Journalism: A Reader on Their Perception in the Third World.* Bonn: Division for International Development Cooperation of Friedrich-Ebert-Stiftung.

Larson, T. J. (1972). *Tales from the Okavango.* Cape Town: Timmins (Howard).

Larson, T. J., and the Botswana Society. (1994). *Bayeyi and Hambukushu Tales from the Okavango.* Gaborone: Botswana Society.

McCall Smith, A. (1998). *The No. 1 Ladies Detective Agency.* Cape Town: D. Philip.

McCall Smith, A. (2002). *Morality for Beautiful Girls.* New York: Anchor Books.

McCall Smith, A. (2002). *Tears of the Giraffe.* New York: Anchor Books.

McCall Smith, A. (2003). *The Kalahari Typing School for Men.* New York: Pantheon Books.

Mitchison, N. (1966). *Return to the Fairy Hill.* London: Heinemann.

Mogapi, M. (1986). *Ngwao ya Setswana.* Gaborone: Mmampodi Publishers.

Nyati-Ramahobo, L. (2000). "The Language Situation in Botswana." *Current Issues in Language* 1 (2): 243–300.

Parsons, N. (1998). *King Khama, Emperor Joe, and the Great White Queen: Victorian Britain through African Eyes.* Chicago: University of Chicago Press.

Rey, C. F., and N. Parsons. (1988). *Monarch of All I Survey: Bechuanaland Diaries, 1929–37.* New York: L. Barber Press.

Schapera, I. (1965). *Praise-Poems of Tswana Chiefs.* Oxford: Clarendon Press.

Schapera, I. (1971). *Rainmaking Rites of Tswana Tribes.* Leiden: Afrika-Studiecentrum.

Seboni, B. (n.d.). Why I Write What I Write. http://www.uiowa.edu/~iwp/EVEN/ documents/SeboniWhyIWrite.pdf.

Vorting, H. (1990). *Lekgapho Khama Memorial Museum Review 1988–1989.* Serowe: Serowe Printers Botswana.

Sampling of Nineteenth- and Early Twentieth-Century Travel Literature and Ethnography

Andersson, C. J.(1856). *Lake Ngami, or, Explorations and Discoveries during Four Years' Wanderings in the Wilds of Southwestern Africa.* New York: Harper & Brothers.

Bryden, H. A. (1893). *Gun and Camera in Southern Africa: A Year of Wanderings in Bechuanaland, the Kalahari Desert, and the Lake River Country, Ngamiland.* London: E. Stanford.

Burchell, J. (1822). *Travels in the Interior of Southern Africa.* London: Batchworth Press.

Campbell, J. (1974). *Travels in South Africa, Undertaken at the Request of the London Missionary Society.* Cape Town: C. Struik.

Chapman, J., and E. C. Tabler. (1971). *Travels in the Interior of South Africa, 1849–1863: Hunting and Trading Journeys from Natal to Walvis Bay & Visits to Lake Ngami & Victoria Falls.* Cape Town: A. A. Balkema.

Duggan-Cronin, A. M. (1928). *The Bantu Tribes of South Africa: Reproductions of Photographic Studies.* Cambridge: Deighton, Bell.

Gordon Cumming, R. (1911). *The Lion Hunter of South Africa: Five Years' Adventures in the Far Interior of South Africa, with Notices of the Native Tribes and Savage Animals.* London: John Murray.

Holub, E., and E. E. Frewer. (1881). *Seven Years in South Africa: Travels, Researches, and Hunting Adventures, between the Diamond Fields and the Zambesi (1872–79).* Boston: Houghton Mifflin.

Lichtenstein, H., and O. H. Spohr. (1973). *Foundation of the Cape [and] About the Bechuanas.* Cape Town: A. A. Balkema.

Livingstone, D. (1858). *Missionary Travels and Researches in South Africa.* New York: Harper and Brothers.

Livingstone, D., and I. Schapera. (1975). *Family Letters, 1841–1856.* Westport, Conn.: Greenwood Press.

Mackenzie, J. (1871). *Ten Years North of the Orange River 1859–69.* London: Frank Cass.

Moffat, R. (1842). *Missionary Labours and Scenes in Southern Africa.* London: J. Snow.

Moffat, R. (1976). *The Matabele Journals of Robert Moffat, 1829–1860.* Salisbury: National Archives of Rhodesia.

Oswell, W. E., and D. Livingstone. (1900). *William Cotton Oswell, Hunter and Explorer: The Story of His Life with Certain Correspondance and Extracts from the Private Journal of David Livingstone, hitherto Unpublished.* London: W. Heinemann.

Passarge, S. (1904). *Die Kalahari.* Berlin: Dietrich Riemer.

Passarge, S., and E. N. Wilmsen. (1997). *The Kalahari Ethnographies (1896–1898) of Siegfried Passarge: Nineteenth Century Khoisan- and Bantu-Speaking Peoples: Translations from the German.* Köln: Rüdiger Köppe.

Theal, G. M. (1899). *Records of South-Eastern Africa.* London: William Clowes and Sons.

ART AND ARCHITECTURE

Ashmore, W., and B. Knapp. (1999). *Archaeologies of Landscape: Contemporary Perspectives.* Malden, Mass.: Blackwell.

Burchell, J. (1822). *Travels in the Interior of Southern Africa.* London: Batchworth Press.

Duggan-Cronin, A. M. (1928). *The Bantu Tribes of South Africa: Reproductions of Photographic Studies.* Cambridge: Deighton, Bell.

Grant, S., and E. Grant. (1995). *Decorated Homes in Botswana.* Cape Town: Creda Press.

Hardie, G. (1994). "Continuity and Change in Tswana Expressive Space." *South African Journal of Art and Architectural History* 4 (2): 34–44.

Huffman, T. (1982). "Archaeology and Ethnohistory of the African Iron Age." *Annual Review of Anthropology* 11: 133–50.

Kuper, A. (1980). "Symbolic Dimensions of the Southern Bantu Homestead." *Africa* 50: 8–22.

Larsson, A., and L. Larsson. (1984). *Traditional Tswana Housing.* Stockholm: Spangbergs Tryckerier.

Miller, D. (1996). *The Tsodilo Jewellery: Metal Work from Northern Botswana.* Rondebosch: University of Cape Town Press.

CUISINE AND TRADITIONAL DRESS

Burchell, J. (1822). *Travels in the Interior of Southern Africa.* London: Batchworth Press.

Duggan-Cronin, A. M. (1928). *The Bantu Tribes of South Africa: Reproductions of Photographic Studies.* Cambridge: Deighton, Bell.

Durham, D. (1999). "The Predicament of Dress: Polyvalency and the Ironies of Cultural Identity." *American Ethnologist* 26 (2): 389–411.

Durham, D. (2004). "Disappearing Youth: Youth as a Social Shifter in Botswana." *American Ethnologist* 31 (4): 589–605.

Hendrickson, H. (1996). *Clothing and Difference: Embodied Identities in Colonial and Post-Colonial Africa.* Durham, N.C.: Duke University Press.

Lichtenstein, H., and O.H. Spohr. (1973). *Foundation of the Cape [and] About the Bechuanas.* Cape Town: A.A. Balkema.

Martin, P. (1972). *The External Trade of the Loango Coast—1576–1870.* Oxford: Clarendon Press.

Miller, J.C. (1988). *Way of Death: Merchant Capitalism and the Angolan Slave Trade, 1730–1830.* Madison:, University of Wisconsin Press.

GENDER ROLES, MARRIAGE, AND FAMILY

Alverson, H. (1978). *Mind in the Heart of Darkness: Value and Self-Identity among the Tswana of Southern Africa.* New Haven, Conn.: Yale University Press.

Biesele, M. (1993). *Women Like Meat: The Folklore and Foraging Ideology of the Kalahari Ju/oan.* Bloomington: Indiana University Press.

Comaroff, J., and J.L. Comaroff. (1997). *Of Revelation and Revolution: The Dialectics of Modernity on a South African Frontier.* Chicago: University of Chicago Press.

Durham, D. (1999). "The Predicament of Dress: Polyvalency and the Ironies of Cultural Identity." *American Ethnologist* 26 (2): 389–411.

Durham, D. (2004). "Disappearing Youth: Youth as a Social Shifter in Botswana." *American Ethnologist* 31 (4): 589–605.

Gibson, G.D. (1956). "Double Descent and Its Correlates among the Herero of Ngamiland." *American Anthropologist* 58: 109–39.

Griffiths, A.M.O. (1997). *In the Shadow of Marriage: Gender and Justice in an African Community.* Chicago: University of Chicago Press.

Hahn, C.H.L., et al. (1928). *The Native Tribes of South West Africa.* Cape Town: Cape Times.

Herbert, E.W. (1993). *Iron, Gender, and Power: Rituals of Transformation in African Societies.* Bloomington: Indiana University Press.

Schapera, I. (1941). *Married Life in an African Tribe.* New York: Sheridan House.

Schapera, I. (1947). *Migrant Labour and Tribal Life: A Study of Conditions in the Bechuanaland Protectorate.* London: Oxford University Press.

Schapera, I. (1970). *A Handbook of Tswana Law and Custom.* London: F. Cass.

Schneider, H.K. (1981). *The Africans: An Ethnological Account.* Englewood Cliffs, N.J.: Prentice Hall.

Vansina, J. (2004). *How Societies Are Born: Governance in West Central Africa before 1600.* Charlottesville: University Press of Virginia.

Vivelo, F.R. (1977). *The Herero of Western Botswana: Aspects of Change in a Group of Bantu-Speaking Cattle Herders.* St. Paul, Minn.: West.

SOCIAL CUSTOMS AND LIFESTYLE

Burchell, J. (1822). *Travels in the Interior of Southern Africa.* London: Batchworth Press.

Comaroff, J., and J.L. Comaroff. (1997). *Of Revelation and Revolution: The Dialectics of Modernity on a South African Frontier.* Chicago: University of Chicago Press.

Denbow, J. (2002). "Stolen Places: Archaeology and the Politics of Identity in the Later Prehistory of the Kalahari." In *Africanizing Knowledge: African Studies across the Disciplines,* edited by T. Falola and C. Jennings, 345–74. New Brunswick, N.J.: Transaction Publishers.

Dow, U. (2000). *Far and Beyon'.* San Francisco: Aunt Lute Books.

Dow, U. (2002). *Screaming of the Innocent.* North Melbourne: Spinifex Press.

Dow, U. (2003). *Juggling Truths.* North Melbourne: Spinifex Press.

Durham, D. (1999). "The Predicament of Dress: Polyvalency and the Ironies of Cultural Identity." *American Ethnologist* 26 (2): 389–411.

Durham, D. (2004). "Disappearing Youth: Youth as a Social Shifter in Botswana." *American Ethnologist* 31 (4): 589–605.

Griffiths, A.M.O. (1997). *In the Shadow of Marriage: Gender and Justice in an African Community.* Chicago: University of Chicago Press.

Guenther, M.G. (1999). *Tricksters and Trancers: Bushman Religion and Society.* Bloomington: Indiana University Press.

Head, B. (1977). *The Collector of Treasures, and Other Botswana Village Tales.* London: Heinemann Educational.

Larson, T. (1985). "Death Beliefs and Burial Customs of the Hambukushu of Ngamiland." *Botswana Notes and Records* 17: 33–37.

Larson, T.J. (1972). *Tales from the Okavango.* Cape Town: Timmins (Howard).

Larson, T.J., and Botswana Society. (1994). *Bayeyi and Hambukushu Tales from the Okavango.* Gaborone: Botswana Society.

Lee, R. (1979). *The!Kung San: Men, Women and Work in a Foraging Society.* New York: Cambridge University Press.

Livingstone, D. (1858). *Missionary Travels and Researches in South Africa.* New York: Harper and Brothers.

Motzafi-Haller, P. (2002). *Fragmented Worlds, Coherent Lives: The Politics of Difference in Botswana.* Westport, Conn.: Bergin & Garvey.

Schapera, I. (1930). *The Khoisan Peoples of South Africa: Bushmen and Hottentots.* London: G. Routledge.

Schapera, I. (1941). *Married Life in an African Tribe.* New York: Sheridan House.

Schapera, I. (1947). *Migrant Labour and Tribal Life: A Study of Conditions in the Bechuanaland Protectorate.* London: Oxford University Press.

Schapera, I. (1970). *A Handbook of Tswana Law and Custom.* London: F. Cass.

Schapera, I. (1971). *Rainmaking Rites of Tswana Tribes.* Leiden: Afrika-Studiecentrum.

Schapera, I. (1978). *Bogwera, Kgatla Initiation.* Mochudi, Botswana: Phuthadikobo Museum; distributed by the Botswana Book Centre.

Schapera, I., and J.L. Comaroff. (1991). *The Tswana.* New York: John Wiley & Sons.

Setiloane, G. (1976). *The Image of God among the Sotho-Tswana.* Rotterdam: A.A. Balkema.

Vansina, J. (2004). *How Societies Are Born: Governance in West Central Africa before 1600.* Charlottesville: University Press of Virginia.

vin Binsbergen, W. (1994). "Minority Language, Ethnicity and the State in Two African Situations." In *African Languages, Development and the State*, edited by R. F. a. G. Furniss, 142–88. London: Routledge.

Wilmsen, E. N., and P. A. McAllister. (1996). *The Politics of Difference: Ethnic Premises in a World of Power.* Chicago: University of Chicago Press.

MUSIC, DANCE, AND THEATER

Andersson, C. J. (1856). *Lake Ngami, or, Explorations and Discoveries during Four Years' Wanderings in the Wilds of Southwestern Africa.* New York: Harper and Brothers.

Biesele, M. (1975). "Song Texts by the Masterof Tricks: Kalahari San Thumb Piano Music." *Botswana Notes and Records* 7: 171–88.

Burchell, J. (1822). *Travels in the Interior of Southern Africa.* London: Batchworth Press.

Chapman, J., and E. C. Tabler. (1971). *Travels in the Interior of South Africa, 1849–1863: Hunting and Trading Journeys from Natal to Walvis Bay & Visits to Lake Ngami & Victoria Falls.* Cape Town: A. A. Balkema.

Gordon Cumming, R. (1911). *The Lion Hunter of South Africa: Five Years' Adventures in the Far Interior of South Africa, with Notices of the Native Tribes and Savage Animals.* London: John Murray.

Guenther, M. G. (1975). "The Trance Dancer as an Agent of Social Change among the Farm Bushmen of the Ganzi District." *Botswana Notes and Records* 7: 161–66.

Guenther, M. G. (1999). *Tricksters and Trancers: Bushman Religion and society.* Bloomington: Indiana University Press.

Katz, R. (1982). *Boiling Energy: Community Healing among the Kalahari Kung.* Cambridge, Mass.: Harvard University Press.

Kirby, P. R. (1968). *The Musical Instruments of the Native Races of South Africa.* Johannesburg: Witwatersrand University Press.

Lewis-Williams, J. D. (1981). *Believing and Seeing: Symbolic Meanings in Southern San Rock Paintings.* New York: Academic Press.

Livingstone, D. (1858). *Missionary Travels and Researches in South Africa.* New York: Harper and Brothers.

Schapera, I. (1965). *Praise-Poems of Tswana Chiefs.* Oxford: Clarendon Press.

Schapera, I. (1971). *Rainmaking Rites of Tswana Tribes.* Leiden: Afrika-Studiecentrum.

Willoughby, W. C. (1928). *The Soul of the Bantu: A Sympathetic Study of the Magico-Religious Practices and Beliefs of the Bantu Tribes of Africa.* Garden City, N.Y.: Doubleday, Doran & Company.

Index

About the Authors

JAMES DENBOW is Associate Professor of Anthropology at the University of Texas at Austin and has written frequently on Botswana.

PHENYO C. THEBE is a Fulbright Scholar in Anthropology at the University of Texas at Austin and Senior Curator at the National Museum of Botswana.